ecolibrium

Be like a bee: Anything it eats is clean, anything it drops is sweet, and any branch it sits upon, does not break. Be like a bee!

Imam Ali

ecolibrium
THE SACRED BALANCE IN ISLAM

Nadeem Haque
Al-Hafiz B.A. Masri
Mehran Banaei

Foreword by Michael W. Fox

BEACON BOOKS

First published in the UK by Beacon Books and Media Ltd
Earl Business Centre, Dowry Street, Oldham OL8 2PF UK.

First edition published in 2021

www.beaconbooks.net

ISBN   978-1-912356-97-3 Paperback
ISBN   978-1-912356-98-0 Hardback
ISBN   978-1-912356-99-7 Ebook

Cataloging-in-Publication record for this book is available from the British Library

Cover design by Joas Ahmed Edward

Contents

About the Authors

Nadeem Haque is a researcher and author of numerous interrelated areas that connect with Islam. His work has thus far focused on the following areas: animal rights and environment/ecology; the origins and nature of consciousness; the unification of physics; macroevolution and history/history of science, and extraterrestrial life and the Qur'an.

Haque is the grandson of the late Al-Hafiz B.A. Masri, who is internationally renowned as the pioneer of Animals and Islam theological research and an ardent animal welfare activist. Besides his Islamic research work and interests, Haque is a registered professional engineer (civil/structural and environmental) practising engineering in Ontario, Canada and also has a degree in Economics.

Al-Hafiz Basheer Ahmad Masri (1914–1992) was born in India and graduated with a B.A. (Hons.) degree in Arabic from the Government College, Lahore, of the University of Punjab. He also attended the Faculty of Arabic at al-Azhar University, Cairo. He was fluent in many languages, including English, classical Arabic, Urdu and Hindi, Punjabi, and Kiswahili. (For our non-Muslim readers we should explain that Al-Hafiz denotes one who has memorized the whole of the Qur'an).

During the 20 years he spent in East Africa (1941–1961), he was the Principal (Headmaster) of the largest Secondary School and also held secretarial and presidential posts on social, educational and Islamic organizations among the African, Asian and European communities—including animal welfare. In the 1960s, he was the (Sunni) Imam of Shah Jehan Mosque, in Woking, U.K., which was the central Islamic centre in Europe at the time, and he was the joint-editor of *The Islamic Review* journal. Masri, also wrote the pioneering book *Animals in Islam*; a new edition will be published in 2022.

Mehran Banaei is an environmental activist, naturalist, independent researcher, blogger and a law enforcement officer in Toronto, Canada. He holds a BA in Social Psychology and MA in Social Philosophy from York University. He is the co-author of *From Facts to Values: Certainty, Order, Balance and their Universal Implications*, as well as many published articles on socio-political thought.

Preface

Background

This book's actual origin is in 1988, after Nadeem Haque discussed with Al-Hafiz B.A. Masri, the idea in 1985, to write a book on the environment and Islam. Nadeem had already written his final year undergraduate thesis in Civil Engineering on International Irrigation Systems Management, incorporating environmental considerations in an integral way, for the first time with respect to this technical subject (there were no books combining irrigation systems and environmental considerations at that time). This was at the University of London, King's College. Whilst strolling on The Strand, near the college, he heard Cat Stevens' (aka Yusuf Islam's) environmentalist song being played on a radio nearby: 'Where do the children play?' The tune stayed with him until he reached Masri's home, where he was headed that afternoon, which he used to visit every few weeks. He was already thinking deeply about the environment and the lyrics of this song inspired him to seek the publication of such a book drawing up knowledge from the Qur'an, as such a work focusing on the Qur'an and the environment was non-existent at the time. *Islamic Concern for Animals* had already been published by Masri and *Animals in Islam* was about to be published. Masri had also written by that time on Islam and vivisection. Inspired by Nadeem's suggestion, by 1992, after four years of reviewing the Qur'an and Hadith, Masri had written a simple and short version of this book *Islam and Ecology*, for the Series on *World Religions and Ecology*, published by Cassels, as part of an anthology on the subject, intended for the general public. His chapter, the keynote chapter in the book, was published just before he died in the same year. Haque continued to work on the shorter simple version until after the year 2000, and then, Mehran Banaei, who was the co-author with Haque of *From Facts to Values: Certainty, Order, Balance and their Universal Implications*, published in 1995, by Optagon Publications Ltd., joined him as the third author.

Mehran and Haque continued to work on the manuscript until 2011. From 2011 to 2019 the manuscript lay dormant. By 2019, fortuitously, however, Haque was able to incorporate further intense work in terms of articles that he had written based on his unique and dynamic international lectures from 2013 to 2018, which dealt with animals, ecology and the environment. Haque removed the chapter on environmental facts and figures as they kept getting outdated and on 'climate change'. Concerning 'climate change' and Islam, the authors do have well-defined views but intend to write a separate monograph on the subject.

Focus of Concern

In view of the immense criticality and scale of environmental destruction, this book is an attempt to suggest a global solution for the socio-environmental-ecological crisis, by examining the root causes of the problems related to the natural environment and human interactions—interactions that have become more acute in this century for various reasons. Our advancement in science and technology, while enabling us to harness the forces of nature more efficiently and wisely, has also placed in our hands additional tools with the potential for great destruction, for we have started chopping off the very branches of the tree of life upon which we are sitting. In this book, we shall discuss humankind's adverse affects on the tree of life, consisting of the ecology and biosphere of the Earth, by taking into consideration the human being as part of the system. The word ecology denotes the study of animals and plants as interrelated systems. Unfortunately, we often tend to forget that all living creatures, including human beings, are subject to the very same laws of nature. These laws operate in such a way that the ecosystem of the planet gets adversely affected when even one animal species is destroyed. Each species is a thread in the web-like chain of life, and this chain is only as strong as its weakest link. It will, therefore, be necessary to include a wider examination of animals too, as an overall consideration of the dynamic balances in nature.

Our proper utilization or misutilization of nature, and our attitudes towards other creatures is dependent upon our outlook towards life. Every human being lives according to a set of beliefs and values—and in this sense, everyone follows a particular philosophy or adheres to a religion. However, most people tend to think that religion is meant to give guidance only in 'spiritual matters'. Islam, however, is proclaimed to be a comprehensive code of conduct in this worldly life. It extends moral considerations toward nature in the true sense of universal ethics, where there is neither distinction between the 'spiritual' and the 'physical' well-being of mankind, nor indeed, between 'religion' and 'secularism'. Islam regards the social and ecological systems as a unit. Our material well-being is interdependent upon and interwoven with the well-being of nature and all kinds of life that exist on Earth. In this book we shall be objectively analyzing the veracity of this claim by going directly to the main sources: We shall examine the way the universe functions, the Qur'an and the authentic hadith that do not contradict the Qur'an or facts. The Qur'an is claimed by Muslims to be the direct communication from the originator of the universe to humanity. The hadith are the sayings of Muhammad, who is considered by Muslims to be a human messenger of that Originator of nature.

Environmental protection and animal welfare are the universal responsibilities of all mankind, but Muslims have an added responsibility in this area. The Qur'an has laid down a well-integrated, consistent and all-embracive philosophy of nature which serves as the nucleus for shaping all attitudes and human behaviour. Furthermore, the statements in the Qur'an and hadith on man's interactions with nature, have formed the basis of Islamic Law for the last fourteen centuries. Such information is readily available for those who choose to avail themselves to it. Our intention, in writing this book, is to transcend ideological boundaries in the hope of reaching out to every thinking human being. We feel that our duty ought to be truly universal, in that, we ought not to be concerned only with ourselves and the future generations of our species, but also to do justice to the welfare of the future generations of all other species that inhabit this universe.

The scope of this book, as the title would suggest, is the following: to present the Islamic view on nature and Muslims' proper attitude towards it. Our thesis is that the only way to solve the environmental problem is to have a globally inter-connective outlook, which takes into consideration the Creator (the one and only singular God) of the system. We would also like to demonstrate, in the nine chapters, that the essence and principles of Islam meet the requirements of that globally interconnected system and hence, correspondingly, yield the universal solution to our rising environmental problems.

It has taken 30 years of struggle to have a say on a topic that is so vast, deep and crucial for this planet, and we hope that this book invites critique, discussion, analysis and creativity in helping to solve our multifarious problems.

Nadeem Haque and Mehran Banaei, 2020
The late Al-Hafiz B.A. Masri (1914–1992)
Part of this preface was written in 1992.

Foreword

I feel honoured by the authors to be given this opportunity to write a Foreword to this book. I currently live in Minnesota, USA, where a religious attitude of reverence for all life was embraced by the indigenous gatherer-hunter peoples long before they were supplanted and the land that sustained them taken over by European settlers. Many of the latter believed in manifest destiny embodied in Biblical scriptures that they interpreted as God's will that they should dominate and subdue the untamed wilderness because they had God-given dominion.

One of these indigenous peoples was Lakota Sioux Chief Luther Standing Bear who wrote in his 1933 book *Land of the Spotted Eagle*: 'The white man has come to be the symbol of extinction for things natural to this continent.' Tellingly, he wrote: 'The animal has rights—the right of man's protection—the concept of life and its relations was humanizing and gave the Lakota an abiding love. It filled his being with the joy and mystery of living; it gave him reverence for all life; it made a place for all things in the scheme of existence with equal respect for all.'

Contemporary religions have taken us away from such affinities with other living beings and the natural world, long condemning such views as primitive paganism, and heretical to the divine order of man under God and man over all else. It is surely time to make amends to all indigenous peoples and species and the ecosystems they share and sustain. This book helps us make amends from an Islamic perspective which informs us that: 'Unlike humans, animals always naturally conform to their environment; in this sense they are "Muslims"— who naturally submit to the laws of the Creator.' As the Qur'an advises, we humans must likewise submit to the laws of the Creator through reverence for all life and respect for the sanctity of Creation. This wisdom of Islam is as relevant today as its conception by the Great Prophet. And it is more urgent than ever that Muslims and others fully understand this bioethical gem of insight. It enables us to understand that to be obedient to the will of God is to conform to the laws of nature. All but human life-forms conform naturally, instinctively. The *telos* (life's final purpose) and instrumental and existential values are at the interface of every living being and the environment and ensures the continuance of the Creative process. For a Muslim, this *telos* includes experiencing, through Nature, God's divine conception, love and will, in the phenomenal world, which is the source of our spiritual and ethical sensibility and what the Qur'an calls true innate nature or pattern—*fitrah*.

The ethical principle of reverential respect for all life and our shared environment is the spiritual and bioethical foundation of One Health for the Earth and all beings. Optimal biodiversity is the keystone of One Health—animal, plant, environmental and human—which Albert Schweitzer MD, was one of the first to recognize in his call for reverence for all life, an ethic that contradicts the ethos of consumptive and destructive cultures. Having respect for all beings and things is one of the seven traditional core values of the Lakota Sioux. The contribution of biodiversity to One Health includes clean air, pure water (now via 'bioremediation'), productive soils and ecosystem resilience: And, therefore, to greater climatic, economic and social stability and food security—provided our needs and numbers are more effectively self-restrained rather than by the adverse, anthropogenic consequences of intensifying planetary dysbiosis. For detailed documentation of the degradation of planetary ecosystems and loss of biodiversity, see the 2019 United Nations' IPBES Global Assessment Report on Biodiversity and Ecosystem Services. (https://www.ipbes.net/assessment-reports/eca). The Report finds that around one million animal and plant species are now threatened with extinction, many within decades, more than ever before in human history.

The practice of Islam, as well as of the two other monotheistic traditions, namely, Judaism and Christianity, has become severely corrupted over the centuries. Linear, hierarchical, dualistic and patriarchal modes of perception, cognition and behaviour have eroded the pristine vision of pure and unadulterated monotheism. However, if we take, for example, Jesus' actual teachings, then what G.K. Chesterton once said about Christianity may hold a grain of truth for most other religious traditions: Namely, that 'there is nothing wrong with Christianity except that no one has ever tried it.'

Yet thanks to insightful books like *Ecolibrium: The Sacred Balance in Islam* this great belief system of Islam, its ethics, compassion and respect for all life, is being restored. Such restoration is vital to the material, spiritual and physical well-being of humanity, and to the ecological integrity and future of the Earth community. *Ecolibrium* is an affirming guide and inspiration, highlighting the teachings of Islam from a God and creation-centered perspective. As the authors reveal, these teachings will help humanity realize the source of its pathology and find how best to heal itself. By way of this concern, we discover our cosmic place in Creation, and our *telos* in God-centered awareness is re-alized.

Until I became familiar with the writings and works of Al-Hafiz B. A. Masri, one of the co-authors of the present work, I was uninformed about the true nature and relevance of Islam. I now appreciate the deep spiritual and practical relevance and significance of what it means to be Muslim—true to one's God-given nature, like animals always are, as our teachers and exem-plars of divine purpose and conception. Human nature is embedded in the entire life-cycle of this solar system that has birthed a consciousness that can apprehend the process by which it came to be: its origin and divine purpose. When humans attain such apprehension and live mindfully, conscientiously and gently, they are Muslim, obedient to their true natures, the *ethos* and *telos* the Creator/Sustainer has bestowed upon them.

When we realize that all wounds are ultimately self-inflicted, we begin to heal ourselves by changing our behaviour so that we stop harming others, be they other humans, non-human beings, natural systems, lakes, forests, savan-nas, swamps and the elements themselves, which we have made increasingly toxic. The waste we burn, the rains that fall, the water we drink and irrigate our crops, like the soil and air, are all contaminated with human created chemical and radioactive wastes, even to the extent that we now have pesticides and micro-plastics in the rain. There is much healing to be done and suffering prevented, and this book is a major call and contribution to these reasonable and just ends.

For those people who are troubled by the word God and are atheists and agnostics, they, along with secular materialists, do not see the word and will of God written and manifest in Nature's laws, processes, and myriad life forms. To be blind to this great beauty and mystery is to be blind to God, deaf to the music and rhythms of life, and thus not yet born, according to the Qur'an, into the light of our natural being-in-awareness. But when we are not so God-Blind and disconnected from Nature and from our own nature and cosmic origin in stardust and starlight, we realize that, 'This *ruh* is by my Sustainer's command: you have been granted but a small portion of the body of knowl-edge,' needed to know its exact nature, as stated in the Qur'an.

We do indeed see through the glass darkly, but what we can see is as life affirming as it is life sustaining. When we do not see, we do not seek, and become separate from our origins, from Nature and the divine source, we separate ourselves from God. Such separation brings (sin and evil) into the world because we are no longer in right-relationship and right-mindedness with God and Nature. Sin and evil are moralistic terms that compassion and understanding see as ignorance and tragedy manifest in many ways from the suicidal nihilism of disaffected teens and dedicated terrorists to the collective destruction of ancient forests and plunder, pollution and infestation of planet Earth. Indeed, crimes against Nature—harming indigenous plant and animal species and their ecosystems—are crimes against ourselves as humanity, and since we and all life are inextricably interwoven, those who have concern for life's biospheric ecological entities, end up suffering a grievous moral injury.

This separated, dualistic state may be a natural developmental stage for *Homo-sapiens*, a kind of spiritual adolescence through which we must all pass. But in our contemporary industrial consumer society, this developmental progression has been arrested, creating a collective condition of destructive adolescent-like alienation, arrogance and selfish indifference. The suffering of sentient life and state of the natural world attest to the pathology of the human condition. We may have some god-like powers, but we think we can play God and turn the natural world into a bio-industrially raped and desecrated wasteland to sate our own exclusive materialistic needs, claims and aims. *Ecolibrium* provides us with the insight and wisdom to help us overcome this developmental impasse for the good and glory of all Creation. The choice is ours: suicide, ecocide and deicide—or adoration.

Dr. Michael W. Fox
Author, veterinarian and syndicated columnist
May 22nd 2020

Chapter 1

The Etiology of Devastation

Beginnings and Endings

From the emerging dawn of human civilization, man has always reflected on the origin of the universe. He has marveled at the resplendent beauty and the order manifested in it. Like an earnest child asking inquisitively why the canopy of the sky has the blue hue, mankind, in general, has always sought answers to such seemingly perplexing questions, pertaining to the origins and destiny of the whole of existence. In a state of deep yearning, he stares at a starry sky and wonders: where does this universe start, where does it end? Does it have an actual edge, and if so, what lies beyond it? He wonders: why does nature behave the way it does? As he contemplates, he sees the pattern of birth and death in the animate as well as in the inanimate world. In addition, he knows that his own body is not immune from this scheme either. But, what about this universe as a whole? Did this vast universe have a beginning in time, and if so, would it ever finally come to an end?

With the progression of knowledge in this century, we have been able to gain a better understanding of the immensity of the cosmos. We have become privileged witnesses to the beginning of creation. It is now well-established that countless galaxies are receding from each other at tremendous velocities approaching that of the speed of light. This would mean that once, the entire universe had been compressed to a singular point, where there were absolutely no spatial distances and absolutely no time, for these were originated in a flashing instant when that singular region exploded to form our conceptions of space and time. For beings like us, who have always been engulfed within this space, it is indeed difficult to visually conceptualize that somehow the universe of space and time was brought into existence from oblivious non-existence.

Further knowledge confirmed this astonishingly unique event, when it was detected on a radio-wave antenna that a constant background radiation permeates the whole of space. This background noise was no doubt the primeval remnant of that explosion which took place less than 14 billion years ago, commonly referred to as the Big Bang—the singular moment in the creation of the

1

totality of the universe. But from this explosive expansion it was not disorder which resulted, but rather a deep penetrating order. But unlike any explosion that results in destruction, this explosion resulted in construction of unimaginable precision and scale. Through the course of time, as the universe cooled, many structures arose: galaxies were formed that were comprised of immensely dense clusters of stars, flowing relentlessly across a vast cosmic ocean of space. In time, planets formed and subtle processes came into effect which allowed the emergence of life on Earth. Subsequently, biological life developed due to the vital presence of the water-cycle and similar processes, producing a great diversity of plants and animals. Without water, there would have been no life springing from the dry Earth. Remarkable balances between the living and non-living components of our planet allowed for the preservation, sustenance and continuation of life. The nurturing rays of the sun provided growth for life. Plants started to give off oxygen, which was necessary for all breathing beings, and animals returned carbon-dioxide which was necessary for the plants. Furthermore, each animal arose to be specialized and functioned to maintain the balances in nature. Without these processes life would not have been possible. By reflecting on the inter-penetrations of origins and destiny, we may fully appreciate that so many are the celestial bodies that permeate space that they remain countless within its ever-expanding horizon. Yet even within this cosmological expansion, strewn with innumerable galaxies, we have not, thus far, been able to empirically determine the existence of any other ecosystems and extraterrestrial life.

It was with the advent of these biological processes on Earth, that there came a time when the most complex organism arose: the human being. Yet in essence, a human being, within his own lifetime, issues from the very processes inherent within the vastness of cosmic order. Human life begins with conception, and then, in just nine months, a nearly microscopic fertilized egg-cell is transformed, through a truly remarkable process into a human infant, possessing heart, brain, eyes, muscles, lungs, and all the biological systems needed for survival outside the mother's womb. It is indeed amazing to envisage that in the combination of such a tiny, minuscule part of a drop of male semen and a female egg there exist specific parts responsible for the development of our complex body, mind and social being. In just a few years after birth, this newborn baby has grown into a human being well capable of learning a multitude of languages, of familiarizing himself with his environment, and has the

2

capacity to be creative, learning to interact with others of his own kind and other species.

As this human being is maturing and aging, the process of intellectual development and questioning continues actively, and as a sense-making creature he ponders on his origins and about his place in the universe. He becomes aware of the fact that the omnipresent face of death is an inescapable consequence of life. He also becomes aware of the rapidity with which the dead body deteriorates, when in time, it will be turned into nothing but a pile of rotting bones, and then face a further reduction from bones to dust—dust to dust ... under the dust to lie! This appears to be our common heritage and unavoidably our common destiny, the transition of man from birth to death, the journey of mankind from noble extraction to a hopefully noble extinction. He came from nothing and, finally, will merge back into nothingness, for in nature, just as things began, so too will they end. He knows that he is residing on this Earth for only a short while and once he is departed, shall return no more. Thus, he curiously looks up at the starlit sky, seeking to know if there is anything beyond his death.

Just as our sun had its own birth billions of years ago, so too is it eventually destined to extinguish itself into a shrunken, collapsed dead star and with it our Earth will be rendered devoid of life, where once it had been so profuse. Life on Earth is crucially dependent on the sun; indeed, had the Earth's orbit been even slightly offset in either direction, water and the resulting forms of life would not have emerged. Yet, our sun is only one tiny speck of light amidst an ordered scattering of billions upon billions of objects distributed throughout the vast reaches of space in time, which are all experiencing the same patterns and throes of birth and death in the cosmos.

But will the universe, which had its birth with the emergence of space and time, also have its fate sealed with the end of space and time? It is now theorized that depending on the density of the universe, it will either fade away into an infinite void as the stars disintegrate into a sea of obsolete radiation, or conversely, it will collapse into a Big Crunch as it reaches the limits of its expansion; notwithstanding these, there may yet be another sudden mode for the collapse of the universe currently beyond our ken. In the Big Crunch, the overwhelming density of matter and energy, or some other mechanism, would have the effect of contracting the universe back into one singular point with a very minuscule finite dimension, due to immense gravitational forces.

Nevertheless, whatever the outcome is, it appears certain that the universe will end up either in the emptiness of space, where time will not be significant, or in the nothingness of absolutely not existing (except as a compressed region), just as it was in the beginning. This is not obscure fantasy nor is it far-fetched science-fiction. It is derived from facts and scientific knowledge, even though it is not visually conceptualizable that space and time will simply vanish into the Nothingness of Nowhere.

We have seen that this universe has originated from the non-existence of 'space' and 'time'. The emergence of life into the intelligent consciousness of man has been facilitated and is dependent on the unfolding of time by precisely arranged, intelligently structured laws of nature. We have also seen that the universe will eventually devolve into a realm of nothingness. But why did it originate in the first place? And then why should it disappear again? From nothing to something and then from something to nothing with no meaningful purpose and no purposeful end? Is this a cosmic joke? Is this all there is?

Meaningless or Purposeful Direction?

The answer to this deep question of meaning and purpose has an impact on everything else in life, both individually and collectively. If one assumes that there is purpose then one's actions will be different than if one assumes that no purpose exists. We therefore ought to reflect as to whether there really is a purpose behind the Big Bang, and ask such questions as what role we ought to play, if any, in the realm that has evolved afterwards? Did nature evolve from the Big Bang merely for subservience to Man?

Indeed, as we engage in our mundane activities, such questions of origin and purpose persist deeply in the recesses of our psyche. Yet the tragically brute fact is that we generally tend to ignore the pursuit of such fundamental questions. If perchance we do, they often times end up being mis-answered. Due to our passion-driven blindness towards sincerely seeking out true answers, we fail to understand the origin, and purpose of existence and, as a result, dispassionately end up destroying both natural systems and ourselves. Many human beings have erroneously assumed that the whole panoply of creation that multifurcated from the Big Bang, was produced by sheer randomness instead of being created by incalculably intelligent non-randomness. We feel that since we have been cast onto the shores of a fortuitously hospitable planet—itself sprouting by chance from the sea of space and time—we simply ought to resign ourselves into making the best of our slot in the grand cosmic roulette. From the tottering academic fortresses spinning labyrinths of aimless vision, we are told to believe that our whole purpose, if any, after billions of years of program-like cosmic evolution, is to merely chase our own shadows on a spinning bluish dot, that calculatingly floats in the abyss of deep space. We are told by some atheists and sceptics that there cannot be answers to the fundamental questions of existence. However, we seem to ignore the stark fact that this unsubstantiated conclusion is itself an answer, and thus a blatant contradiction. We have opted for selective amnesia, from a remembrance of things past, of humble beginnings, such as our origin from recyclable stardust and the primeval elements and compounds therein; indeed, we have forgotten the meaning of true sublimity, no longer walking humbly on the dust of the Earth, our former and future physical state.

Such it is that, being decapitated from our cosmic roots, we have managed to cocoon ourselves in an utterly purposeless vision. In this vision, we perceive our fractured selves as being at the centre of the expanding universe. Trying to compensate for the concomitant alienation we feel in this cosmos, we think that *we* are all that matters, since we have arrogantly appointed ourselves as the chosen species. As unaccountable executive functionaries in an 'accidental universe', we act as if the plenitude of nature exists merely for the capricious whims and false securities of our insatiable consumption and plundering appetites. Indeed, we have rendered ourselves obtuse to the harmonious polyphony of nature, and what it perennially points to. Yes, we can certainly take pride in the fact that we have become Masters—but Masters of what? Masters of our own fate and that of the environment, and slaves of the desires that nurture such an invidious fate!

To avoid such an invidious fate, we need to be cognizant of the fact that the proper utilisability of the resources of nature depends upon our understanding the overall purpose and scheme of things, that is, of being cognizant of where everything naturally fits in nature and the source of that purpose. However, before this is discussed at length, in Chapter 2, we shall firstly review man's dismal report card on interactions with nature and the damage that has and is being wrought and after this, we shall examine the underlying ideological reasons for the abuse of nature.

The Judeo-Christian Legacy

By examining the origin of Western thoughts and attitudes towards the natural world, we notice the adverse influence of the Judeo-Christian tradition, emanating directly from various selective passages in the Bible. These passages convey a concatenation of callously domineering ideas, such as the *ipso facto* dominion of man over the entirety of creation. Here, domination is itself a God-given gift to man—the chosen species. From this slanted view of the misinterpreted Christian perspective, man considered himself as the master of the universe, created by God Almighty to wield the sceptre over the world. In the book of Genesis, we are told:

> And God said, Let us make man in our image, after our likeness: and let them have dominion over the fish of the sea, and over the fowl of the air, and over the cattle, and over all the Earth...[1]

Indeed, one of the major sources responsible for this environmental nightmare emanates from the Old Testament, a view which is proclaimed bluntly, even by reflective thinkers who emanate from Christianity itself, to have problematic passages. For instance, Prince Charles, who has been well-known for his concern for the environment, in the preface to the book, *Save the Earth*, succinctly expresses the implications of domination on the behaviour of those who have consciously or unconsciously been affected by such traditions:

> In Western terms, one of the underlying factors which may have contributed (by being taken literally) to the desire to dominate nature, rather than live in harmony with it on a sustainable basis, is to be found in the book of Genesis where it records that, 'God said unto man, be fruitful and multiply, and replenish the Earth and subdue it: and have dominion over the fish and sea and over the fowl of the air and over every living thing that moveth upon the Earth.' To me, that Old Testament has provided Western man, accompanied by his Judeo-Christian heritage, with an overbearing and domineering attitude towards God's creation. It may not have been a conscious realization, but it has contributed, nevertheless, to a feeling that the world is somehow entirely man's to dispose of—as income, rather than a capital asset which needs husbanding.[2]

1. Genesis 1:26.
2. HRH The Prince of Wales in Porritt, Jonathon. (1991), *Save the Earth*, p. iii.

These Biblical passages came to shape an ontological chain of hierarchy. Starting from the bottom, with inanimate objects like rocks, the chain then ascends to plants, animals, man, angels, ending with 'God'. According to this continuum, an animal is something just more than a plant, since it possesses some extra capacities and abilities which do go above and beyond merely vegetative functions. Although, in this scheme, animals are given some intelligence, this intelligence is not always viewed as something positive. For example, early Christians believed that some animals like snakes, bats, owls, black cats, crow and wolves possessed evil spirits or demonic powers, which had to be obliterated. For religious reasons, absurd characteristics and values of good or evil were attributed to animals. It may seem strange and ridiculous to us today, but in medieval times, in Europe, animals were actually put on trial by some members of the Church hierarchy and made to suffer horrible deaths when found supposedly guilty. There is a morbid, yet eye-opening account, of this insanely justified practice in Jeremy Rifkin's book, *Biosphere Politics*—during the Medieval times in Europe:

> During the Inquisition, church leaders tortured and burned to death nearly three quarters of a million people for witchcraft. In many of the cases, bestiality was alleged to have occurred.[3]

> Men and women, along with their cows, sows and donkeys, were regularly tried and burned at the stake for bestiality. ... Many times older women would be convicted of bestiality and burned as witches simply because they lived alone with only a pet animal to keep them company.[4]

A great many cats were also burned with the 'witches'. Indeed, so many were liquidated in this way, that the rats must have had a field day, because of a decline in feline density during the period when the plague swept through Europe, decimating the population.[5]

The unworthiness of the animal kingdom is also echoed in some verses of the New Testament. For instance, in the Gospel according to Mark, Jesus supposedly annihilated 2,000 higher mammals in order to save one human

3. Rifkin, Jeremy. (1991), *Biosphere Politics: A New Consciousness for a New Century*, p. 200.
4. Ibid. p. 201.
5. The plague or the 'Black Death' as it became known, swept across Europe reaching England by 1348. In effect, at least a third of the population of Europe was decimated. It has, however, become a controversial issue as to whether this was some disease other than plague caused by flea-infected rats, due to the considerations of the unique symptoms exhibited that are unlike the pneumonic plague postulated.

being from affliction.[6] It is unlikely that Jesus—supposedly a divine role-model—could have committed such a senseless and brutal act of animal-cleansing, or animal-genocide; however, in this particular Christian scripture, such behaviour is indeed attributed to him. It is most regrettable that the general outlook that developed in European civilization was not along the lines of several passages in the Bible that are eco-sensitive and caring.[7] Animal rights researcher and advocate Lisa Kemmerer has asserted that Christianity through Jesus, as an exemplar, emphasized love and that this love was universal and not limited to love for human beings alone, but to all entities; such researchers see the narrow domineering outlook held by many Christians in the past and present as nothing but a neglect and distortion of the true message of Jesus Christ.[8] Is it any wonder then why the state of affairs has descended into such a pit of seeming hopelessness for animals and the rest of nature, with a neglect of such a universal outlook?

Such an incredulous view of nature caused a great deal of alienation between man and the animal kingdom. The late Thomas Berry, a Canadian eco-theologian, lamented that:

> While none of our Christian beliefs individually is adequate as an explanation of the alienation we experience in our natural setting, they do in their totality provide a basis for understanding how so much planetary destruction has been possible in our Western tradition. We are radically oriented away from the natural world. It has no rights; it exists for human utility, even if for spiritual utility.[9]

Frederick Ferre, in his essay, 'Theodicy and the Status of Animals', states that the Judeo-Christian perspective towards animals is problematic in the sense that there are inherent internal contradictions regarding the attributes of a 'Creator-God of perfect goodness' and the epistemology or the lack of it with respect to animals.[10] It was only after the environmental movement of the latter half of the twentieth century, that a somewhat awakened public opinion

---

6. Mark 5:1–2,5–9,11–13.

7. See, for example: Psalms 8 and Psalms 104; Isaiah 24:5.

8. Kemmerer, Lisa. (2018), 'Africa, animals, and the Almighty: A Christian call to the cause of animal liberation', *Africa and her animals*, Ed. Rainer Ebert and Anteneh Roba, pp. 85–95. See also Kemmerer, Lisa, (2012), *Animals and World Religions*, p. 205–223.

9. Berry, Thomas. (1990), *The Dream of the Earth*, p. 80.

10. Ferre, Frederick. (1991), 'Theodicy and the Status of Animals', *Contemporary Classics in Philosophy of Religion*.

became reticent towards the prevailing Judeo-Christian view. We deal with theodicy in Chapter 6, in great detail.

Mysticism and Occultism

Mysticism in its broadest definition pertains to ascribing both existence and powers to objects, phenomena and/or entities without establishing even elementary causal connections. As the name itself would suggest, the connections are mysterious and not subject to rational comprehension. In addition, there is an inconsistency either in the basic precepts and/or with the evidence(s) that exist in nature and history. In this section, some mystical ideas that have proven harmful to nature and man will be discussed.

During the Dark Ages, exorcism was in wide practice throughout Europe. For example, a dose of exorcism was believed to cure many a dubious ailment. The practice of senselessly killing animals for mystical rituals was widely prevalent. Nature was not recognized as a natural system of cause and effect, functions and structure, but was looked upon in purely symbolic terms, to explain, justify and represent a motley number of irrational mystical belief systems.

After the Renaissance, the swing of the pendulum towards dominance had the effect of profoundly disenchanting many individuals who were trying to get away from the dogma of exorcism and the Judeo-Christian tradition. In search for a desperate remedy, new and alluring ideas were emerging, which, in reality, were no better than their predecessors. One of such substitutes was occultism. In fact, since then, in the West, there has been an inordinate trend towards Eastern mysticism and various other syncretistic forms of mysticism, evolved as a form of backlash, particularly against the dogma of the entrenched Judo-Christian perspective on nature. There are some adherents of the New Age movement, for instance, who have gone to the opposite extreme, where they espouse the belief that man is subservient to nature. Nature is animalistically sacred and must be 'loved'. Some of them actually devolved into worshipping nature or certain phenomena in it, whereas others, like the mystics of Eastern mysticism, started worshiping specific animals. Cows and rats, for instance, are worshiped by some Hindu groups. However, giving these species royal treatment has caused their overpopulation and the concomitant spread of deadly diseases in various parts of India. In a region atrociously suffering from the pangs of poverty, where serious food shortages are the norm, the sewer rat—a notorious scavenger—seems to enjoy a better status than humans.

9

While by virtue of supposed divine rights, such overpopulated rats are left to rummage with open access to limited food supplies, the destitute masses miserably scrounge for food in garbage dumps. These are indeed clear cases of two species erroneously inter-placed, with serious consequences to the stability of a fragile ecosystem. The fact that some animals are highly elevated to the point that they are depicted as deities, whereas others are portrayed as devils incarnate, is, in itself, an extreme form of irrationality with adverse environmental consequences. Indeed, mysticism is plagued with such troublesome irrationalities, which adversely affect society and the environment, directly or indirectly.

Out of all the Western environmental thinkers and activists, Murray Bookchin seems to be one of the very few who have noted the fallacious aspects of mysticism in connection with socio-environmental reform. He reflects upon his own society and notes that:

> We [in the West] thereupon find ourselves in something of a quandary. It is obvious that we cannot do without many technologies (not even the technologically sophisticated binoculars with which we watch birds or whales or cameras with which we photograph them); nor can we do without conventional reason in our everyday transactions. We thus tend to live in a rather schizophrenic way: we are obliged in the ordinary course of life to use the much-despised tenets of conventional reason in order to survive, and then take refuge in an irrational, mystical, or religious private world to support our moral and spiritual beliefs. Often, this withdrawal yields a state of social quietism that is more dreamlike than real, more passive than active, preoccupied more with personal change than with social change, and concerned with the symptoms of our powerless, alienated lives more than with their root causes.[11]

Although there are some mystics, such as the followers of the New Age movement, who respect the environment, many of them being commendably ardent and dynamic activists, there is an Achilles' Heel that delimits and eviscerates the effectiveness of their sincere activism. Their lack of realization that the unique belief in one Creator envisages a rational system that can transform society, consequentially fosters personal irrational doctrines, that may simply be of the 'touchy-feely' kind, that cannot affect a global systems' change in the foundations of society. In contrast, those who are truly and seriously conscious

11. Bookchin, Murray. (1990), *The Philosophy of Social Ecology: Essays on Dialectical Naturalism*, p. 19.

of the Creator, will act both locally and globally and try to affect a systems change.

Secular Views on Nature and the Animal Kingdom

The cross-cultural and various philosophical views regarding the designation of animals as mere machines and automata, made either by God or evolution, implied that only human beings have a soul and consciousness. Non-animal nature, such as trees, were not considered as sentient and living beings. Man lives according to what he is convinced of, and the belief that animals are machines legitimizes his mastery and domination over the animal kingdom, and they are seen merely as man's mechanical possessions.

One of the most influential philosophers of the Western World who pushed the idea of the mindlessness of animals, was René Descartes. In fact, in Christendom, the ontological chain of hierarchy was unchallenged up until the 17th century, when Descartes attacked the continuum by bringing dualism into the picture. In his *Discourse on Method*, Descartes sharply separated body and soul. He gave the soul complete autonomy, in that he believed that thinking was only the property of the soul. He denied the soul to animals. Unlike an animal, it was only the human body which possessed an immaterial and rational soul. Descartes argued that an animal does not possess sufficient intelligence to be classified as a 'moral agent', for animals lack the faculty of speech, which, for him, was the criterion for intelligence. Therefore, he believed that they could not be included in the inner sphere of morality. He simply viewed animals as automata or non-thinking biological machines, without any volition and totally lacking conscious perception. Descartes believed that animals were able to sustain themselves in their daily affairs merely by reflex actions and by being responsive to stimuli. He even went as far as arguing that since animals do not possess any soul, they cannot, therefore, feel even the sensation of pain, the implication of which is that they cannot suffer.

Descartes' view of a mechanical Nature paved the lane of cruelty towards animals in the West, particularly in sports hunting and in the scientific domain, where the idea of animal rights became the subject of sarcasm. Animals were being sacrificed in the most inhumane ways for the good of humanity, all in the name of sports, entertainment, scientific experimentation and the expansion of knowledge. The irony is that such cruelties were promoted and perpetuated, not by the average layman, but by high-browed spiffy aristocrats of scholastic institutions. The result was that the belief that animals do not feel pain became widely accepted. In research institutions, scientists started to compete with each other in devising ever-new means of torture and the exploitation of helpless and innocent creatures—all in the name of scientific research and experimentation. Francis Bacon, a prominent British scientist believed that the purpose of science was to control nature, that is to force nature to serve humanity. The domination of the scientific community over nature and its animal kingdom was no better than the attitude fostered by mainstream Christianity of the time. This can be seen in the 19th century French physician Claude Bernard's comment in support of vivisection:

> Another question presents itself. Have we the right to make experiments on animals and vivisect them? As for me, I think we have this right, wholly and absolutely. It would be strange indeed if we recognized man's right to make use of animals in every walk of life, for domestic service, for food, and then forbade him to make use of them for his own instruction in one of the sciences most useful to humanity.[12]

The sad fact is that for centuries, classical and modern philosophers, scholars, naturalists and scientists had a low opinion of animals. To them, animals were, and to many still are, mere commodities, a means to a human end, having no intrinsic value.

Gradually, the West started to emancipate itself from irrational teachings of the Church, steeped in a mystical mindset, towards new ways of thinking. After Descartes, a large collection of other ideologies shaped the foundation of secular humanism, where the idea was to allow individuals and parliamentary governments to pursue their various goals unimpeded. In this respect, one of the acclaimed views shaping neoteric thoughts is utilitarianism. Utilitarianism is an ethical doctrine, which predominantly emphasizes that the happiness and the needs of the majority always outweigh the happiness and the needs of a smaller group. Accordingly, right and wrong is purely determined by the consequences of acts which bring about the best total outcome for everyone (the majority) affected. Thus, the welfare of a smaller group can be sacrificed for the prosperity of the majority. This, of course, means that nature can be exploited, if it brings benefits to the majority, which is, of course, the human majority.

Utilitarians candidly acknowledge that the interests of animals are unimportant when compared to human interests. Indubitably, animals ought to be

12. Bernard, Claude. (1957), *An Introduction to the Study of Experimental Medicine*, p. 102.

treated with kindness, but not necessarily with justice. For example, they believe the harm done to animals in pursuit of scientific knowledge, is perfectly justifiable, if, and only if, the benefit of aggregated gains for all those affected by the outcome supersedes the pain of animals involved. Destruction of the rainforest with all its human and non-human habitants is well justified, if it improves the state of the economy of some major countries. That is to say, in such contexts, the end will always justify the means. One of the consequences of such self-centered perspective on the environment, as coined by Peter Singer, is 'speciesism'. Singer emphasizes this notion repeatedly: that man of the rainforest with all its human and non-human habitants is well justified, if it improves the state of the economy of some major countries. That is to say, in such contexts, the end will always justify the means. One of the consequences of such a self-centered perspective on the environment, as coined by Peter Singer, is 'speciesism'. Singer emphasizes this notion repeatedly: That man sees himself as a special species, with the right of unfettered domination over other species, a view analogous to racism and sexism—the veritable domination of one over another. Never can the interests of other species of flora and fauna be equated with the interests of humanity. In fact, the philosopher Immanuel Kant stated blatantly:

> But so far as animals are concerned, we have no direct duties. Animals are not self-conscious, and are there merely as a means to an end. The end is man... Our duties towards animals are merely indirect duties towards humanity.[13]

According to Kant, it is due to our duties towards humanity that we should not treat animals with cruelty, since those who treat animals with cruelty, will eventually devolve into cruelly treating humans at some point. From the Kantian ethical perspective, the underlying assumption is that man is the sole object of moral concern. Other species have no intrinsic value and thereby have no rights to life. Respecting the non-human natural world for its own sake is not a good enough reason—always and only human interest is included within the scope of the majority.

In the debate of what has rights and intrinsic value and what does not, Francis Herbert Bradley, another European thinker, rejected animal rights because, he claimed, animals do not possess sufficient intelligence. The lack of ability to distinguish between ideas and perceived reality is an indication

13. Kant, Immanuel. (1963), *Lecture on Ethics*, p. 239.

which was used as the criterion to dismiss all animals as un-intelligent be-ings, and that which lacks intelligence cannot be considered a moral agent. Subsequently, that which cannot be a moral agent cannot possess any inherent rights. Jeremy Bentham, a trained lawyer, tried to resolve this unsettled issue by bringing the animal kingdom into the moral fold through a legal channel. As a staunch positivist, he tried to protect animals by the virtue of legislation and parliamentary laws. Bentham believed that only the institution of legal rights can safeguard nature. For example, parliament can protect animals from vivi-section, sports hunting and other forms of cruelty. For him the issue was not whether animals can talk, think, reason or be self-conscious or moral agents, but rather the issue is: Can they suffer? Can they feel pain? In the case of cruel treatment, they naturally do suffer, and must therefore be protected by legal law. However, Bentham certainly failed to establish what would be the basis of any legal law, universally acceptable by all. What universal guidelines, if any, ought to be used in the House of Commons' decision-making? For instance, if the criteria becomes pain and suffering, does this mean that that which does not suffer cannot possibly possess any intrinsic value? Further, as is evident, there have always been numerous national and international conflicts in the legal domain over who has the rights over certain natural resources. When two opposite legal laws clash, conflicts begin and rise. In fact, by putting the par-liament in the position to wield absolute authority and full decision-making capabilities, Bentham and his proponents made themselves vulnerable to criticisms coming from value relativists. These relativists argue that determin-ing right and wrong arises out of the self-interests of the society to which it serves its purpose and seems useful. Thus, any environmental protection laws are subjective and are merely designed to serve those who construct them. Furthermore, if animals do not have inherent rights, and the protection of the entirety of nature is dependent solely upon the mercy of the voters, their decision could also easily be reversed and the given protection could easily be taken away. In fact, so far, what many parliamentary governments have done is to pass legislation to exploit nature.

The unwanton deforestation around the globe, the captivity of animals in zoos, commercial crocodile farming, seal hunting and slaughtering of other marine mammals are not illegal activities in many Western countries. These policies are governmentally concocted, and serve as proposed solutions, by elected politicians, for high levels of unemployment and poverty. Thus,

Bentham's proposition was not much of a solution; rather it served as a participant in fomenting the degradation of nature, despite noble intentions.

Emergence of Relativistic Pluralism

In addition to particular notions on rights, our atrophied view of nature was influenced by much wider currents of thought. Indeed, European civilization as a whole was deflected away from a properly conceivable approach towards nature, because of an overreaction of those brought up in Judeo-Christian traditions, against their respective religious institutions, comprised of self-authorized clergies, and the intransigent irrationality of mystical thoughts. In search for a better system, the shift towards secularism coalesced from multiple philosophical, sociological and scientific angles. From the scientific perspective, the notion of haphazard evolution by natural selection was used to sway people away from calculated creation or even evolutionary creation, by those who were disgruntled with the Church for one reason or another, particularly by its authoritarian and elitist hand against challenges to its basic doctrines arising from within Christian society itself, and possessed a counter power agenda through shaping views for humankind. Yet with this counter-reaction, what subsequently became the dominant view was a mechanical universe governed by randomness and luck, having no beginning and end—a view having no author of existence for the seemingly infinite celestial library. The sociological attitudes of competitiveness, domination, survival of the fittest, so prevalent in such societies, were grafted onto a particular theory of evolution, based on randomness and chance underlying natural selection, which then enshrined and recursively justified the very same notions as its central driving force in the economy, sociology and philosophy. Since the 19th century, this view, which is termed *relativism* has been gaining ascendancy, where even the notions of relativity (in physics) and quantum mechanics (observation connected issues) have been misutilised or misunderstood to justify the notion of the relativity of truth and the unobtainability of certainty in human knowledge. Cultural relativists claim that there is no such thing as objectivity; everything is subjective, including values, truth and knowledge. The notion of justice and its foundation are all relative and circumstantial. Right and wrong are just a matter of opinion, depending on one's perspective and interests. 'Do as you like, truth is in the eye of the beholder', has become the vacuous motto of the era. Such an attractive view appealed to easy-going individuals and societies. This was ammunition for the corporate agenda, and for the socio-economic and environmental policies of governments, who were already well predisposed to ravage the Earth's natural resources. If right or wrong is the subject of a belief system, we could have a belief system which sees it fit to wreck the planet and terminate all criticisms from the outside by treating them just as another existing viewpoint, or model. Under the banner of pluralism all views are tolerated and treated with equal validity and respect, a condition which relativism and perspectivism thrives on. Under such circumstances, by what principle, can bullfighting, the rodeo and sports-hunting be criticized and banned, when nothing has any *absolute* foundation? How can any rational individual prove that his or her opinion is based on solid facts, as opposed to that of his or her opponents, which is based on myth, theory or unfounded speculation?[14] Relativistic pluralism has created a mental and legal ambivalence by holding that two opposing views can both be justified.

Although pluralism does have valuable aspects, it is its relativistic nature which has prepared us to tolerate every hue of cry of sheer nonsense; it has tragically accustomed us to a prolonged flight of insanity without any seatbelts or landing strip. Relativism has prepared us to ignore the connections between the cause and effect, and natural laws: indeed, the very foundation upon which nature itself is functioning. The end result of this obdurate blindness is, for instance: the depletion of the ozone layer, acid rain, poaching, clear-cut logging, nuclear and toxic dumping, the destruction of human and non-human habitats and even that which we do not know we are damaging, due to the lack of knowledge.

Corporate Colonialists

Another major contributing factor to the destruction of nature is that of unfettered radical capitalism and the encroaching attitude of transnational corporations. This is a system in which the goal is transfixed on profit maximization and cost minimization; a prime objective which must be achieved by any means necessary.

Such an ideological system suffers from ill-defined concepts of growth, development, progress, modernization and value. If you get these basics wrong, you then get everything else wrong. Under this system, profit is obtained by economic growth. The survival of capitalism depends upon ongoing economic

14. This is all dealt with and resolved in *From Facts to Values: Certainty, Order, Balance and their Universal Implications*. (Refer to the Bibliography).

growth and the promotion of materialism. A common strategy to achieve and maintain a continuous growth, is to create more wants and artificial desires, which consequently lead to higher consumption and market opportunities. Sandage and Fryburger acknowledge this strategy:

> Modern society emphasizes the right of every person to be employed. To achieve this, high-level consumption is essential… This will require persuasion. This is the function of advertising.[15]

Mokhiber and Weissman add:

> … the credit card industry sends out 2.5 billion solicitations each year; credit card advertisements urge consumers, simply, to spend; and the consumer culture encourages extravagant purchases and constantly upgrades the measure of what is an 'essential' versus a 'convenience.'[16]

At first glance this strategy may seem innocuous to many; however, a few major problems insidiously lurk behind this nefarious approach, waiting to pounce upon the unwary and embark upon a course of strangulation—this is just a more sophisticated version of the Little Red Riding Hood story!

The first is the way in which consumption and market opportunities are pursued, and how their outcomes on ecology are mishandled. For instance, to consume more, means inevitably to produce more; to produce more, we must have access to more resources. At the same time, the increased consumption has a net effect on waste production. Pollution of various kinds is the residual by-product of a production process. A positive correlation always lurks near at hand; while resources are being depleted, just as consumption increases, waste by-product also increase. The increase in waste by-products and its continuous release into the environment, in turn, aggravates the threat to the natural environment and causes its further deterioration. In this vicious cycle, the environment pays the ultimate price for our soaring consumption. The only cycle we have here is the cycle of mounting contamination.

Of course, there is really nothing wrong with rapid production, consumption and making profits, so long as the resources are used efficiently and justly, and so long as developmental projects are maintained at sustainable level, and waste outgrowth is minimized and managed properly. However, with radical capitalism that is not the case at all, due to erroneous goals, mixed-up

15. Sandage, Charles and Fryburger, V. (1960), *The Role of Advertising*, p. 149.
16. Mokhiber, Russell and Weissman, Robert. (1999), *Corporate Predators: The Hunt for Mega-Profits and the Attack on Democracy*, p. 33.

priorities, devious approaches, and illusory concepts of growth and development. The number one priority is to maximize the profit at a minimum cost. Corporate policies are profit-motivated not need-oriented. The reason for the multinational corporations' constant vehement opposition to the development of any rational operational and environmental policies is based on the frantic fear of the fact that by implementing such policies, their profits would be curtailed. For instance, consider the General Motors case: Back in 1949, GM was convicted of conspiracy to destroy America's mass transit systems by purchasing and dismantling electrical transit systems in more than 45 major U.S. cities. 'A jury convicted GM, Standard Oil of California, Firestone, and E. Roy Fitzgerald, among others, for criminally conspiring to replace electric transportation with gas-and diesel-powered buses and to monopolize the sale of buses and related products to transportation companies throughout the country.'[17] Or consider the notorious case of General Electric involving the discharge of toxins. For years GE was dumping PCB straight into the Hudson River from two of its plants, while this river is used as the main source of water supply for New Yorkers.[18] GE is certainly not alone in polluting water, air and land as most industries are in habit of engaging in this ongoing fatally hazardous practice and do their best to conceal their hazardous activities. Many transnational corporations exert their power on the print media in order to circumvent exposure to their detrimental environmental policies. For example, in the case of a renowned environmental magazine—*The Ecologist*—it became clear that fearing legal action from Monsanto, the printer for this magazine, Penwells, in 1998, shredded 14,000 copies of a special issue by this highly renowned publication, criticizing the corporation; it was then given to a different printer to publish the issue! Indeed, as has been pointed out by Mokhiber and Russell:

> The Monsanto issue carries tough attacks on the St. Louis-based biotech giant, including reviews of its links to major corporate disasters involving Agent Orange, polychlorinated biphenyls (PCBs), genetically engineered bovine growth hormone (rBGH), Round-Up herbicide, and the terminator seed. (Get this: When you plant this seed, you get a plant and sterile seeds. That way, farmers cannot save the seed for the

17. Mokhiber, Russell. (1988), *Corporate Crime and Violence: Big Business Power and the Abuse of the Public Trust*, p. 227.
18. Ibid. pp. 363–364.

next planting season—they have to go back to Monsanto to buy more seed).[19]

The corporate polluters are surely aware that the honest way of doing business, including the preventative approach, clean-up programs, or a sound waste management are not cost-free. Implementing green policies affects their profit margin—which is the sole bottom line. One common adopted solution is to move the polluting industry to the 'third world' countries of the southern hemisphere, where there are either no environmental regulations, or if there are any, they are lax and subject to manipulation and corruption. For instance, the World Bank encourages more migration of dirty industry to the south. Former Deputy Prime Minister of Canada, writer and activist, Paul Hellyer, recently deceased, tried to knock some sense into Canadians and others, by quoting Laurence Summers who was the World Bank chief economist and responsible for the 1992 *World Development Report*, the report which was de-voted to the economics of the environment. Summers justified such migration on three grounds, when a new type of 'chips' had been put on the market:

> Firstly, since wages are low in the Third World, economic costs of pollution arising from increased illness and death are lowest in the poorest countries... Secondly, since in large parts of the Third World, pollution is still low, it makes economic sense to introduce pollution... Finally, since the poor are poor, they cannot possibly worry about environmental problems. The concerns over an agent that causes a one-in-a million change in the odds of prostate cancer is obviously going to be much higher in a country where people survive to get prostate cancer than in a country where under five-years old mortality is 200 per thousand.[20]

Summers, blinded by profits, ignores the basics of environmental studies, which is that environmental degradation knows no man-made borders. As is evident, to avoid the problem, noble and critical considerations are not on the corporate agenda, unless they happen to be imposed and rigorously enforced by some governmental rules or international regulations. It is very seldom that a corporation voluntarily adopts a 3Rs approach or reduces pollutive emis-sions for Earth's sake; this happens only when recycling or when the use of

19. Mokhiber, Russell and Weissman, Robert. (1999), *Corporate Predators: The Hunt for Mega-Profits and the Attack on Democracy*, p. 105.
20. Hellyer, Paul. (1999), *Stop: Think*, p. 44–45.

alternative energy, for instance, becomes profitable. Saving the planet for its own sake is not a good enough reason.[21]

Progress or prosperity is confused with globalization, free market expansion, technological advancement, and is measured by social rank, financial power and the ability to freely produce and consume more deluxe goods. This, of course runs head-on into the parameters of what constitutes a healthy society. It causes not only environmental deterioration, but also social discontentment and inter-resentment within the various strata of society. Nancy Snow argues that prosperity in essence has become: 'the condition by which corporations can function free of any government regulation of their bottom line, while relying on government intervention in form of tax breaks, corporate welfare, and related business assistance'.[22] Globalization should not mean that we ought to live in a boundless global system of free market economy solely defined by the Western corporations but rather it should mean that we ought to live in a free global society where our economic logic includes indiscriminatory well-being for both human and non-human members. Instead of saying that corporate globalization is occurring at a rapid pace nowadays, perhaps a better word to use would be rampant *corporatization* of the planet.

Development in a radically capitalistic landscape is tantamount to the destruction of splendid and purposeful natural habitats, by a replacement of concrete jungles, highways or dams. Yet it is totally missed that, that which is destroyed, is a thing whose existence has been essential to our existence, and was already well developed, indeed far more advanced and beyond what the best human technology could ever produce or muster. Indeed, that which exhausts, pollutes, destabilizes, disembodies, depletes, distorts, creates ugliness and undermines the life-supporting systems of a marvelously self-sufficient planet, is inimical to any development worthy of the name, let alone 'sustainable development'. How can that which has destructive consequences—which destroys the development of life—be deemed 'sustainable development'? Even from a business point of view, how could a project be considered a worthwhile development, when its long-term losses distinctly outweigh its short-term petty gains?

Trying to establish a proper notion of value in a society which is highly influenced by relativism, serves no purpose, since values do not then depend

21. Romm, Joseph J. (1999), *Cool Companies: How the Best Businesses Boost Profit and Productivity by Cutting Greenhouse Gas Emission.*
22. Snow, Nancy. (1998), *Propaganda: Selling American Culture to the World*, p. 38.

on the absoluteness of truth. Everything is judged to be relative. The end result of this consideration is that value is measured by problematic notions. Under capitalism, value is most often measured by money, which is neither a true indicator of real value nor of the well-being of society and the state of the economy. In a world plagued with rampant relativism, the value relativists of the corporate world behave like absolutists, where absolute value must always be measured by the almighty Dollar, oblivious to eco-sensitive schemes.

Growth is often perceived by those using their critical faculties, as wastefulness and extravagancy, for spoiled avid consumers, who consume way beyond their comfort-providing needs. They waste by overindulging in excesses and create further problems in the process! Natural resources are viewed merely as a means to an end and are the subject of man's exploitation. They are not only considered to be exclusively ours, but infinite. There is a doctrine that we can live better, by destroying more. Greed and accumulation of wealth have become all that matters for such tunnel-visioned capitalists, often getting rich at any cost, by any means necessary. This voracious system has made people addicted to over-consumption. Radical capitalism has created a throwaway society. Products that were purchased not long ago and are still in good functioning order, must be replaced with the brand new, latest models, just because the enticing ads tell us that we can afford to buy them, and we should do so fast, lest we let ourselves be diminished into insipid nonentities. Consumers are manipulated to become voluntarily slaves of ever-changing fashions. Shopping has become a recreational activity for people in countries like the U.S., the birthplace of multiple-level shopping centers, department stores, huge malls and 'all-you-can-eat' restaurants. In terms of total consumption habits, the United States, for instance, with only 5% of world's population, consumes over 40% of world's resources. Development researcher Susan George, in 1980, elaborated on Americans' consumption habits, which now has proliferated to other so-called first world and so-called second world nations:

> Americans are perhaps the only people on Earth privileged to buy unbreakable perfectly calibrated, dehydrated, rehydrated parabolic potato chips packed in vacuum-sealed tennis ball cans—at dozens of times the cost of the original, long-forgotten potato.[23]

In fact, the product she refers to is now, in 2020, available in many countries. In a recent study on the attitude of Americans on consumption, it was

23. George, Susan. (1980), *Feeding the Few: Corporate Control of Food*, p. 30.

revealed that Americans 'cherish the ability to consume more than people elsewhere, and many perceive their ability to consume at high levels as an earned privilege'.[24] The so-called luscious 'American Dream', envied by outsiders, has sadly become a model to be emulated in the 'underdeveloped' and 'developing' world. But, is this really an enviably sweet dream, or an un-enviable horrific nightmare? As George Carlin put it so brilliantly and succinctly: 'You have to be asleep to believe in the American dream.' Indubitably, this supposed sweet dream for consumers is being overshadowed by a horrific nightmare for nature, in which all consumers make their home and are invariably rooted. Would one like to be rooted in such a nightmare?

Furthermore, in this system, aside from how it has endangered the entire planet, the so-called economic growth and prosperity enriches only a few, at the expense of impoverishing so many. Affordability to consume is obviously not everyone's reality, as the majority of the world's population cannot even fulfill their basic needs. Consequently, many dwell under conditions impossible for human existence. Millions of children die every year just because of starvation and malnutrition. The root problem here is not that of food production, but of deprivation and unjust food distribution. All children have equal needs, but their needs are not equally met in a planet overwhelmed with renewable resources. It has been conclusively demonstrated that the current environmental crisis has resulted in the further poverty and emaciation of the 'third world', as they are called. Their poverty is the created outcome of selfish and deficient economic and political systems, which seek unjust exponential 'growth'.[25] Many must be deprived in order for a few to soak in the filthy froth of illicit over-abundance. Transnational corporations pollute the air, water, land and exterminate other species for the sake of supposedly creating 'a better standard of living' for selected groups. The price to pay by all is transnational pollution and the destruction of nature, which imminently affects the vulnerable nations of the 'third world'. The massive influx of environmental refugees across the globe, shows that indigenous people are forced to leave the emaciated regions, because their homeland is no longer able to provide them with the means of sustenance.[26] Deteriorating topsoil and lack of water for irrigation have caused farmlands of Africa, Asia and South America to vanish. As the food supplies are tightened and traditional jobs disappear, the indigenous

24. *Perspective of American Voters on the Cairo Agenda: A Report to PrepCom III.* (1994), p. 13.
25. Douthwaite, Richard. (1993), *The Growth Illusion.*
26. Lassailly-Jacob, Veronique. (1992), 'Environmental Refugees'.

people are left with no choice, but to migrate to the big cities. The very little that they had is also taken away from them. Their lives have been shot to pieces and now they may be shot at the forbidden borders.

At the same time that the magnanimous West continues to financially flourish, the 'third world' countries are continuously struggling to pay the interest on borrowed money and installments for imported Western goods. They are forced to borrow more and more, since their raw materials invariably devalue and do not pay off the bills. Susan George, a renowned authority on this subject, states that 'many third world countries are now so deep in debt that their new loans are devoted *entirely* to servicing old ones. The unenviable roster of countries unable to pay interest otherwise is growing ominously long.'[27] Their lack of ability to pay off the loan obliges them to keep selling out their own under-priced natural resources to avoid default and maintain their immediate survival. Not surprisingly, there is a striking correlation between debt and deforestation. Susan George points to this connection:

> Of the 24 largest debtors, 8 never had, or no longer have forest reserves significant on a world scale. Of the 16 remaining major debtors ($10 billion or more) all are to be found on the list of major defrosters. The correlation is particularly strong for mega-debtors such as Brazil, India, Indonesia, Mexico, Nigeria (among the top 8 debtors) all of which rank among the top 10 defrosters according to both the World Resources Institute and Myers.[28]

Indeed, there is a major problem related to the so-called international developmental projects, which has had a profound bearing on socio-ecological issues. This problem is none other than the fact that the Western nations have continued to produce a debt crisis among the poorer nations in which interest payments alone ridiculously exceed new loans. Often, the interest rate charged is higher than their economic growth. These payments on interest are a significant proportion of GNP of the country in debt. The net transfers from 1984 to 1987 into the Northern banks from poorer Southern countries totalled an astronomical US$106 billion.[29] Even as far back as 1992, according to the U.N.'s Human Development Report, markets denied to these poorer countries by the richer Western nations totalled $500 billion. This was ten times more

27. George, Susan. (1988), *A Fate Worse Than Debt*, p. 13.
28. George, Susan. (1992), *The Debt Boomerang: How the Third World Debt Harms Us All*, p. 10.
29. Bennett, John and George, Susan. (1987), *The Hunger Machine*, p. 41.

than the 'generous' loans these richer nations give out in terms of foreign aid. Vandana Shiva, a leading Indian environmental activist states:

> The economic inequality between the affluent industrialized countries and the poor Third World ones is a product of 500 years of colonialism, and the continued maintenance and creation of mechanisms for draining wealth out of the Third World. According to the United Nations Development Program, while $50 billion flows annually from the North to the South in terms of aid, the South loses $500 billion every year in interest payments on debts and from the loss of fair prices for commodities due to unequal terms of trade.[30]

It has been calculated by Ahmad Abubaker, an African economist that 'for every dollar the United States, for example, gave in aid, to West African nations, it received back two dollars and fifty four cents.'[31] In Latin America, between 1962 to 1966 the average annual assistance from the United States to this region amounted to $1.2 billion, while within the same period the average annual debt repayment was $1.6 billion, a net profit of 0.4 billion dollars for the U.S. Who is really 'aiding' whom? Is this an act of charity or a brutal rip-off? The President of the World Bank in the late 60s candidly admitted to this hypocrisy:

> ...when all [debts] are taken into account, the back-flow of some $6 billion from the developing countries offsets about one half the gross capital inflow which these countries receive. These payments are continuing to rise at an accelerating rate and in a little more than 15 years, on present form, would offset the inflow completely. In short, to go on doing what the capital export countries are now doing will, in the not too long run, amount to doing nothing at all.[32]

Paul Hellyer points to another tragic aspect of borrowing:

> In addition, and in a sense even worse, the IMF attaches conditions to its loan agreements requiring recipient countries to adjust their macro-economic policies in order to conform to the ideological imperatives of the Washington consensus. Almost always these changes are tailored to the interests of official and commercial creditors and almost always to

30. Shiva, Vandana. (1997), *Biopiracy: The Plundering of Nature and Knowledge*, p. 11.
31. Abubaker, Ahmad. (1989), *Africa and the Challenge of Development: Acquiescence and Dependency Versus Freedom and Development*, pp. 91–100.
32. Woods, G.D. (1966), *Foreign Affairs*, January Issue.

the considerable discomfort and impoverishment of the majority of the people living in debtor countries.[33]

The conditions attached are usually: privatization, cut in government expenditure on health, education and social programs, 'developmental' projects which must include direct involvement of certain specific corporations, prohibition of domestic wage increase where foreign owned industries are located, etc. As former U.S. presidential candidate Jesse Jackson puts it, the colonialist and imperialist powers today no longer use bullets and ropes; they use the World Bank and IMF.

In any case, tragically, despite the heavy loss of borrowing, foreign aid is after all often misspent by the ruling classes in the poorer nations, by inflating project costs, striking deals with foreign contractors, purchasing arms and pocketing the extras. The build-up, diversion and funneling of capital toward the military-industrial complexes in the rich nations is neither helping their own nations nor the 'third world'. The military and even non-military regimes in these economically poorer countries end up buying obsolete weapons to decimate their very own countrymen or neighbours due to petty tribalistic attitudes of divide and rule created and fostered by those elites in the richer nations who are obsessed with and utterly blinded by power, money and the hegemonic control and the insalubrious siphoning-off of the indigenous resources. Noam Chomsky elaborates on the devious relationship between food, loans and arms sales:

> As noted, the World Bank now estimates that protectionist measures of the industrial countries—keeping pace with free market bombast—reduce the national income of the South by twice the amount of the official 'development assistance.' The latter may help or harm the recipients, but that is incidental. Typically, it is a form of export promotion. One notable example is the Food for Peace program, designed to subsidize US agribusiness and induce others to 'become dependent on us for food' (Senator Hubert Humphrey), and to promote the global security network that keeps order in the Third World by requiring that local governments use counterpart funds for armaments (thus also subsidizing US military producers).[34]

33. Hellyer, Paul T. (1999), *Stop: Think*, p. 27.
34. Chomsky, Noam. (1993), *Year 501: The Conquest Continues*, p. 106.

It is calculated that at least fifty percent of arms sales are to these economically suffocating countries.[35] Between 1960 and 1987, the economically suffocating nations of the South, were loaned almost $400 billion to purchase arms from the industrialized nations, keeping both Western banks and arms industry content, and making the 'underdeveloped' nations more economically dependent, while creating a bogus image of Western generosity. Total aid offered by the U.N. from 1946 to 1981 amounted to $134 billion—just over nine weeks for international military expenditure.[36]

Another approach employed by Western corporations to take over the resources of economically developing and underdeveloped countries is that of the so-called foreign investment and foreign ownership. Once a country loses its economic sovereignty, it concomitantly loses its political sovereignty. A prime example of this is Canada, where the overwhelming number of corporations operating in Canada, in every field, are big American companies, or subsidiaries of American companies. Paul Hellyer reports:

> At the time [of signing the U.S./Canada Free Trade Agreement], Canada was already the most foreign-dominated of any industrialized country in the world; 100 percent of its tobacco industry, 98 percent of the rubber industry, 92 percent of the automobile industry, 84 percent of the transportation, 78 percent of electrical apparatus industry, 78 percent of the petroleum and coal industry, 76 percent of the chemical industry and 75 percent of heavy manufacturing were foreign, largely American, owned. In contrast, foreign ownership of the U.S. economy was only 3 percent; of Britain's 3 percent; Japan's less than 2 percent and 3 percent in France. If the U.S. and Canadian figures on foreign ownership had been reversed there is no way the deal would have been acceptable south of the border.[37]

In this way, by opening a country to foreign ownership, not only is the environment affected, but so too is cultural sovereignty, where the government helplessly loses its control on national and international affairs, becoming totally obedient to the policies of what the master dictates, so that whatever concerned attitudes about socio-environmental issues that do exist in the dominated nation, are effaced into oblivion. What is left of the usurped country is

35. Myers, Norman. (1984), *Gaia: An Atlas of Planet Management*, p. 247.
36. Ibid. p. 246.
37. Hellyer, Paul T. (1999), *Stop: Think*, p. 56.

nothing but a meaningless flag and the hollow drone of the national anthem. Canadian writer Mel Watkins states:

> Once the most dynamic sectors of our economy have been lost, once most of the savings and investment is taking place the hands of foreign capitalists, then the best prediction is a steady drift toward foreign control of the Canadian economy with the only certain upper limit being 100 percent.[38]

Secondly, stiff competition is absolutely imperative in radical capitalism. That is because, in such capitalism, the rule is that market opportunities ought to be dominated by the clan bully. Therefore, a tight Darwinian competition in the economic sense, among the competitive corporations and nations ensures that only the best, the biggest, the strongest and the fastest growing businesses or nations survive, while the weakest ones are doomed to extinction by the impact crater of bankruptcy caused by the gigantic asteroid of radical capitalism. To get ahead, competing corporations engage in a wide range of legal and illegal activities, ranging from competitive intelligence to corporate espionage, software or hardware sabotage, industrial theft, smuggling and even orchestrating and financing a *coup d'etat* to topple a foreign government which is in favour of nationalizing its resources.[39]

Often times, the competitive struggle for markets or resources becomes the underlying cause of war between competing nations. The 'perpetual growth or disintegration' option, forces corporations of the Western world to wreck the Earth with no mercy, in order to have competitive edge and prolong their preservation. This rapacious predatory attitude kills the human within and takes away any sense of mercy one may have towards dispossessed and powerless human and non-human members of a global society. The deforestation of rainforests, destruction of Earth's atmosphere, over-numbered and overloaded landfills, plundered oceans and acid rain are just a handful of the plethora of cases in point. This is a natural result of the evils of radical technocracy.

Indeed, radical capitalism has given birth to radical technocracy. The advancement of science and technology is solely geared towards the acceleration of 'growth' and higher profits. With that intention, an advanced mechanized world has been created, where technology has become a new god, replacing

38. Watkins, Mel. (1971), in the preface to Kari Levitt, *Silent Surrender: The American Economic Empire in Canada*, p. xi.
39. Perkins, John. (2004), *Confessions of an Economic Hit Man*.

the old gods. Concomitantly, without the proper belief in God—an immaterial and non-anthropomorphic Originator and man's accountability to this Supreme Entity—the concept of a global empathetic family has also vanished. The worshipers of this new god have not raised their heads out of the sand to recognize that this sense of accountability to a Singular Creator, now lost, is not at all at odds with true technological advancement, but would, rather, enhance it further. If God created man in His own image—metaphorically and not anthropomorphically—then a Machine God, according to Mechanical Scripture—would inevitably produce the Mechanized Man, incapable of the empathy and compassion so essential for human and environmental development and holistic interrelationship. As Lewis Mumford, the American writer on social history remarks:

> Modern man is the victim of the very instruments he values most. Every gain in power, every mastery of natural forces, every scientific addition to knowledge, has proved potentially dangerous, because it has not been accompanied by equal gains in self-understanding and self-discipline.[40]

This transformation towards undisciplined callousness, in turn, has unavoidably resulted in deterioration of human values, morality and the human sense of sharing and caring; a deterioration that has emanated from the absolute vacuum of 'spiritual' emptiness. The younger generation is increasingly becoming the lost generation: where will this lost generation lead mankind when it reaches adulthood? Further into the abyss? In the current state of capitalism, one is not hard-pressed to notice that the prevailing system suffers from a severe lack of sharing and cooperation within the human society, and between human and non-human species, unless it is for some tax-break, or where the giving is part of a promotional gimmick. Western capitalists in particular enjoy and no doubt intend to carry on forever to enjoy a monopolistic control of world's raw materials: both of what is theirs, and what is not. British historian, Brian Easlea comments on the radical capitalist's attitude in this respect:

> ...[exploitation of underdeveloped countries], however regrettable, it is 'necessary' since we live in a world characterized by the scarcity, or possible future scarcity, of vital raw materials with regard to which the capitalist countries enjoy, and intend to continue to enjoy,

40. Edwards, Tryon. (1959), *The New Dictionary of Thoughts*, p. 380.

monopolistic control. Furthermore, it would appear that Western interests are best served by maintaining privileged élites in power in underdeveloped countries who have little genuine interest in the kind of industrialization that would benefit the poor of these countries but who are prepared to enrich themselves by exporting the natural resources of these countries to the advanced capitalist nations, thereby sharing in the high profits of the investing Western companies, while squandering this income mainly in conspicuous consumption and in the purchase of that military equipment from the West without which the continuance of their privileged status in the midst of so much suffering, hunger and disease could not be ensured.[41]

Given all these factors, we can see that competitiveness, greed and the desire to control have removed the spirit of humanity, genuine care, giving, sharing and cooperation for their own sake. The corporate identity and attitudes have become a reflection and personification of the arrogant, self-centered and avaricious nature of its irresponsible controllers. Indeed, nothing else matters when this point is reached, for the element of concern for both the environment and humanity in corporate boardrooms; it is just a numbers game where compassion is totally effaced. This system has led to an alienation of capitalists and technocrats from the rest of society and nature, which, in turn, has exacerbated the lack of concern and responsibility towards these elements. The organic relationship that should ideally exist between the corporations and society has been totally cut off, as the roots of a tree are cut off from the soil. As a result, the ideal symbiotic developmental relationship between society, corporation and the perennial corporate body of non-human nature, has ultimately suffered. This is often manifested in continuous downsizing, workers—the breadwinners of families—being callously and injudiciously replaced with robots, machines and computers to enhance productivity and profit margin without thought of the human factor. There seems to be no end to 'how much profit is enough'; year after year, corporations (such as pharmaceuticals, insurance companies etc.) and financial institutions, are not just competing with their competitors, but also happen to be madly engaged in a race against themselves, in order to break their own last year's earnings record. Indeed, radical capitalism is a sick system caught up in a mad spiralling obsession to outdo itself, thereby heartlessly liquidating humanity and human values. It

41. Easlea, Brian. (1973), *Liberation and the Aims of Science: An Essay on Obstacles to the Building of a Beautiful World*, p. 210.

both creates and is a product of a culture of greed, which is maintained so long as the goal is transfixed on the maximization of profit and minimization of cost, by any means necessary. With this narrow mindset there will be no room for proper giving, sharing and cooperation. Radical capitalism is concerned with growth—something not in and of itself harmful—but, unfortunately, its concept of growth is like the growth of cancer, destroying the inter-connectively holistic and organic environment around it, in the physiognomy of the Earth. The pathological behaviour of corporations has been well documented and, as such, described. If we applied the same laws to corporations as we do to human beings, such organizations would be in lock-up and/or (metaphorically speaking) be receiving psychiatric treatment![42]

The Dialectical Culture of Greed

We are now in the position to assess the unsavory concoction brewed by the systems that have been discussed in the previous sections. (Irrational) mysticism, value relativism, radical capitalism and secular humanism, are all intertwined and complementary to each other. Moreover, these four strands of human predilection have had dialectical relationships in various permutations and combinations over the ages. In a nutshell, the basis of this motley amalgamation is human greed and selfishness. However, at various times and places in history, there has been an ascendancy of one system over another. For example, for centuries in most parts of Christiandom, mysticism, through Trinitarianism, prevailed authoritatively; the chief beneficiary was the Church—the upholder of mystical doctrines—which acted much like a capitalistic corporation in unholy communion with the feudal monarchy to suppress freedom of thought, exploit resources, the means of production and to bring about a society in which the gap between rich and poor was vast. This is clear from Medieval Society where serfs were subservient and exploited by the king and the ecclesiastical leaders. However, there was a counter-reaction against this domination which led to borrowing in part from ancient Greek ideas of man being at the centre of the universe, not accountable to the Church and of ideas from the Islamic world infusing through Europe to use reason (i.e. the Averroists, through Muslim philosopher Ibn Rushd, for example). But the domination of one type of elite, instead of being eliminated, was converted into the domination of another type of elite, who did not profess belief in any

---

42. Bakan, Joel. (2005), *The Corporation: The Pathological Pursuit of Profit and Power*, Free Press.

higher power and felt that man was unaccountable to anything other than his own wishes and desires. In fact, paradoxically, many such relativistic capitalists would identify wholeheartedly with ideas from the Bible of *ipso facto* domination over the Earth, be it consciously or unconsciously. Therefore, it can be seen that one of the direct consequences by which irrationality in the form of mysticism has brought about socio-environmental devastation is through its being a catalyst for the emergence of relativism and secularism, as many of those who rejected mysticism—but still maintained greed, power or selfishness already present in some strains of mystical thought and practice, opted for a system without any accountability to a higher power—leading to arrogance and anthropocentrism through their feeling of unconditional human superiority over a desacralized nature. These four convoluted elements of thinking have caused social injustice, which, in turn is the cause of environmental destruction. Indeed, environmental destruction is a subset of social destruction which itself is a subset of the destruction of proper rational thought that underlines true magnanimity and compassion. These issues cannot be separated. We can see the social and ecological interconnections in a straightforward manner. As animal ethicist and veterinarian, Michael Fox remarks:

> ... to promote humane sustainable agriculture will indirectly help protect wildlife and habitat ... to a large extent restoring and protecting wildlife refuges require the development of sustainable agriculture. When indigenous peoples can farm for their own subsistence, they do not need to traffic in wildlife. Humane, sustainable, and socially just agricultural... programs... will... play a major role in protecting the wildlife, natural resources, and people...[43]

We can see that the greed of unfettered capitalism leads to socio-economic problems in many countries, with externally dictated policies adversely affecting the well-being and very livelihood of indigenous peoples, who, in turn, end up wreaking havoc on nature, many times out of the desperation of pure necessity. A parallel concern for both the welfare of human-beings and the environment needs to be implemented and creative solutions for parallel beneficence are required, rather than one at the expense of another.

Yet, can distorted thinking patterns brought about by the ideologies of greed and their concomitant social and financial structures, lead to such sincere

43. Hoyt, John A. (1994), *Animals in Peril: How 'Sustainable Use' is Wiping out the World's Wildlife*, p. 185.

and rational efforts to develop humane and sustainable modes of living? There is a growing yet presently disparate, realization that the beautification of the world in all its original glory is not possible without recourse to the reformation of the human mind towards a worldview that emancipates itself from these errant ways of thinking—from these time-proven, age-old ideologies that allow devastation.

We have analyzed the root problems in terms of problematic beliefs, attitudes and behaviour among humankind, which has created environmental devastation. Obviously, a change in attitude and vision is imperative. Among those concerned, there is unanimity in our need for a new way of dealing with nature and society. Yet, how can we transcend this careless attitude and realize a sound vision that would serve as a panacea for our self-inflicted wounds. Indeed, can humanity and nature co-exist amicably? If so, what is it that is needed to extricate ourselves from this quagmire and how shall we achieve a wholly harmonious co-existence with nature? If the force of avidity, and a relativistic and mystical stance towards nature has been at the root of our instabilities, then could viewing the totality of nature and man in terms of the absoluteness and foundation of cause and effect relationships be imperatively in order? Let us delve into the foundations of nature itself to see if such a worldview is justifiable and based on reality, in that, if an absolute system for living with nature exists, then could absolute rights be derived from it?

Chapter 2

The Foundations of Animal
and Ecological Rights

Introduction

In this chapter we shall try to illustrate that the proper use of nature requires that one must be aware that animals and the rest of ecology do indeed possess inherent rights, and that these rights must be upheld. How do we arrive at this universal conclusion for the existence of inherent rights? And where do these rights originate from? Would it be possible to derive such rights from first principles, using our mind and the signs in the universe, endowments readily accessible to any human beings, anywhere on this planet, at anytime?

On a daily basis around the world, thousands of animals of all kinds are being brutally sentenced to deprivation and extinction, due to the insensitive activities of humankind. Indeed, the very ecosystems which serve as the basis of life are being devastated as never before. Yet, in this atmosphere, although there is a great deal of 'lovey-dovey mumbo-jumbo' about 'saving the planet', it appears that more than such sentiment is going to be necessary to make amends. An attitudinal shift is required so that our attentions are translated into the performance of the most useful kinds of actions possible. Sincere emotional concern is not sufficient. What needs to be examined is our attitude towards how we ought to relate to nature as human beings. Indeed, what is needed is the realization of a globally beneficial and integrated worldview.

The obvious question which comes to mind, in connection with such issues is that of the concept of rights. Are we human beings justified in categorizing ourselves as the 'chosen species', given the fact that animals existed long before even the first homo-sapiens ever set foot on the Earth? Do we possess the autonomous authority to override animals and nature for the fulfillment of our egocentric whims? Or are we, on the contrary, violating the rights of animals, together with the rest of nature?

The opponents, and even many of the proponents of animal rights, assume that the concept of rights must originate in the minds of human beings. They presume, that these rights are not absolute, but rather, arbitrary. According to this view, all rights extendable to animals, by humans, are determined by vested interests and socio-cultural factors. But what needs to be pointed out is that the very assumption that the source of all rights is an institution of human beings, is itself fallacious: it is, indeed, just another anthropocentric (human-centred) notion as to where rights emanate from. In fact, this premise is a prime example of a faulty argument known as the 'fallacy of dubious assumption' or 'fallacy of problematic premise.'[44] This fallacy surfaces when the foundation of one's argument is based on a premise or on a set of premises which are not validated and are open to question. Therefore, what we should ask in the first place is: Is it indeed legitimate to assume that all rights are conventional?

John Locke, the seventeenth century thinker, was among those over the centuries who noticed this erroneous form of argumentation. Locke argued for natural rights discoverable by reason, as opposed to those imposed by the changing institutions of social convention. He asserted that the state of nature is the state of liberty not of license and that therefore, the state of nature has the 'law of nature' to govern it. These laws are absolute and independent of governmental legislation. This led to the view that the rights derived from a recognition of these laws, are neither relative nor the products of human convention: everything is unnatural about the captivity of wild animals, just as everything is natural about their inborn freedom in the state of nature.

The State of Nature

In the natural domain, when the relationship between members of the same species and coexisting participants is examined, we realize that within such interspecies' and intra-species' interactions, the prevalence of rights is associated with their behavioral patterns. For example, many mammals, birds and even some fish are highly territorial as they explicitly mark off the extent of their boundaries. In the event that the markings are missed, any unwelcome visitors would be immediately chased out. The defence of a territory does not usually involve fighting. Most often, for example, the invader respects the displays of a resident bird's vociferous squawks or threat displays. Such communicative objections are usually sufficient to cause the invader to withdraw peacefully. The explicit unwritten right here is tantamount to. This is my tree—keep off! Another example, is of hyenas abruptly terminating the chase

---

44. Johnson, R.H. and Blair, J.A. (1983), *Logical Self-Defence*.

of a promising prey animal as soon as they reach the border of neighboring hyena territory, even though no other predators are in sight.[45]

Some mammals such as the dominant bull elephant seal and the sea lion, are highly possessive of the females in their polygynous entourage. The dominant male fights off any rival male who approaches his females, making sure that the intruder understands that he alone has the right to mate with the females.[46] The message being conveyed in this case, is equivalent to: Stay away from my relations! It can also be observed, that in some specific instances, hyenas and wild dogs give up their hard-earned kill without even putting up a fight, as soon as a lion approaches the carcass. There is a social ranking among the various species that have gathered while the lions feast. When they have consumed enough, the attendant species proceed one by one in a specific order towards the remaining flesh. The sequential order of approach is as follows: firstly, the hyenas, followed by the wild dogs, then the jackals and lastly, the vultures. All of this suggests the existence of well- established relational ranking among species: the lions appear to have a priority, in this instance at least, over the meal, than their ravenous audience.[47] This 'power' and priority in nature is directly linked to the sustenance of equilibrium, however, and not to 'greed'.

Competition or Cooperation?

There are various perspectives in ethology, on whether there is cooperation or competition among animals. Some of those who posit that animal interactions are all purely cooperative state that because the above-cited examples of animal behaviour are mistakenly held as being competitive, it is then assumed that rights automatically exist (because only when there is competition in the human world are there rights associated with competition). Such cooperationists feel that when the proponents of competition theory refer to such observations, they are anthropocentrically equating rights with competition. In fact, some of these radical cooperationists, hold that there is no actual competition among wild animals, and that therefore, one cannot even talk about rights when it comes to the wilderness.

---

45. Kruuk, Hans. (1972), *The Spotted Hyena: A Study of Perdition and Social Behaviour*, p. 160.
46. Attenborough, David. (1990), *The Trials of Life*. An example of this incident is captured on film under the BBC television series entitled: *The Trials of Life*.
47. Suzuki, David (Host). (1991), *Running for their Lives*. Season 31, Episode 6, *The Nature of Things*, aired on CBC.

Although the above-mentioned observations may not be sufficient to conclude the presence of competition among species, they are nonetheless an indication of territorial ownership. Whether the behavioral patterns exhibit competition or cooperation is, in fact, absolutely irrelevant here, since even in the case of cooperation, there are associated constraints. After all, cooperation does not exclude respect for mutual ownership. Indeed, we cannot escape the fact that cooperation itself includes the fulfillment of the respective functions contractually or verbally assigned to mutually cooperating parties. This fulfillment is an expectant right of the mutually opposite members of the same cooperative unit. Animals, in actuality, appear to be engaged in more than our simplistic anthropocentric notions of either 'cooperation or competition'. Each species conducts itself by rules, within myriad 'infrastructures' and dwellings which are optimally suited to their own particular needs.[48] Indeed each species is in 'submission' to something higher, the exact nature of which will unfold during the course of this book.

Animal species also engage in various forms of communication,[49] in what could best be described as communities.[50] In order to flourish, any community, be it human or non-human requires a set of regulatory principles based on natural law, which ensure the collective stability of social order taken as an ensemble. Indeed, examples of such animal behaviour are profuse.

The Source of All Rights

By reflecting on the expanding universe, and the diversity of lifeforms within it, we can certainly observe a panoramic display of remarkable order and consistency in its laws. Such harmonious order is maintained throughout the domains, by the structure of the extremely delicate balances in the physical universe, as for instance in the ecological realm of existence, where plants and animals have been designed to be ingeniously adapted to their respective niches. There is indeed a fragile equilibrium within nature's economy; even a minute change would disrupt the balances in this dynamically interrelated scheme of existence.

Consider a notorious case of human folly, which occurred in Australia. Not too long ago, a famous movie star appeared a number of times on camera,

48. Hansell, Michael H. (1984), *Animal Architecture and Building Behaviour*.
49. Bright, Michael. (1984), *Animal Language*.
50. Giller, Paul S. (1984), *Community Structure and Niche*. Also see Forsyth, Adrian. (1989), *Togetherness: The Logic of the Herd*, Equinox, pp. 48–57.

wearing an outfit made of snake-skin. As a result of this blatant exposition, the outfit became the prevailing fashion of the day. To keep up with an increasing market demand, the suppliers raided the bushes, killing as many snakes as possible, not realising that the snake has a function in the complex food-web. It preys on rats. Since the inherent property of this physical universe rules that every cause is followed by effect(s), and that for every action there is a concomitant reaction, the subsequent callous mass slaughter of snakes resulted in an explosion in rat population. The prairies were destroyed, as the multitudinous rats consumed all their favorite crops. This culminated in a man-made food shortage in parts of Australia and further led to increased habitat destruction through the continuation of ecosystemical dislocations. These were induced by none other than a network of cause and effect interdependencies. The example just cited is not simply an isolated case; indeed, the world is plagued at present by the elimination or reduction of many species, interconnected to the precious web of life by similar or worse catastrophes.

In fact, this disastrous episode graphically reveals that in order to maintain the balances in nature, the snake has the inherent right to remain unmolested and free in its natural setting. This right is not derived by an arbitrary or selected social convention; rather, it is the snake's natural right, as defined by the universality of cause and effect relations, manifested in the equilibrating checks and balances within the countless structures and processes in the universe. Universal laws of cause and effect dictate natural rights with well-defined parameters. Take the case of the Galapagos Islands and various other national parks around the world where inherent natural rights based on the conservation of the balance of nature are fully recognized and upheld by the international and local governmental institutions. The pristine ecosystem has to be preserved and untouched. In the Galapagos, as bizarre as it sounds, animals, no matter what species, have more rights than the wealthiest humans. All natural inhabitants of the Islands enjoy the rights not to be disturbed, while animals from the outside have no rights even to enter the Islands (brought in). The question is: Why should this sound policy be limited to just a few places on Earth? In fact, in some cases, the natural laws would themselves dictate that the animal in question should have more rights than the human, in order for the system to move toward the restoration of the natural balance. For example, if the human and the animal shared a common food resource and there was a shortage of supply, the animal would have precedence over the human, in the consumption of that resource, for the human would have many alternatives, whereas the animal would be tightly bound by its niche.

With this kind of an overview, it is observable that it should not be humans who should be inventing this right. Rather, it should be humans who recognize these unique rights, by observing the interrelationships within the processes inherent in the universe on Earth. Humans should therefore choose to intra-connect these discoveries within the communities in nature, be those communities human or non-human, as naturally integral components of already pre-existing universal laws. In a sense then, it is nature which projects the realization of these rights onto the sense of the human, if the human is observant of those very balances in nature in the first place. This will transpire only if the human mind is an unfiltered, pure or clear receptacle of information and evidence extracted and analyzed from nature. These rights can be termed *Equigenic Rights*[51] in the sense that they are not only founded upon and originate from the equilibrium of nature, but they are also realized through this.

It has been necessary to establish such terminology to distinguish it from the connotations of 'natural rights', which tend to convey nature as being a brutish realm, thanks to such philosophers who talked of 'natural rights' as Spinoza and Hobbes. Given all these factors, an obvious thought which comes to mind, is that so called 'Mother Nature' is not in itself a conscious entity, and one could still pose the logical and legitimate question: What exactly is the real source of the originated laws and the natural rights derived therefrom?

The realization of 'natural laws' on all levels, then, is diametrically opposed to the concept of the human's own manufactured notions of rights derived by social convention. In fact, social conventions must be in complete congruence with natural universal laws in order for the whole system to function beneficently. For if man-made conventions traverse against the natural flow of universal laws, they cause crippling dysfunctionalities which ultimately lead to an inevitable collapse of the integral systems of life. For example, take the case of governmental policies regarding deforestation: clear cutting in the Amazon and elsewhere around the world, has led to the death of forests, destroying their roles as the harbingers and maintainers of the crucial life support systems of our biosphere. The tragic fact is that not much regard had been paid to their complex ecological characteristics. Now, more attention, though certainly not enough, is indeed being paid due to a clear-cut realization of the adverse effect

51. From Latin *equi* means 'equal' (alluding to balance) and again in Latin, *genic* means 'start of change' conveying origin.

of such devastating conventional 'policies' on the various creatures and their ecological niches. Any disruption in the natural order is not only harmful for florae and faunae, but also devastating for man. After all, man is not apart from nature, but a part of nature.

A Worldview with Co-Integrated Rights

It has been discussed as to where rights should in actuality emanate from. However, if the term 'rights' in connection with animals and nature still conjures up a perception which appears incongruous for many, it is because humans have unnaturally disconnected themselves from the realization of the proper interconnectivity between the entities in nature and human society. For in essence, the issue of animal rights, and by extension, the ecosystems, boils down to how humans ought to treat them. What needs to be done is, therefore, to look beyond—to the core of the issue. Humans need to delve deeper and remember that if the concern here is truly about animal welfare, including the plight of the whole ecosystem and the future of humanity, then one must not get bogged down by some trivial semantic objections as to what it really means to give rights to animals and the rest of nature. It is necessary to look to the essence of things. Instead, the words treatment policy or simply treatment for rights could be used, for this is the very basis of what anything of value converges to.

Any human society is based on a particular worldview, which, perceptibly or imperceptibly, molds the attitudes governing the treatment of things within its space. The present tragic state of affairs is stark living, or in fact dying proof that most human societies around the world have lost touch with the balance. However, if a society were to be comprised of individuals who would base their outlook on the reality of the principle of balances, from which all laws at any level could be deducible, their society would necessarily evolve to a stage where it would promulgate not only a balanced Charter of Human Rights, but also a co-integrated Charter of Animal-Ecological Rights. As established, the balances in nature put a limit to the extent of human rights, so that they are not utilized at the expense of animal and ecological rights. That is to say, human beings have no right to harm an animal for ostentatious personal luxuries. In fact, individuals in such a society would recognize such rights within the very framework of their own governing constitution and would naturally implement any such inherent rights. This implementation would be the result of the realization that the human being is not at the center of the universe, but anything in the natural world is at the center of the universal concern, whenever the balances impinging upon it are threatened. With this worldview, nothing of significance, whether it be in the universe or on the Earth, be it large or small, would be looked upon with neglect or disdain. For in such an atmosphere, any entrenched homocentric view would be superseded by a teleocentric view which would include a deep concern and sensitivity for every living and non-living element within its embrace. *With this concern, it would be realized that everything has a purpose and that there is indeed no redundancy in biodiversity.*

Human beings, in such an evolved society, would form an integral part of this natural legislative process. They would be cognizant that humans are the only uniquely reasoning multi-adaptive carbon-based creatures on the face of the Earth and would be responsible for their myriad interactions. Such individuals would, in actuality, be the only ones who would not be blinded by the beasts within; rather, they would realize the existence of such rights with wholesome sensitivity. No doubt, they would deeply understand that, so far as is known, this is the only planet where the interface of fate between the global community of humankind, and that of the established communities of animals in the rest of nature is necessarily interlocked in a state of mutual dependency. In the final assessment, it is only as a direct result of this development, that a sustainable and enhancing future for all humans, animals and their ecological/environmental niches can be assured, on the singular global niche of our precious Planet Earth. Yet, how long will the plea of the Earth go unheeded, as a solitary cry in the midst of depleting wilderness?

The Equigenic Principle

The implication of the previous section has been the appropriate use of nature, inherently concludable from nature itself. This has been termed as *Equigenic Rights*. Let us now precisely define this principle. To establish a truly egalitarian society, the concept of rights needs urgent re-appraisement. From the Islamic perspective, it is not enough to think in terms of only human rights ignoring the rights of other creatures. Of course, the cause of human rights is of utmost importance, but so too is the cause of animal and ecological rights. These domains are ultimately indivisible.

In the section 'The Source of All Rights', the foundation for animal and ecological rights was introduced, and a new term encapsulating that foundation termed *Equigenic* was used, meaning: origin in balance (or equality). This concept is so important—as it serves as the fulcrum of the entire outlook towards nature presented in this book—that it seems fitting to give a precise and concise definition of what could be termed the Equigenic Principle. This should also help explain what we mean by the 'indivisibility of rights'.

The Equigenic Principle refers to the use of nature as the foundation of rights realized when human beings, using reason, that is, by properly interconnecting things, recognize the dynamic balance in nature. The rights realized as belonging and applied to any component of nature, are those which would help maintain the balance, without which disequilibrium would necessarily ensue. Recognizing this balance entails recognizing the way things in nature have been designed in terms of their structure and function and ultimately realizing the ultimate origins of the components including the universe as a whole. Recognizing the designs that facilitate the balance means simultaneously recognizing the extent and mode by which things in nature ought to be used, or ought simply to be left alone as they naturally are. The Equigenic Principle is also applicable to all the affairs of man, since man is an integral part of nature. As such, the Equigenic Principle is a unifying principle by which human society ought to be structured and by which all animal societies are already naturally structured, in order to achieve the balance, which is the basis of justice and concomitantly, the basis of peace. Since the Equigenic Principle is based on the absolute nature of cause and effect in the reality of this universe, it is not a relative, man-made principle but an absolute one, and, since it is based on the nature of the universe it is the absolute foundation of rights and justice—the principal principle. In fact, our deviation from the Equigenic Principle is the cause of our multifarious problems. Indeed, the measure of the health of society is a function of how close we are to the application of this principle. Humanity, based on this outlook, appears to be approaching an all time low—a historical global *minima*—in this respect, for the vast majority has failed to grasp this foundational concept, even if it be from an intuitive perspective.[52]

52. Banaei, Mehran and Haque, Nadeem. (1995), *From Facts to Values: Certainty, Order, Balance and Their Universal Implications.*

Does the 'Balance of Nature' Really Exist?

It is pertinent to ask a fundamental question. Is there truly a balance upon which all fundamental rights are to be based? There has been a growing controversy about the nature of the balance of nature. Among ecologists, this has come to be referred to as the diversity-stability debate. Prior to the 1970s, there was the view that greater diversity enhanced ecosystemic stability. In 1973 however, ecologist Robert May, using mathematical models, found that diversity tended to destabilize the ecosystem's communities. It was subsequently discovered that the intensity of feeding interactions between predator and prey, that is, 'the interaction-strength' was crucial to stability. It has been further realized that it is diversity that maintains and lays the foundation for ecosystem stability. However, it is not only diversity that maintains stability; the ability for communities to respond to changing environmental conditions plays a central role. It is now hypothesized that an ecosystem that has less diversity, would need species in it to be able to respond to varying conditions better than if there was more diversity. Some predators have a strong interaction strength with particular prey, whereas with other prey, they have a weak interaction strength. It has also been discovered that indeed most interaction strengths between predator and prey are weak. For example, if predator A kills prey X more frequently (i.e. a strong interaction strength) and prey X's population were to drop drastically, predator A would switch to prey Y (with which it had less interaction). This would allow the population of prey X to recuperatively increase. Such a mechanics, based on differential interaction strengths, offers a safety factor and stabilizing effect for the ecosystem—a natural insurance policy, as it were. Since this is the case, removing species will disrupt the ecosystem by *increasing* the overall interaction strength on average. To draw upon an analogy, the eradication of species is like making an elastic and flexible system become brittle—subject to cracking and complete shattering by impacts.[53] For example, ecologists have now realized that such creatures as sheephead fish, spiny lobsters, and abalone in more variegated Californian kelp forests had the effect of keeping sea urchin populations stable until these predators and sea urchin competitors had also been extirpated.[54]

---

53. McCann, Kevin Shear. (2000), *Nature*, 'Review Article: The diversity-stability debate', pp. 228–233.
54. Jackson, B.C. Jeremy, et al. (2001), *Science*, 'Ecology Through Time: Historical Overfishing and the Recent Collapse of Coastal Ecosystems', p. 636.

In the book *Africa and Her Animals*, with a chapter co-authored by Haque and Banaei, further points concerning the balance of nature are discussed:

> There has been increasing recognition in ecological studies that diversity maintains and lays the foundation for ecosystem stability (Pimm 1991:355–356). However, it is not only diversity that maintains stability; the ability of communities to respond to changing environmental conditions also plays a central role: According to the most widely accepted usage, those ecological systems are in equilibrium [ie the balance] which fluctuate around some stable point, i.e. return to it after disturbance due to 'self-correcting mechanisms' (see Rohde 2013:1, as referenced from Hutchinson 1948:221–246). The 'balance', dynamic and complex though it may be, does indeed exist and a contrarian position is both misdirected and harmful. Indeed, a balance exists from the cosmological level (the pencil-point-like balancing between expansion and contraction forces in the Big Bang to allow for overall creative expansion) to the dynamic interactions between predator and prey ('interaction strengths', for example, that maintain diversity). The dynamism and complexity, as well as evolutionary development of flora and fauna, should not lead to a devastatingly irrational conclusion that no balance exists, currently being espoused by many ecologists, or that it is an outdated or archaic notion. The irony perhaps is that the balance itself is not perceived in a balanced way![55] ... From the Qur'an is clear that there is a balance and Muslims who follow the Qur'an trust this book's information, in particular since it has shown remarkable convergence with scientific facts, pre-empting them by over 1300 years, for example, the now famous Big Bang verse (Qur'an 21:30), and the expanding universe verse (Qur'an 51:47). Muslims who have studied the Qur'an deeply on the issue of science and belief systems would, therefore, find it implausible that the Qur'an could be wrong on this account, but are willing to look. The Creator, they would argue, knows His creation well enough! Secondly, the Qur'anic notion of balance does not mean it is a simple static balance but rather a dynamic and complex balance, since it takes the whole universe into account (Qur'an 55:7–9). We have briefly cited basic ecological observations on this subject that are facts, including the fact that the universe and humankind have evolved from a common origin, although it is directed evolution according to

55. Haque, Nadeem and Banaei, Mehran. (2018), 'The Equigenic Principle and *mizan*. Islamic foundations for animal welfare in Africa', Ed. Rainer Ebert and Anteneh Roba, *Africa and her animals: Philosophical and Practical Perspectives*, p. 104.

the Qur'an; this makes the balance even more complex and intricate, as a long-term time dimension is involved. Thirdly, Muslims see the denial of the balance of nature as akin to atheism, in that they see no evidence against the balance in nature, just as they can see no evidence against an ordered universe. Also, they feel that since the balance implies strong teleology and design, pointing to a singular Creator, the trend to base science on a lack of order or randomness, and 'anthropocognition' (a human-centred way of perceiving structures and processes in nature) in current mainstream academia, works its ways into such 'theories' that spout that no balance exists, perhaps even unconsciously permeating the minds of those who formulate such hypotheses or theories as legitimate and having evidence.[56]

In a discussion on the Equigenic Principle we noted that all animal species are in submission to the laws of something higher than mere co-operation and competition. What is this 'thing'? Is it chance and self-regulation or is it indeed an intentional external directive force emanating from some Intelligence as described above? When one ascribes things to chance, one still has to account for intelligence. If the Singular Intelligence that originated the cosmos is not acknowledged, then the property of intelligence has to be relegated to inanimate objects in order even to verbally sound intelligible, at the very least, to describe how things function. For example, in a book written by a group of scientists, there is a rather apologetic introduction about the usage of the word 'design' in their title, *The Mechanical Design of Organisms*:

> The idea that biological materials and structures have functions implies that they are 'designed'; hence the book's title. We run into deep philosophical waters here, and we can do little but give a commonsense idea of what we mean. In our view, structures can be said to be designed because they are adapted for particular functions. They are not merely appropriate for these functions, because that could happen by chance.[57]

Some evolutionary biologists such as the late Stephen Jay Gould, are under erroneous assumption that nature is chance based and often times *ad hoc*. For example, Gould believes that the panda's thumb is a clumsy contraption and uses it as a metaphor for a rather disjointed view of the universe.[58] However, Panda specialist, such as Stephen J. O'Brian has astutely noted that: '... [an]

56. Ibid. *Africa and her animals*, p. 110.
57. Wainwright, S.A. et al. (1982), *Mechanical Design in Organisms*, p. 1.
58. Gould, Stephen Jay. (1980), *The Panda's Thumb: More Reflections in Natural History*, pp. 19–26.

opposable thumb, formed by an extension of the wrist-bone… [is] an adaptation enabling the panda to strip leaves from stalk of bamboo'.[59] This peripheral view of natural objects, based on pure *anthropo-functionalism* as espoused by Gould (where we would define this term as: all is judged by the way human beings would do things, in this case, strip leaves!) extends to the whole of nature, among the majority of scientists today. While not all those who deny a teleological view of nature deny the balance it is true that a denial of the balance is most often linked to such 'Godless' views of structures and function in nature. Sometimes it is difficult to see an ordered pattern in nature; but that is due to our ignorance. Such it is with the dynamic balance of nature. Since it has been now realized that there is a strong *relational* relationship between the various wild species, that slight perturbations can cause various patterns in population increase or decrease (chaos theory), and that consequently, it is not a simple balance, many are making the error of proclaiming that the notion of balance does not really exist, as discussed previously.[60] By so doing, such ecologists are actually throwing the baby out with the bathwater. There are more sophisticated laws operating that were not hitherto anticipated and the dynamic balance is globally inter-connective—that is, it is both spatially extant and temporally teleological. To illustrate the error that is being made, consider the following analogy: If you have a scale with the fulcrum at the centre, with equal weights on either side then the scale will be balanced. Now if you move one of the weights closer to the fulcrum the scale will no longer be in balance and will tilt upwards on the side where the weight has been moved towards the fulcrum. What we now need to do to restore the balance is to put a larger weight on the other side to balance the system. Suppose that this is done by the weigher. Would it be rational for someone to now say, upon looking at the new set-up for the balance, that it is not in balance because one weight is closer to the fulcrum? One has to look at the whole system to know that a balance exists.

Another related problem where there is a great deal of confusion concerning the issue of the balance of nature, is that it is felt by many that the extinction of species over the aeons undermines the notion of balance, let alone perfect adaptation, because it implies that when the environment changed, some species were not adapted to it and could not therefore cope with the change. Many neo-Darwinian biologists presume that the balance was broken and with such

59. O' Brian, Stephen J. (1987), 'The Ancestry of the Giant Panda', *Scientific American*, p. 105.
60. Leakey, Richard and Lewin, Roger. (1995), *The Sixth Extinction: Biodiversity and its Survival*, pp. 149–170.

a change they became extinct! The problem with this view is that it is rooted in the conception of the present state of nature as having been a result of evolution based on chance and randomness, where things happen by trial and error. These notions are taken as the premise, in which a goal directed system (teleological) is pedantically rejected. However, it should not be difficult for any person to see that this universe has directionality, from its very emergence with the Big Bang to the present. The development of this universe is such that it is as if it were 'pursuing an intention'; this was candidly confessed, in fact, during the Eighth International Conference on the Origin of Life, held at Berkeley, California, by the keynote speaker, Nobel Laureate George Wald of Harvard University. He was commenting on the growing realization that the parameters by which the universe has been arranged over time are so precise, that the development of life is dependent on a whole chain and network of crucial precursors. As it is often pointed out by even the champions of randomness and chance in the areas of evolutionary biology, if the dinosaurs had not gradually or cataclysmically phased into extinction, mammals, and thence humans, as the ubiquitous species would not have surfaced and become so predominant.

In summation then, the notion of the balance of nature therefore in reality has two components. The first is the component of stasis or stability to maintain the existing order. The second is the balancing of the relations by the elimination of one species after its having existed for some duration due to a change in the ecological order by, say, a change in the global weather pattern. Therefore, it makes sense that both the equilibrium state of stasis and the dynamical equilibrium state of macroevolution, form one system in space and time functioning with directionality and an external and independent intentionally. If there was no external will, then there would have been no universe, let alone functionally optimal development of the universe.[61] This is why it makes absolutely no sense to make such remarks as: 'This is Mother Nature's grand design!' When such statements are made it is certainly most legitimate and logical to ask: what is 'Mother Nature'? What or who is the designer? After all, nature is only a process, consisting of interrelating and interrelated structures. It is not a conscious entity with a large central brain located somewhere in the cosmos! It would, therefore, be only logical that in the development and evolution of

61. Banaei, Mehran and Haque, Nadeem. (1995), *From Facts To Values: Certainty, Balance, Order and Their Universal Implications*. See also, Haque, Nadeem. (2009), *From Microbits to Everything: Beyond Darwinism and Creationism: Volume 3: The Evolutionary Implications*. For new proof of God arguments see: Haque, Nadeem, and Muslim, M. (2007).

ecological systems, a director for the direction of the whole system must be an absolute logical necessity.

Due to such growing realizations, design arguments for cosmology, ecology and biology are now appearing under various guises such as 'anthropic principles', for fear of association with 'God'. However, be that as it may: let us now turn to the Islamic view of nature and see how it corresponds to the realities of nature that have been discussed in this chapter and the central notion of 'God' from the Islamic perspective.

Chapter 3

The Islamic View of Nature

Understanding the Uniqueness of the Human Being

Unless we, as human beings, know of our proper place in nature, nature itself will continue to be degraded and destroyed, and we too will hence suffer the consequences. Therefore, in order to ascertain the position of the human being within the natural order, from the Islamic perspective, we need to examine its source, which is the Qur'an. The Qur'an consistently and explicitly mentions, in numerous verses, that the entire natural world belongs to God and God alone (3:189). However, humankind is given only temporary successorship/stewardship (*khilafah*) of the natural world. Therefore, humankind is responsible and accountable in this capacity for any abuses of the Earth's life forms or natural resources as a test (6:165). This responsibility is instilled upon humankind because humanity is capable of reasoning. In Arabic, the word used to signify reason in the Qur'an is *aql*, from the root *aqala*, which is based on *iqal*, a word that denotes a cord used to tie a camel's legs so that the animal does not run away. It therefore means 'to bind' and hence 'to secure something.' Reason, therefore, secures reality by interconnecting information.

Reason is the foundation of Islam, and it is claimed in the Qur'an that no contradictions exist between nature (the work of God) and the Qur'an (the word of God); i.e. there is supposed to be 100% congruence between the Qur'an and nature. In the Qur'an, the gauntlet is cast to challenge us, using the Principle of Non-Contradiction, which is the basis of rationality:

> Have they not pondered on the Qur'an? If this book were from other than a Singular God, then surely, in it, you would find many inconsistencies (Qur'an 4:82).

By using reason properly, we can maintain the *mizan*, an Arabic word used in the Qur'an. But what is the *mizan*, and what is its connection to Human Uniqueness?

The universe itself was created as a test to see who would perform the best in deeds (67:2); that is, who would abide by the laws of God, the first of which is not to upset the pre-existing balance:

> It is He [God] who has created the expansive universe and established the balance [mizan], so that you may not disrupt the balance. Therefore, weigh things in equity and do not fall short of maintaining that balance (Qur'an 55:7–9).

> He (God) has appointed, precisely established and positioned the Earth [both the planet as a whole, and the Earth's crust] for the maintenance and development of sentient life forms [both humans and nonhumans] (Qur'an 55:10).

> We have surely sent messengers with clear evidences, and sent them with the Book [the Qur'an] and the Balance [the Equigenic Principle], so that human beings may behave with equity (Qur'an 57:25).

In the Qur'an 55:10, the word *wada-aha*, has been translated as 'appointed, precisely established…' to convey its entire range of meanings as derived from its root meaning and its contextual use elsewhere in the Qur'an.

Animals also know their purpose, but their usage of reason constrains them to only following the laws of God and not deviating from those laws. How animals interconnect in their natural state corresponds with the *Equigenic Principle*: meaning equilibrium in and realized from the dynamic balance of nature, from *equi* (equal) and *genic* (origin) (Banaei and Haque 1995: 120–235). Since nonhuman animals also interconnect with things to attain goals, they also use *'aql*, that is, reason, from this core definition. However, the human being's intellectual flexibility and greater degree of freedom to connect/disconnect things, intellectually and manually, allows him or her to disconnect what ought to be connected and connect what ought not to be connected in nature. This disruption in the *equigenic flow* and pattern designed by God leads to harm. In other words, the human mind can choose to embark on actions that disrupt the dynamic balances in nature, flagrantly violating the Equigenic Principle.

The uniqueness of humans is that they are able to deviate from the purpose by their choices. This 'choice' and the *mizan* (balance) has implications for all facets of existence which we shall discuss in the following sections, to gain a complete understanding of Human Uniqueness—of the question of the 'specialness of humans', that is, of what makes us special, and the unique implications of such a status. All of these facets are inextricably connected to the *al-mizan* (the balance):

1. Uniqueness of Consciousness

According to the Qur'an, human life continues after death because we possess consciousness, depicted by two words: *ruh* and *nafs*. *Ruh* is brought into existence by God's creative commandment and is sustained by His will. Both *nafs* and *ruh* are connected to the created consciousness that arises from the infinitely rich imagination of God—that is, from His transcendent, ever-existing consciousness, since, logically speaking, created consciousness (according to the Qur'an) can only come from, and be sustained by, a higher consciousness. *Ruh* relates to the created and sustained consciousness and *nafs* to the personality and individuality that develops, based on the life experiences associated with that consciousness, created as a sustained command from the mind of God.[62]

According to the Qur'an, then, humans and animals are self-aware and possess consciousness as fractionalized from the source of all Consciousness—an indivisible God.[63] The human being, therefore, is not unique in respect of possessing consciousness and self-awareness. It is the use of his/her consciousness tied to the *mizan* that is crucial.

2. Uniqueness in Salvation

Individuals who have companion animals often wonder and ask what happens to their dogs, cats, turtles, and so on after they die. Just as the Qur'an accurately and remarkably described the Big Bang, far in advance of contemporary science, so, too, the Qur'an tells us that when this universe is terminated by the Creator in a Big Crunch (21:104) it will be replaced by a new and different type of universe (14:48 and 36:81) in a second Big Bang. In light of the continuance of the *nafs*, or *ruh*, from the Qur'an it can be deduced that all animals will be gathered unto their Creator after death in another universe as a holding place until the final hereafter is recreated in a second Big Bang.[64] It is the will of God that determines whether or not individual consciousness continues in the next life in a new and different, albeit similar, form (56:61). This is why the Qur'an declares that all creatures will be gathered unto their Sustainer, not just human beings (6:38).

62. Haque, Nadeem and Muslim, M. (2007), *From Microbits to Everything: Universe of the Imaginator: Volume 2: The Philosophical Implications*, pp. 227–229.
63. Ibid. pp. 179–205.
64. Ibid. pp. 225–258.

Human beings are therefore not unique in having an afterlife, according to the Qur'an. Whereas all animals will have some form of afterlife, not described by the Qur'an for animals *per se*, the afterlife of humans is either a permanent paradise (various levels) or a temporary reformatory place of severe torment (various levels), described in great detail in the Qur'an—a new universe with different laws (14:48 and 36:81), not experientially knowable but analogically described in the Qur'an by the extra-universal entity that created it and the Qur'an itself.

3. Uniqueness of Personhood

According to the Qur'an, all nonhuman animals possess personhood, and not just human beings. Human beings tend to regard themselves as being special because they feel they are uniquely endowed with intelligence, self-awareness, higher communication abilities, and a soul. Using these assumptions about uniqueness, humans often trample callously upon other species because they think that nonhumans either do not possess these abilities or faculties, or, if they do, that they exist in a primitive state. Indeed, humans tend to justify their actions according to these unsubstantiated assumptions. The Qur'anic—and hence Islamic—outlook reveals to us, however, that these assumptions are incongruent with reality and that if the attributes of nonhuman animals are understood properly, great untapped and all-embracing knowledge exists that could lead to a revolution in the largely discordant relationships between humans and other species.

The Islamic perspective acknowledges animal communication in ways not yet recognized by science, though recent research is in fact shedding more light on animal communication. Fourteen centuries ago, the Qur'an mentioned numerous animals and their relationship with human beings in unique contexts: the Qur'an, for instance, describes ants communicating meaningfully with one another. It mentions an ant that is on the lookout and warns fellow ants of impending doom; they had better evacuate immediately, lest Solomon and his entourage crush them unwittingly:

...then they were led forth in orderly ranks, until, when they came upon a valley of ants, an ant[65] exclaimed: 'O you ants! Get into your dwellings, lest Solomon and his hosts crush you unawares' (Qur'an 27:17–18).

65. Note the accuracy of the Qur'an in describing these particular ants as female; all worker ants are female.

52

The ant identifies the danger of being crushed, due to the march-ing of Solomon and his group, and her own ant community, and seeks to avoid being killed. Solomon, we are told, not only understood this communication but took delight in the discourse (27:19). Perhaps most noteworthy is the fact that the female ant (field observations attest to female ants being on the lookout) is aware of Solomon's awareness; this type of meta-awareness requires a very high degree of social intelligence. Present-day researchers note that ants communicate by pheromones, tactile sensors, vibrations, and so on.

As a result of these factors, it becomes obvious from the Qur'an that animals also communicate to various degrees like human beings, and each has personhood; in this sense, humans are unique only to the extent that they are able to wreck the equigenic flow, hitherto discussed, by a misuse of communication.

Perhaps most noteworthy is the fact that the ant is aware of Solomon's awareness; this type of meta-awareness requires a very high degree of social intelligence. Present-day researchers note that ants com-municate by pheromones, tactile sensors, vibrations, and so on. E. O. Wilson encountered a variety of chemicals in his observations of ants: One message means 'Follow me.' Another: 'On guard! A threat to the public good is present.' (This was the message in the scent that Wilson had evoked by picking apart the tree stump in Rock Creek Park; the alarm pheromone [chemical signal] of [the ant species] Acanthomyops is essence of citronella).[66]

From the example of the ants, we can draw the following conclu-sions: In the Qur'an, nonhuman animals are self-conscious and have a highly sophisticated language. They have what we refer to as words and sentences—that is, highly developed syntax and semantics. This does not mean that they communicate just as we do. Whatever their form of communication, however, ethological evidence is fast piling up that it is meaningful in their own modes. In chapter 27, verse 16 of the Qur'an, animal language is not considered a special miracle, but a law of nature akin to human language because it can be learned. If, therefore, according to the Qur'an, animal communication is based on the laws of nature, albeit designed by God, it is neither difficult nor unreasonable to extrapolate that creatures other than birds and ants, with similar ner-vous systems, are also endowed with similar communicational abilities.

66. Wright, Robert. (1988), *Three Scientists and their Gods: Looking for meaning in an age of Information*, pp. 128–129.

4. Uniqueness of Community

Not enough attention has been paid to the fact that the Qur'an seals the biological parity between humans and the rest of the species, first elaborated in modern times, at great length, in the now classic book *Animals in Islam*, by the pioneering Islamic thinker and author Al-Hafiz B.A. Masri (1989), and encapsulated by the Qur'anic passage which states that:

There is not a nonflying and two-winged flying [water/carbon-based] creature, but they are in communities like yourselves… in the end they will all be gathered to their Sustainer. (6:38)

Humans and animals have communities and they all communicate in their own modes, but human beings are unique with respect to being able to disrupt the balance by creating dysfunctional communities, whereas the communities of animals, on the contrary, maintain the balance.

5. Uniqueness of Sentience

According to Islam, we are certainly not alone, for in the Qur'an it is explicitly stated that:

Among His signs is the creation of the galaxies and the Earth, and whatever corporeal creatures (*dabbatin*) that He has dispersed throughout them both. He is able to gather them together, when He so chooses (*idha yashao*) (Qur'an 42:29).

Remarkably, the Qur'an also states that there are other Earth-like planets, which consequently means that they are hospitable to life. In connection with the following verse that speaks of extrasolar planets like the Earth, it is important to note that the number seven in the Arabic language it is often synonymous with 'several', but it may also mean exactly seven. The Qur'an says, 'It is God who has created seven heavens (*samawati*) and of the Earth their like' (Qur'an 65:12). This verse explains that the universe is clustered with countless earths, just as the stars are in clusters, forming galaxies and galaxies themselves are clustered and so on and so forth: in other words, 'similar Earth' clustering, mirrors hierarchical stellar clustering. This is discussed in great detail in one of this writer's other works.[67]

67. Haque, Nadeem and Shahbaz, Zeshan. (2015), 'Extraterrestrials in Islam', *Nexus*, Vol. 22, No. 5 (August–September).

Surprisingly, the Qur'an does not state that we are the topmost species in the realm of the universe, in our overall attributes, be they intellectual and/or physical:

...indeed We have honoured the children of Adam, and We carried them by land and sea. We have provided them with wholesome things, having specially favored them above many of those whom We have created (Qur'an 17:70).

Yes, favored 'above many,' but not all! When viewed in the context of the existence of *jinn* (non-carbon based sentient entities) on Earth and various forms of higher sentient life on other planets, human beings are not unique but rather, are a class of species in the cosmos who can either be creative or destructive in nature.

6.   Uniqueness of Revelation

Animals also receive revelation (*wahi*). The Qur'an speaks of bees receiving *wahi* (16:68) to guide their behaviour, etc. It is more at the instinctual, programmed level for optimal foraging, hive building, hive location selection, communication, etc. Other animals, like the Monarch Butterfly, receive *wahi*, since their navigation system is calibrated through their brain wiring.[68] It directs animals towards sustenance etc. Likewise, the Qur'an is a *wahi* for humans, which is humanity's guidance system as were the originals of other scriptures. Therefore, humans are not unique in receiving *wahi*, but their form of the *wahi* is unique, at least on this planet. Animals follow *wahi*, but humans are severely lacking in this department!

Uniqueness of the Implication of Human Uniqueness

It has been illustrated through recent research on the Qur'an and a model of the origination of life[69], that all life, including that of humans, has evolved from water and clay, with clay as a cooking receptacle/vessel for the evolution of nucleotides, etc. As a consequence, everything is related to each other, through the convergence of origin, and shares in the same consciousness as willed by God. Human beings are the most complexified in the evolutionary process on Earth, together with the *jinn*, who share in the attributes of human uniqueness, though the *jinn* cannot normally be seen by humans. These two

68. Reppert, S.M., Guerra, P.A. & Merlin, C. (2016), 'Neurobiology of Monarch Butterfly Migration', *Annual Review of Entomology*, 61:25–42.

69. Haque, N. 2009. *From Microbits to Everything: Beyond Darwinism and Creationism, Volume 3: The evolutionary implications.* Toronto: Optagon Publications Ltd.

concepts—a common source of evolution of carbon-based life, and its sustenance (both body and consciousness)—are captured remarkably by one Arabic word in the Qur'an: Rabb, meaning the evolver or developer of a thing from one stage to another until it reaches perfection, or completion, while also encapsulating the meaning 'Sustainer' (refer to footnote 74). This realization of a common source tying everything together, yet everything at the same time being separate, leads to empathy and compassion, that can be summed up by one word: affinity.

The entire universe, therefore, has indeed been created for testing highly mentally capable carbon-based and non-carbon based entities (humans, *jinn*, and higher extraterrestrial lifeforms) to see if they can choose to minimize going against the equigenic flow and to see who would choose to develop affinity. It is recognized in the Qur'an that human beings are unique in their ability to interconnect things and to create and name things (creation of artistic/scientific, abstract concepts and technology), on a quantitatively much higher level than animals, according to the Qur'an and as evidenced by more recent research. However, human beings are not unique in terms of the basic principles and attributes of having consciousness, using reason, receiving revelation, communication, personhood and creating communities, according to the Qur'an.

How then are we unique and special? If the ability of humans is understood as being a precarious predisposition of having the potential to disrupt the dynamic balances in nature (the equigenic flow), then it becomes a mode of awareness and sensitivity synonymous with being cautious. This cognizance of the precariousness that constitutes human uniqueness should make all humans sensitive, cautious, circumspect and more creative in the non-disruption of equilibrium in all the interrelated spheres of life.

Although the human being is indeed an animal, categorized by the Qur'anic word *dabbah*—a water- and carbon-based[70] creature that can move spontaneously, as described in verse 24:45—a *conditional hierarchy* prevails in the Qur'an. This hierarchy elevates human animals above nonhuman animals when we treat nonhuman animals and the rest of nature and fellow human

---

70. The Qur'an describes life as having been made—and originated—from water. Although it naturally does not mention carbon, we know that all water-based life is carbon-based. The reason 'carbon-based' has been explicitly expressed in this description is that the Qur'an states that there are other entities made of a more subtle energy form, which we would argue are not carbon-based; these are the *jinn*.

beings properly, but reduces the human person to a mere shell with a mere human façade, when we fail in our rightful role.

Though human beings are unique, God is Unique with a capital U, as captured by the following Qur'anic passage: 'There is no thing like Him' (112:4). In fact, the word *ahad*, translated as 'one' in the Qur'an, in 112:1 not only means one, but means that which is indivisible in any manner. From the Islamic perspective, it is thus realized that once we understand the uniqueness of God and, as such, God's relation to creation, and thereby instill in ourselves awe for God, we can then understand the level of human uniqueness in its true essence and perspective. Once this is understood, then our relations to God and creation can be set aright, in the refulgent equipoise that it was ideally meant to be. The Islamic view, therefore, fosters a teleocentric understanding of the universe, whose centre point is a singular, unmatchable God, so that a more interconnected and caring society can evolve for the holistic betterment of both humans and the rest of creation, of which humans are an integral part.

Conceptions of God

The conceptions of 'God' are indeed numerous and varying in different belief systems. Some people think that 'God' is a human-like entity residing somewhere in space and time, was 'incarnated', or is co-eternal with the cosmos. Others think that there is some sort of 'power' regulating the cosmos. They give this power various names, such as 'cosmic energy', 'universal intelligence', 'cosmic mind', etc. It is crucial to be clear about what Muslims mean when they say 'God' for this is not just a nominal point as Shakespeare puts it, when it is aphoristically remarked in one of his plays that: 'That which we call a rose by any other name would smell as sweet.'[71] Therefore, to fully understand the Islamic position on nature, it is imperative that a proper understanding of the attributes and sovereignty of the Creator of this universe are conveyed. The term 'God' for Muslims refers to the one and only Originator of time, the sole Creator of matter and energy, the Sustainer and Cherisher of this universe of which we are an insignificant part.

The basic difference among belief systems on this issue lies in what attributes and qualities we ascribe to that 'God' or 'power' and whether we shall be held accountable for our actions. Our very attitudes towards life are shaped by our views on this very issue. For example, if it is believed that there is no

71. *Romeo and Juliet*, Act II, Scene I.

power, save the power of this world as the 'be all and end all' of our existence and there is no accountability, then some would tend to act in a selfish way—without caring about how our actions affect others. If we believe in many different powers, then we would end up serving contradicting commandments of various masters, each with their own conflicting interests. It is such contradictory conceptions of God and His dominion over creation and the lack of accountability that has led to the symptomatic socio-ecological devastation, human misery and animal plight that we face today, perhaps as never before.

Muslims firmly hold that according to the Qur'an, and indeed as is realizable by any rational investigation into nature, even without the aid of the Qur'an, the only real and unique power that humans must ultimately depend upon has the following primary attributes:

> Say: He is God [the singular God], the One and Only; God is independent of all, yet all are necessarily dependent on Him; neither has He any offspring, nor is He the offspring of anyone, and no thing/ no-one in existence, exists that is like Him. (112:1–4)

> Say: Verily, it has been revealed to me that your God is indeed the One and Only God: so will you enter into submission unto Him? (21:108)

The Qur'anic concept of submission to the Creator means accountability to that Creator: This accountability is to a God that is transcendent of our conceptions of space and time, yet He is also with us, though not in the pantheistic or physical sense, since God is not bound by His creation.[72] In other words God is not aloof, uncaring or an abstraction; rather, He is just the opposite:

> When my devotees inquire of you about Me, tell them I am indeed near at hand; I respond to the call of every supplicant when he calls Me. (2:186)

> … We [God] have already created the human being and We know what his self whispers to him. We are closer to him than [his] jugular vein. (50:16)

The power and knowledge of this Creator with reference to nature is referred to in numerous verses, three of which are as follows:

---

72. In chapter 112 of the Qur'an it states that no thing like Him exists, in that there is no likeness like Him, but so too, all of us depend on Him for our very moment to moment existence. This only makes eminent sense because He is the Creator and not therefore, logically speaking, part of creation and hence not like creation.

... with Him are the keys to the unseen. He knows whatsoever there is on land and in the sea. There falls not a leaf but He knows of it; neither is there a seed-grain in the darknesses of the Earth, nor anything fresh or dry, but all is [recorded] in a clear record. (6:59)

He has knowledge of all that goes into the Earth and what comes out of it; of all that ascends to or descends from the sky. He is the most merciful and forgiving. (34:2, see also 57:4)

Have they, then, never beheld the birds above them, spreading their wings and drawing them in? None but the most gracious upholds them: for, verily, He keeps all things in His sight. (67:19)

One of the prime attributes of God in Islam is that He is also the Sustainer:

And how many a creature is there that takes no thought of its sustenance, while God provides for it as He provides for you—since He is the all hearing and all knowing. (29:60)

This prime attribute of the Creator and one which has been used the most number of times in the Qur'an is the Arabic word *rabb*. This word has been translated as 'Lord' or 'Sustainer' depending on the context. However, when we look to the root of the word, we see a deeper and profounder meaning: *rabb* actually means 'the fosterer of a thing from one stage to another until it reaches its goal of completion'.[73] This would undoubtedly apply to all systems in the universe through time, including co-evolution (the evolution of the various components of the system happening together) within ecological systems. It must be noted that the quality of gender is not applicable to this Creator; call Him God, Jehovah or Allah, for 'He' is unlike anything in 'His' creation. The use of masculine term is only due to the limitation of the language. This pronoun is merely used for communicational purposes and is not supposed to convey a male anthropomorphic (human-like) deity.

Ecological Regulation

Our Sustainer is He who gave everything its form and nature, and thereupon guided it. (20:50)

It has been emphasized in this book, that the revolution in thought by which one becomes conscious of the Singular Creator, who alone has dominion over creation, is the starting point concerning our beneficial behaviour towards

73. Al-Isfahani al-Raghib Al-Husain Abu-l-Qasim, *Al-Mufradat fi Gharib al-Qur'an (Dictionary of the Qur'an)*, Dar Ihya Al-Turath Al-Arabi.

it. However, the present popular notion that the universe is self-regulating, ideologically attempts to exclude the existence of a Creator. Such an atheistic notion has a direct implication not only on how we view nature, but also on how we gauge our responsibilities towards it. The Islamic contention is that not a single shred of evidence or proof exists for a self-regulatory universe in the ultimate sense, because nature never created itself. Clearly and obviously, nature does not have a conscious self by which it is organizing its 'self' toward some future state. The myriad processes of nature fit together in a coherent way to assure that life is maintained and perpetuated. Such order could not have been the product of blind chance or random organization. It has, on the contrary, unfolded due to an infinitely intelligent and orchestrated plan, based on natural laws, which were installed at the very moment of cosmic origination—a beginning given substance from the limitless creative mind of a Singular Intelligence and sustained thereafter.[74] This is the clear Islamic and Qur'anic position.

Indeed, many thinkers have now started to freely acknowledge that the Earth's processes are very interrelated—so much so that the Earth appears to behave as if it were an organism. This concept has been popularized and brought into the 'mainstream of science' as the Gaia Hypothesis.[75] However, there are many detractors, who are quite sceptical that the Earth could be so remarkably well regulated. In general, there is a tendency to counter the principle behind the Gaia Hypothesis because it has a teleological (goal-directed) underpinning; that is, that the entire universe has been designed for a purpose. However, it should also be noted that a great many of the Gaia supporters do not link Gaia with creation by an Intelligence; they also tend to resort to the notion of 'self-regulation'. The more one looks into nature, though, the more one will realize the fact that the Earth is indeed like an organic unit and that the whole universe,

74. In the Qur'an, the planet Earth is personified in the following context, where it states that the Earth will also reveal information of all that has occurred, on it: 'When the Earth is shaken with its [final] quake, and throws up its burdens, and man cries out: "What has happened to it?"—on that Day it will recount all its [accumulated] information, as inspired by our Sustainer' (99:1–4). Here the basic form of the word used for inspiration to the Earth—*wahi*—is the same as that used for the Creator inspiring the bees as in the following verse: 'And your Lord *inspired* to the bee: *Choose* for yourself hives among the mountains, trees and that which they [human-beings] build' (16:68). Verse (99:1–4) clearly describes the Earth's revelation of information, where information is stored and recalled when this universe is destroyed. Indeed, the recollection of Earth's memory is similar to that of our skin, which the Qur'an states in 41:20–22, will also testify on that day against us, implying the storage and some type of future projection of information, the skin being an external sense organ. This, in turn, implies that we should be as sensitive in following the laws of God when it comes to the Earth, as we ought to be for our own bodies, because the Earth, like our bodies, according to the Qur'an, will recount all the happenings that have occurred on and to it.

75. Lovelock, James. (1988), *The Ages of Gaia*.

let alone just the Earth, is designed in such a way that it indeed functions as if it were pursuing an intention.

The way the Earth is spread out is correlated with the dispersal of animals. In other words, geographical conditions and species diversity are tightly correlated. These are geared to the pre-existing equilibrium of cosmological and geological dynamics. In short, it is not just the Earth that is operating like an organic unit with a purpose; rather, *the whole universe is* according to the Qur'an. It is hard to categorize what area of knowledge such verses belong to: 'Cosmo-biogeography'? This hierarchy of concomitant development and regulation, from the cosmic structures, thence geology, to life on Earth (for example, plate tectonics control the biosphere and not vice versa) is being realized now, in ever greater detail.[76] This becomes clear when we correlate two passages in the Qur'an, which have been fragmented into sections for analyzing the hierarchy:

> (A1)...do they not look at the starry firmament, how it is raised up? (B1) At the mountains, how they are stabilized? (C1) And at the Earth, how it is spread out? (88:18–19)

> (A2) He created the cosmic systems without any visible support structures and (B2) placed stabilizers (mountains) on the Earth so that you may dwell at ease as it revolves; (C2) and dispersed on it all varieties of creatures, and He sent rain and grew all kinds of splendid things on it. (31:10)

Conclusion: The hierarchy of balance and control is that C1 governs C2.

With the Islamic approach, the basis of which is the Eugenic Principle, man is not anthropocentrically judged to be at the center of the universe. Rather, the intentionally based actions of man in the universe are ultimately what are at the center of the judgment. Indeed, in the Islamic outlook, things are not relative or mystical, because the universe is viewed in terms of cause and effect relationships, absolute and inherently beneficial to man and nature. Nature is seen as a teacher, teaching us reflexively how we should treat it. Things are not decided by *ad hoc* parliamentary legislation, and neither are individual and collective whims pursued. Monolithic corporations are not given sway to rule and dictate policies, but are subject to the dictates of the laws inherent in nature. Consequently, there is no quarter for the emergence of radical capitalism,

76. Veizer, Jan. (1987), *Origin and Evolution of the Universe: Evidence for Design,* 'The Earth and Its Life: Geologic Record of Interactions and Controls', p. 190

since the Qur'anic injunctions are a reflection of cause and effect relationships, mapped on human language, one of the foundations of which is the fact of the dynamic balance of nature. Such a view does not leave room for detrimental ideas that can be used as a springboard to augment the darker side of human nature, such as that 'Man has been created to conquer nature, etc.' By pointing to the prime attribute of the structure of the balances in nature, which are a product of the overall cosmic scheme, in the Qur'an, socio-environmental responsibility is placed squarely on the shoulders of the human being, who is categorically told by the Creator to recognize this fact and implement justice based on the balance.

The Psychology of Ecological Thought

According to the Islamic and the Qur'anic perspective, excluding this Creator from the centrality of our lives is considered to be most dogmatic and illogical. It may have a detrimental impact, disintegrating the consistent and integrative outlook towards nature and disconnecting man from nature. The process by which this disconnection proceeds may often be gradual and subtle. It is initiated when the deeply felt responsibility for one's actions disappears due to the concomitant loss of realization of the concept of the ultimate Ownership of Nature by God. This process of dissociation then continues unhindered if the global reasoning pattern—which naturally develops when one is trying to confirm the dominion of the Creator—is willfully blocked. This disconnection is further exacerbated when things are not interrelated simply because they go against one's narrow self-serving desires. Such desires become more practicable when such a Creator is left out of consideration, by either omission or some form of anthropomorphization of God. Consequently, it can be seen that adhering to any system of thought which neglects the existence of a Single Originator or distorts this Originator's singular conception could make one gravitate towards the position of either dominance or subservience toward nature. A departure from the natural state, *fitrah*,[77] is characterized by a failure to establish a harmonious balance with the rest of nature.

In contrast to such a dissociated thinking pattern, the Qur'an implores and urges man to view things naturally as a means of re-connecting oneself to the knowledge of one's origins and destiny in this vast universe. The very direction

77. *Fitrah* means the original and natural state as designed by the Creator through which the human being is naturally/automatically cognizant of a singular creator. See Qur'an 30:30 and the hadith of Bukhari 2.440. See also Qur'an for the original communication all human beings have had from God.

of the human mind towards the Creator has an integrative revitalizing effect by which one is able to review the natural world reflexively, without any irrational inhibitions whatsoever. A person with such a well-connected thinking pattern cannot possibly fall prey to the destruction of nature, for the interconnections and interdependencies within nature and between humanity and nature will be clearly seen. An ocean of sensitivity and concern towards all the elements that comprise the Earth, would flow from a recognition of man's finite status in the universe. Only then would our place in the vastness of the cosmic order of space and time be truly realized and appreciated.

When we break the pattern of such ecological thinking by disconnecting ourselves from the awareness of the reality of the Originator, then we may utterly disconnect ourselves from the global concern for both ecology and humanity. When the ties of realization linking oneself to the awareness of such a creative source are severed, the rational basis of moral sustenance disappears and the death of sensitivity towards the natural world becomes imminent, no matter how 'sentimental' or eloquent we may project ourselves in our 'concern' for nature. Such are the immutable laws of human thought according to the Qur'anic concepts.

Nature and Belief Systems

In the West, there is a general tendency for many individuals to put the blame for all the environmental problems we are facing on the belief in a 'personal God'. In *Diogenes*, the journal of the International Council of Philosophy and humanistic studies, the Mexican philosopher Luis Villoro essentially expresses this view in his discussion on Aztec civilization:

> Time and space were determined in terms of the sacred; the sacred pervaded their institutions, their daily lives, their artistic creations, and formed the basis of their beliefs... The gods are a tangible presence in all things; in trees, rivers, mountains, time and space, and in the daily lives of men... The desacralization of nature and of society began with transcendental monotheism. The alienation of the sacred was accentuated in the renaissance. Nature began to be seen as a manipulable object, destined to be dominated and molded by man.[78]

How valid is this assertion? As was discussed earlier, the main problem is the belief in the conception of 'God' and what is purported to be revelation, coupled

78. Summer 1992, No. 159, pp. 58–60.

with the behaviour of its adherents. And as was also pointed out, our conception of 'God' has an impact on our behaviour as much as our denial of the existence of any conception of God. In fact, this idea is consistent with what we see happening around us. If, for example, belief in a personal Singular God is what has caused the problems, then why is it that many of the North American Indian tribes, who have a concept of God similar to the Islamic concept, are, relatively speaking, so advanced in their treatment of the environment? It is precisely because their belief system embraces the concept of a Singular God and the notion of the family of mankind together with the rest of the species. It is their concept of humility towards the Creator that has been so benefactory for human relations with the Earth:

> Early travelers often said that the Cherokees had no religion. They saw no temples, no idols, and no priests but the 'conjurers' who cured the sick and divined the future. In truth, the Cherokees were so deeply religious that there was no seam between holy and profane. The breath of Life Master, the Great Spirit [the One God], was in all things: townhouse, field, and home were all temples to him and the Earth.[79]

It is indeed true that the belief in a 'personal God' is harmful if and only if the concept of God diverges from the concept of oneness of the Creator. For if such a concept is accepted but one fails to live with this type of God's awareness, then it will be ineffective in modulating behaviour. On the first point, a deviation from the oneness of the Creator leads to and is a product of an irrational belief system. However, in stark contrast, the concept of the oneness of the Creator and the family of humankind and the rest of nature, leads to and is also a product of a rational belief system. What is so harmful about 'irrationality'? Irrationality breaks the natural pattern of the human social fabric by creating artificial hierarchical structures in society, class divisions, arrogance, and 'us' versus 'them' mentalities. These dysfunctionalities, in turn, have a negative impact on the rest of the environment because man does not live in a vacuum; for example, wars for greed, because of false divisions created by powers with selfish vested interests, have been and are being created among humanity (i.e. the fabrication of racism). However, wars ultimately destroy the environment. In addition, in an irrational belief system based on selfishness, there is a lack of understanding of causal relationships which inevitably causes harm.

79. Wright, Ronald. (1992), *Stolen Continents: The New World Through Indian Eyes Since 1492*, p. 101.

The concept of *tauhid* or the indivisible oneness of the Creator is therefore the most important concept having a bearing on our relation toward the universe according to Islam. In the Qur'an, when the word God is used, it refers to the one universal God—not some tribal Arab god. The Qur'an points out that all the Messengers of God over time even before the Qur'an were in submission to God. For example, Jesus is considered as a prophet of God, like Moses, Abraham and many others who appeared to the various tribes and nations over the millennia with the *same* basic message; they were all Muslims and therefore following Islam. It is a great fallacy to state that Muhammad was the founder of Islam, which gets repeated over and over again in non-Muslim media. Whether one agrees or not whether Muhammad was a prophet is beside the point; the fact is that according to the Muslims, based on the Qur'an, he was not its 'founder'.

It is interesting to note that Jesus (Isa) himself emphasized the concept of the oneness of God, with himself as a subordinate created creature merely obeying the Creator. It is not well-known by most Christians and Jews, who have been engulfed by Medieval and Hollywood inspired Eurocentric notions of Jesus, that Jesus spoke Aramaic, as his mother tongue, and not Greek or Hebrew. In Aramaic he used the word *Alaha*,[80] which denotes oneness or Uniqueness for God, as it does in Arabic (*God*). However, it must be recognized that it is not the word which is significant, but the concept, because concepts shape attitudes, attitudes mold behaviour and behaviour is action—action in relation to the elements of the rest of nature.

In the West, there has been an inordinate trend towards Eastern mysticism and various other syncretistic forms of mysticism as a reaction to the domination of nature. There are other disgruntled individuals, however, who do not feel that any ideology can solve our problems, be it Hinduism, Buddhism, Judaism, Christianity or Islam, because they feel that these systems are hypocritical in various ways. Each of these systems have scriptures which lay down instructions and guidance on how to treat the environment with care and the animals with compassion and fellow-feeling. However, many of the Pandits, the Rabbis, the Priests, and those who speak for Islam have started vying with each other to prove that their respective Books have the best to offer in this respect. Yet, under their very noses, their followers are competing with each other in devising ever-new means and methods of torture and exploitation of helpless and innocent creatures and the destruction of habitats.

80. See, for example, the Ancient Aramaic New Testament translated from the ancient Khabouris Manuscript (https://archive.org/details/Khabouris).

As discussed in *Animals in Islam* by one of us,[81] in the East, many of the supposed followers of such traditions cannot follow the 'idealistic' interpretations of their very own Eastern religions in their daily lives. This is because the over-stringent rules are uncompromising with the laws of nature and lack the regard for human capacity. They often lead to the hypocritical simulations of virtue. Let us take a few examples from Jainism, the practitioners of *Ahimsa* (non-injury).[82] Jains believe that all creatures are equal and possess a soul. Their doctrines, such as non-injury to creatures no matter how small—in the general sense of *Ahimsa*—are no doubt very benefactory to animal welfare. However, for fear of killing germs and insects, Jains are not supposed to eat root vegetables such as potatoes, or to pulp and grind grains. One of the five tenets of *Ahimsa*, is that one should eat only during daytime, before sunset. From a health point of view, it is a very wise proposition. Even modern dieticians recommend that it is not healthy to retire for the night on a heavy stomach. However, the reason given in the religious sources for this tenet is that, after dark, there is a greater possibility of insects in the air getting in the mouth along with the morsels of food.[83] One should not travel too far from home lest one should cause harm to beings in an unfamiliar place.[84] Worms and insects in the soil get injured by digging or ploughing and therefore farming is considered as one of the contra-*ahimsa* occupations.[85] One Jain sect, called the Digambaras, denounce even such activities as bathing, the use of fire, wearing clothes, farming, etc., for fear of hurting the creatures in air, water or earth.[86]

Though it might sound too critical for those who advocate a relativistic ecumenical approach, it must be pointed out bluntly, that from the Qur'anic perspective, such extreme *ahimsaic* attitudes are the direct result of doctrinal misunderstandings or misrepresentations that have accrued over the ages. The Qur'anic view is that at one stage in history, mankind had one belief—that of submitting voluntarily to the Creator of the universe.[87] This changed over the course of time as man began to live a sedentary life in towns and villages in

81. Masri, B. A. (1989), *Animals in Islam*, pp. 50–51.
82. Chapple, Christopher. (1986), 'Noninjury to Animals: Jaina and Buddhist Perspectives', *Animal Sacrifices: Religious Perspectives on the Use of Animals in Science*, p. 215. *Ahimsa* comes from the Sanskrit root *hims*, and with the prefix '*a*' is best translated as 'absence of the desire to kill or harm'.
83. Wadia, Koshlya. (1974), cf. *The Conception of Ahimsa in Indian Thought*.
84. cf. *Purusartha—Siddhupaya*, p. 140.
85. *P.S. Jaini*, p. 171.
86. Jacobi, Herman. (1973), cf. *Jaina Sutra*.
87. Qur'an 2:213.

farming communities. A hierarchical system or class system consisting of kings, priests, warriors and labourers, thereafter gradually emerged. To maintain such hierarchical control systems and to enforce them, many people strayed from this rational way, eventually giving rise to many divergent and contradictory belief systems or 'religions'. When, as a corrective measure, the messengers of the Creator of the universe were sent to teach people—of every nation and tribe on Earth—to live with nature, rather than over or under it, they mistook and misapplied the messages over time, often times wittingly. For example, when they were told to take care of their animals, over the years, they eventually started worshiping them; when they were advised to bathe in the river for hygienic measures, they started to misconstrue the practice of dipping their bodies into the river as a means by which to gain eternal salvation. With the passage of time, a multitude of such practices became institutionalized and enshrined. These ideas were then put to ardent practice, without question, from generation to generation to this very day, causing unnecessary hardship and untold oppression in the hierarchical schemes or the societal structures which became established.

We can therefore see that according to Islam, various other pre-Qur'anic revealed scriptures were also sent down as a guidance to humanity from the same source of Infinite Wisdom. However, these scriptures have been altered in many ways over the ages and are no longer in their pristine forms as they had been originally revealed thousands of years ago. Yet, despite this major drawback, by sifting and sorting, one can still determine what information is likely to have been compatible with the basic ethical teachings that the Prophets must have taught. By critically examining the pre-Qur'anic scriptures in this manner, we can still discover precious gems of relevant and benefactory advice which may be inspirational in solving our present day ecological/environmental problems. Given this history, it should not come as a surprise to hear the echoes of a belief system based on submission to the Creator, in various 'religions' on Earth. The purely monotheistic statement of Chief Seattle of the Squamish Tribe in 1854—before his tribe's particular land in North America was usurped by the Europeans—is highly significant in this context. In the text of his long speech from which this extract is given, Seattle was expressing—from a conceptual perspective—a purely Islamic position, when he said that:

> Whatever befalls the Earth, befalls the children of the Earth... The people did not weave [this] web of life but are merely a strand in it. [Hence] whatever we do to the web we do to ourselves... Continue to

contaminate your bed and you will one night suffocate in your own
waste… the Earth is precious to God, and to harm the Earth is to heap
contempt on its Creator.

It seems that the dispossessed Chief Seattle's prediction of the future state of
affairs is unfolding with great rapidity! Just over one and a half centuries later,
his words pierce through the armour of our irresponsible technological society.

Despite the many divergences and alterations from the rational concept
of One God and its implications, the quintessence of all such pre-Qur'anic
scriptural messages boils down to the reality that the fates of the human and the
animal creation are interlocked. In fact, even our contemporary naturalists have
started preaching fidelity to life and nature as an aggregated whole—in stark
contrast to the European scholastic nominalists of the Middle Ages.

The Islamic Concept of Custodianship

For Muslims, it is God who has made the Earth facilitative and yielding.
man can go around in all its regions and partake of the sustenance, but God is
the ultimate provider. According to the Qur'an, human beings are to be neither
dominant nor subservient to nature. Rather, they are to act as integral parts of
the patterns in the fabric of nature. They are responsible for the safekeeping of
the intrinsic balance of nature. The Qur'an reminds humankind that all the
components of the ecosystem have a unique function; each part is playing a
particular role in the ecological cycle. Hence, extermination or disruption of one
element has a net-effect on the entire chain through the causal nexus.

Many environmentalists today have learned about the Qur'anic position in
relation to the Earth's resources and have acknowledged this qualitative difference
which has led them to criticize the Bible for decades. It was mentioned earlier
that Prince Charles in the preface to *Save the Earth* has stated that: 'Genesis
provides a license to exploit the environment by implying that the world was
created to be at man's disposal. By contrast, the Koran specifically mentions the
fact that the natural world is loaned from God.' Likewise, Peter Timmerman, a
professor of environmental studies states:

It is clear that this [the Qur'anic position] is a restatement in much
stronger and more explicit language of what is found scattered here
and there in the Old and the New Testaments of the Bible, and which
modern theologians in the West have had to patch together into a
workable environmentalism. The Qur'an states emphatically and

repeatedly humanity's special role as stewards of the world. In Islam, the world is seen as a test of humankind's ability to govern wisely, and it is therefore held only in trust.[88]

Unlike the Bible, the Qur'an consistently, that is, without any contradictions and explicitly, mentions in numerous verses that the entire natural world belongs to God alone.

> And unto God belongs the dominion over the celestial/galactical systems and the Earth: God has the power over all things. (3:189)
>
> Certainly, to Him belongs all that the universe and the Earth contain ... (22:64)
>
> Blessed is He to whom belongs the dominion of the entire universe and the Earth therein; He who begets no offspring, nor has any associate to share in His dominion; He who created everything, and ordained for each and everything its specific function. (25:2)

Humankind is given only temporary stewardship of the natural world. Furthermore, humankind is both responsible for the proper use and is accountable for the abuse of the Earth's natural resources.

> And whatever is in the universe and whatever is on the Earth is God's; and certainly We enjoined those who were given the Book before you and We enjoin you too that you should be careful of your duty to God. (4:131)

How we use nature depends on where we place ourselves in nature. Is humanity abiding with some grand illusion about its unconditional importance, or is it entrenched in reality? The Qur'an does indeed tell human beings that God 'did create human beings in the best of make' and He has appointed man to exercise limited and temporal authority on Earth, but at the same time, in clear, unequivocal language tells us that those who breach the trust sink further and fare worse than the 'lowest of the low'. This limited authority on Earth is meant to be a 'custodianship' of the florae and faunae on Earth as an earthly representative of the Creator who has a far greater love for His creatures than a mother's love for her child.[89] This is the actual meaning of the Qur'anic term *khalifah*[90] translated as steward. *Khalifah* certainly does not mean feudatory over-lordship,

88. Timmerman, Peter. (1989), 'God is closer to you than your jugular vein', *Probe Post*.
89. Abu Dawoud, Sunun, Ibn al-Kathir, al Jami, Vol. 4, pp. 529–530, Hadith 2634.
90. *Khalifa* (Plural: *Khala 'if*) is mentioned in the Qur'an in: 2:30; 6:165; 7:74; 10:14; 10:73; 27:62; 35:39; 38:26.

either linguistically or contextually—or indeed in any other way. In fact the root meaning of *khalifah* is successor and not deputy vicegerent, vicegerent or trustee;[91] however, in this context the function of the successor is the custodianship, which we can understand from the verse in the Qur'an (33:72–73) which states that man has accepted the trust from God but is ungrateful, whereas the celestial objects, Earth and mountains rejected the trust because of the heavy responsibility and were cautiously fearful of accepting it. Note that God is able to give consciousness to anything if He wills, and to ask that question to inanimate objects, like the stars, Earth and mountains for the brief moment.[92] The Islamic view, therefore, is that human beings, unlike animals, have been endowed with the capacity of higher levels of reasoning and abstraction does not in the least entitle us, *ipso facto*, to any undue privileges over so-called brutes. On the contrary, this volitional power puts on us an added responsibility to defend the *Equigenic Rights*, as defined earlier, of those who are incapable of voicing their protests in the most reasonable manner. Bereft of volition which leads to the consciousness of the Creator as Ultimate Owner, and of that which is harmful and beneficial, man degrades himself to a level lower than a brute, and forsakes his rightful place as *khalifa*.

There is another relevant concept in the Qur'an, known as *sakhkhara*, which needs to be discussed. *Sakhkhara* literally means 'subservience' and is mentioned on numerous occasions. For example, there is a verse in the Qur'an which asks:

> 'Are you not aware that it is God who has made subject (*sakhkhara*) to you all that is on the Earth, the ships that sail through the sea at His behest—and the celestial bodies, so that they may not fall upon the Earth otherwise than by His leave?'[93]

This verse is bracketed between two verses, the preceding one reminding us that the universe and everything in it belongs to God, and the succeeding verse admonishing the ingratitude of man towards God, despite man having been well-bestowed with all the beneficent processes in life. In fact, whenever the word *sakhkhara* is used[94]—in relation to the rest of nature—it implies the functional utilizability of all things in creation by man due to the ultimate

91. Tlilli, Sarra. (2012). *Animals in the Qur'an*, Cambridge University Press.
92. Qur'an 33:72–73.
93. Qur'an 22:65.
94. The perfect active verb *Sakhkhara* is used in the Qur'an in the following verses: 13:2; 14:32; 14:33; 16:12; 16:14; 21:79; 22:37; 29:61; 31:20; 31:29; 35:13; 38:18; 38:36; 39:5; 43:13; 45:12; 45:13; 69:7.

subservience of everything to the laws of the Creator, for it is 'God who has made subject to you...'. In other words, it is only by God's permission that we are given the potentiality for control over natural phenomena. Indeed, man has been endowed with the ability to utilize nature with his mind and hands, with far greater dexterity and capacity than any creature on Earth. *Sakhkhara* then, does not mean overbearing subservience or exploitation—rather it means the subservience of nature to the laws of the Creator in which man is part of nature and in which man has been endowed with the potentiality to subject all things in nature under the behavioral laws of the Creator—an approach which can only begin when we are grateful to the Creator. Indeed, the Qur'an stipulates that this utilization must not be at the neglect of God—rather one must remember God by contemplating on universal design. Failing this, the created natural laws related to human psychology—of *moral entropy*—will reduce the human being to something else:

> Certainly, We have created man in the best of make and, save the ones who believe through verification and do good works—whose reward will be never-ending—all others will be reduced to the state of the lowest of the low. (95:4–6)

To avoid this degeneration, then, the Qur'anic view is that we must not lock ourselves up in a cave and automatonically chant on the 'sound of one hand clapping', but must constantly keep cognizant of creation interactively. To *paraphrase* a section in the Qur'an (3:190–191): 'In the creation of the universe and the Earth, and in the sequence of night and day, there are manifest evidences for those who reflect. These evidences are for those who constantly celebrate the praises of the Creator—while standing, sitting, or reclining— keeping in mind that it is the Creator who has originated, designed and created the cosmos. When they then reflect seriously on the wonders of nature created in the universe and the Earth, they cry out: "Our Sustainer! You have not created all this without a meaningful plan and purpose; all praise is due to You; Yours is all the glory; save us from the dire consequences of harm in the next life (the fire), if we fail to apprehend all this."'

Teleology

Muslims thinkers have been cognizant of teleology, since the 8th century, as for instance the Muslim writer and evolutionist, Al-Jahiz (776/7 to 868/9 C.E), author of *The Book of Animals*, who emphasized the source of everything

71

created to a unique Creator, who is One and non-anthropomorphic, as discussed previously. He remarked that:

> I would have you know that a pebble proves the existence of God just as much as a mountain, and the human body is evidence as strong as the universe that contains our world: for this purpose the small and slight carries as much weight as the great and vast.[95]

Al-Jahiz had specifically written about animals to prove the glory of God's creation and wisdom. The Islamic concept of custodianship begins with and is founded upon the realization of this teleological outlook and the Creator of teleological inter-relationships. Before Islamic societies became ever more engulfed with mysticism and dogmatic thinking, against the teachings of the Qur'an, thinkers such as Ibn Rushd discussed teleology and the route to certainty, the unity of knowledge and the concordance between faith and reason based on evidence. This understanding is a far cry from the notions of many Muslims about Islam today, and indeed from the perception of non-Muslims about Islam. For Ibn Rushd states that:

> We say: If the activity of 'philosophy' is nothing more than study of existing beings and reflection on them as indications of the Artisan, i.e. inasmuch as they are products of art (for beings only indicate the Artisan through our knowledge of the art in them, and the more perfect this knowledge is, the more perfect the knowledge of the Artisan becomes), and if the Law has encouraged and urged reflection on beings, then it is clear that what this name signifies is either obligatory or recommended by the Law.[96]

The Qur'an on the Signs in Nature

The Qur'an points to a Singular Intelligence as the Originator and Creator of the universe—a universe with special properties: In this all-encompassing architecture of reality, we see that the diversity of life and non-life covers a vast spectrum ranging from the submicroscopic world of experimentally theorized quarks to the macroscopic world of clusters upon clusters of galaxies and beyond. We realize from the examination of this universal order, that everything in space and time is interwoven into an intricate fabric which is both incredibly complex

95. Pellat, Charles. (1969), *The Life and Works of Jahiz: Translation of Selected Texts*, p. 152.
96. Averroës. (1967), *On the Harmony of Religion and Philosophy*, (translated by Hourani, George Faido) p. 44.

as well as fully integrated. We see the sun, Earth, moon and planets ceaselessly orbiting within an ordered system. We also see the water-cycle bringing rain onto the dusty parched ground, onsetting the growth of luxurious foliage. We literally observe countless signs surrounding us, yet in our daily lives we may be completely oblivious—due to over-familiarization—to the miracle of their very existence, let alone their purpose and design.

Through research, we are now fathoming the depths of the microworlds and macroworlds of the present and the past. We are gaining insight into the origins, transformations and termination of such things, ranging from the graceful metamorphosis of a chrysalis into a butterfly, to the explosion of a star into a supernova. The Qur'an itself expounds on this theme in a great many places. For instance, it states that:

> In the creation of the universe and the Earth, in the sequence of night and day; in the vessels that ply through bodies of water carrying beneficial cargo for mankind; in the rain that God causes to descend from the clouds—thereby regenerating the dead soil and dispersing all manner of animals—in the regulation of the air-currents and the clouds that circulate between the sky and the Earth—surely in all these, there are manifest pointers for those who would take thought. (2:164)

> Have they never cast a glance at the firmament above? How we have structured and adorned it and it is without rifts! And the Earth—We have spread it out; have cast forth stabilizing mountains and caused to grow on it, beauteous kinds giving insight and reminiscence to every penitent votary. (50:6–8)

> It is God who has raised up the cosmic canopy without any visible support. Then He established Himself on the throne [of power] and made the sun and moon subservient [to His laws]—each running its course to its appointed term. It is He who regulates all affairs and explains clearly His portents, so that you may be certain of your eventual meeting with Him. (13:2)

Recent findings should, in fact, leave no doubt in our minds that everything on Earth, in space and time, is interwoven into a beautiful natural tapestry patterned by the extremely intricate and complex balances in nature. Investigations of the universe at large have revealed that it has originated from the absolute non-existence of space and time. It has evolved over time to make life possible on Earth, and is precisely structured for existence itself. For example, had the gravitational and expansional forces not been arranged perfectly, the universe would have either collapsed or expanded too fast for the formation of galaxies, depending on which of the two forces was even minutely greater.

On Earth, animals and plants are optimally adapted to the environment and are, similarly, spatially dispersed, by means of which the balances in the ecosystem are maintained. We know that the introduction of a non-indigenous species into a natural ecosystem has devastating effects as does the elimination of an indigenous one by the interference of humans. Non-living elements also participate in this grand network of dynamic interactions which allow life to continue and flourish on our unique planet. Although, for example, the energy output of the sun has increased over a few billion years, the proportion of the vital gases in the atmosphere has remained steady as even dead matter, in the cyclical scheme, contributes towards producing this equilibrium which is so crucial for life. In Qur'an chapter 55, verses 7 to 10, quoted previously, where it is stated that the balance is not to be upset, it is further added that:

> And the Earth (both the planet as a whole, and the Earth's crust itself)! He has appointed and precisely established and positioned it for the maintenance and development of creatures. (55:10)

And:

> ... the Earth! We have spread it out and set on it stabilizing mountains, sprouting from it, all kinds of things in due balance. (15:19)

The true complementary meanings of the word *wada-'ahaa* in Qur'an 55:10 is appoint, precision placement, establish and bear. This can be realized by analyzing various verses in the Qur'an, where the same word is employed in different contexts. In 55:7 and 88:14 it means to set-up, structure or establish; in 18:49 and 39:69 it means to place; in 3:96 it means to appoint; and in 3:36 it means to bear or deliver (where the context is the womb), that is, the womb supports, maintains and develops the embryo/fetus after which it is born. The idea of precision and proper positioning/placement comes from verse 4:46 and 5:13. The rendition above reflects all these concepts co-joined in an integrated manner to get the full meaning of the verse. The implication of this verse is that given that God has set up the dynamic equilibrium in which the animals and Earth are 'in sync' and that the Earth is also positioned precisely from the sun to produce carbon-based life, we must do our utmost to preserve that 'sync'.

This Creator then does not just sustain things haphazardly, but has created this universe with a higher purpose that is reflected in nature. The Qur'an is profuse with teleological statements about the nature of the cosmos where God and His designs are always at the focus. Here are a few samples:

> It is He who created the universe and the Earth therein, in the truth. Whatever He wills to Be, it is. (6:73)
>
> It is He who has created for you all things that are on the Earth—His design comprehended the universe, for He gave order of perfection to its multi-leveled cosmic systems;[97] and of all things He has perfect knowledge. (2:29)
>
> Extol the Glory of your Sustainer—the Most High! Who creates and establishes proportion; who determines the potential of things and then guides them accordingly; who brings forth the pasturage, and then reduces it to duskish stalks of stubble. (87:1–5)
>
> It is God alone who upholds the cosmic order, lest it should fall into chaos. In case the celestial bodies were even to deviate from their orbits, there is none to put them back on course. Verily! He is most clement and forgiving. (35:41)
>
> It is He who has created the many celestial systems in full integration with one another: You will find no flaw in the design of the most Gracious. Indeed, observe again! Can you see any flaw? Look again and again! Your sight will end up being dazzled and strained. (67:4)
>
> Or who is it that originates creation to begin with, and then repeats the process; and who is it that provides you with sustenance out of the sky and the Earth? Could there be, then, another deity besides God? Say: Bring forward your proof, if you are truthful! (27:64)
>
> There is not a single thing in existence, whose depositories are not with Us, and We do not expedite them except in a known measure. (15:21)

The hundreds of centuries of experience of life on Earth has most certainly fostered the development of our intelligence, yet all of it will be of no help

---

97. The word *sama* means 'that which is above' and is contextual in nature. Its plural is *samawati*. The translation *saba samawatin* is best rendered using our present knowledge about astrophysics, which is that: this universe is built up on the basis of the clustering of stars and galaxies 'one above the other' as the Qur'an also states in 67:3 and 71:15. It should be noted that the word *saba* (seven) in Arabic also is often used to denote a limited plurality, not unlike the word 'several' in English. It could though perhaps also mean exactly seven levels of clustering and in another context the space surrounding exactly seven stars (i.e. each star has its heaven, or literally, that which is above it).

when we fail to grasp the basic fact that each and everything on Earth, be it visible or invisible, large or small, exists for some specific goal, as part of an artistic and beautiful expression of the will of the Supreme Designer, thoughtfully designed to serve a specific purpose. Certainly, in this design, we observe countless miracles around us, and in awe do we admire them; but we fail to see and admire the miracles happening within ourselves. We see a small egg and wonder how it could possibly contain the blueprint of such an enormous bird as an ostrich. We see a little acorn and wonder how it could contain instructions giving rise to such a lofty tree as an Oak. On the Earth, so many different species of animals flourish that we are unable to fathom just how many there really are. Yet out of these millions of kinds of life forms, man is the only earthly creature who has the potential to use the mind to choose between what is harmful and beneficial in the intellectual sense and it is only because of this 'freedom of choice' that man can be considered to be potentially higher ranking than the animals. Animals also possess minds, and can also differentiate between that which is good and bad for their needs. However, animals naturally follow set patterns of behaviour, and do not, in that sense, possess the freedom of choice associated with either virtue or corruption. Our ability to choose, based on knowledge and intelligence, puts on us the added responsibility toward the rest of the natural world. Indeed, it is these very resources which help to sustain and promote life on Earth. Some of those resources, however, be they animal, vegetable or mineral, are hidden to us so far, due to our lack of knowledge. However, these undiscovered components in the vast complex of the environment, certainly also deserve equal protection lest we unwittingly destroy them.

It is we, the descendants of *homo sapiens*, branching out from common primeval origin, who have been chosen to carry out that will by running the affairs of this world in an orderly way, that is by not disrupting the inherent order it possesses. Due to our capacity to reason at a higher level of abstraction, and the complementary manual and linguistic dexterity, we have been entrusted with the responsibility to participate within the processes of nature. We have been assigned the key role as cardinal players within the spectrum of myriad life-sustaining interactions on Earth. Having evolved in stages until we grew into complete human beings, we possess intelligence capable of interfering and utilizing the forces of nature. Yet how are we to view nature, given our double-edged sword of exploitative faculties?

Ownership of the Balance

The realization that the universe has indeed been designed and originated by an Intelligence, draws attention to two essential facts realizable from nature—the facts of ultimate ownership and of the balance.

> Say: Whose is the Earth and whoever is therein, if you know? (23:84)
>
> Surely the Earth belongs to God, and He bequeaths it to such of His servants as He pleases; and the future belongs to the God-conscious.[98] (7:128)
>
> Certainly, to Him belongs all that the universe and the Earth contain; and verily, God alone is self-sufficient, the One to whom all praise is due. (22:64)

We human beings, are finite and dependent creatures; therefore, we cannot lay claim whatsoever to being the ultimate owners of things in nature; the natural world is tantamount to a loan from the originative singular Creator of the universe, who alone is its Ultimate Owner. This view certainly has a profound implication: in order to avoid a disruption of the Earth's inherent natural balances, that which is loaned, must not, under any circumstances be abused or misused. In fact, our right to use the natural resources, is only in the sense of usufruct—as if one had been given the right to use another's property with the clear understanding that one would not damage, waste or destroy its substance. Indeed, the elements of nature such as the land, water, air, fire, forests, sunlight, for example, are the common property of all creatures—not only of human beings:

> He spread the Earth (i.e. continental drift) and has brought forth from it [the Earth] its waters and its pastures, and stabilized the mountains firm—as a source of provision for both you and your (domestic) animals. (79:30–33)
>
> ... We cause pure water to descend from the skies so that We may bring dead land to life thereby, and give to drink thereof to many, animals as well as humans, created. (25:49, also see 80:32)

In verse 79:30–33, water is mentioned in connection with mountains; in fact in most cases when mountains are mentioned in the Qur'an, then so

---

98. The word translated as 'God-conscious' is *taqwa*, the implication of which is protection from harmful actions in this universe and protection from punishment in the hereafter which necessitates an awareness of God watching all actions.

is water. The reason for this is that 50% of freshwater emanates from glaciers which are on mountains. It must be remembered in passing that the Prophet Muhammad being no glaciologist or geologist would not have known of this fact in an era when inductive science was almost non-existent!

If we were duly conscious of our own origins and the fact that we do not own the natural world and its resources in the ultimate sense, then we would not allow ourselves to be steered towards either a domineering, or a helplessly subservient attitude in relation to the rest of the natural world. We would, for instance, not be subservient to the wilderness in the sense that we would not allow the forces or elements of nature to dominate us, by the misdirection of superstition. Instead of being paralyzed or intoxicated by fear, or wayward by the arrogance of domination, we would strive our utmost to live our lives as rational individuals within the matrix of the variegated patterns displayed by the rest of nature. We would not disrupt any of its inherently structured checks and balances. Deeply ingrained within the very consciousness of our being, would be the realization of our place in the whole of the cosmic scheme—a state of peaceful, participatory coexistence with the rest of the natural world. There are, in fact, many verses in the Qur'an which deal with man's abnormal tendency towards domination over nature. It is our arrogance and forgetfulness, which precludes the possibility of such a harmonious coexistence with the rest of the animate and inanimate world. The Qur'an reminds us to avoid such an attitude:

> It is He who has made the Earth compliant. So walk in its tracts and partake of the provisions laid out by Him—bearing in mind that unto Him is the ultimate return. (67:15)

> Do not walk on the Earth in overbearance—for you can neither split the Earth asunder, nor can you rival the mountains in stature. Such arrogance—the wickedness of it all—is hateful in the sight of your Sustainer. (17:37–38)

Purpose in the Natural World

The Qur'an repeatedly emphasizes that everything, large or small, has been created for specifically designated purposes; we cannot, therefore, go about destroying things haphazardly simply because we do not see any existential purpose. The Qur'an conveys that God did not create this universe without a meaningful purpose, but it is man who created a meaningless purpose without God in the universe. In fact, we may not recognize any such purpose in both the universe as a whole and in its countless structures and processes because of a lack of knowledge or wanton unheedfulness, not because there is none. In the natural realm, everything has a purpose, which is manifested by its structure and function, a fact which is clearly pointed out by the Qur'an. The universe is the scheme of the Creator, who knows what is needed to run it—a Creator who weighs and measures everything accordingly:

> Behold! We have created everything with a pre-determined measure. (54:49)[99]

> We have built this universe with a force; indeed, We are most certainly expanding it. And We have spread the Earth out wide—how well We have ordered it! (51:47, 48)

The principle of conservation in Islam rests on this very foundation: that everything in nature has a purpose and is not redundant or otiose in its natural setting. It is man who creates the disorder and imbalances. Therefore, the onus falls squarely on man to rectify any inversions of the balance. In the rectification process, the following Qur'anic juristic rules, which will be comprehensively discussed in Chapter 5, should be kept in mind:

- No damage can be put right by inflicting a similar or greater damage.
- Prevention of damage takes precedence over the achievement of interests or the fulfillment of needs.

For example, if human needs are non-critical then one cannot damage nature to gain such needs. There are no compromises on these principles in Islam. If there is an imbalance in nature, due to the inadvertent or advertent migration of animals, or due to the increase of one species over others as a result of man's activities, man cannot go about killing the species in question to try to restore a balance. The Islamic system would ensure that there be a proper management, redistribution or relocation of species or the introduction of various other species to redress the imbalances which would have been created in the first place by man's callous calculations or miscalculations.

In certain situations the best action is no action. However, the Islamic position, being logical and practical, allows for flexibility in particular or special circumstances where there are absolutely no better alternatives: *If two harms conflict, choose the lesser harm to prevent the bigger harm.* However, this can only

99. See also Qur'an 5:3, Qur'an 13:8, Qur'an 25:2.

be done with the proviso that one is certain that one is not dishonestly justifying one's actions for dubious vested interests: *All false excuses leading to damage should be repudiated.*

The main problem is the pervasive usage of false justifications, constructed in order to be able to engage in various improper practices, in an attempt to appease inner consciences and increase some form of profitability. The construction of such false justification systems usually involves the use of special pleading, where only that data or information is cited which supports one's own view at the expense of any other data which goes counter to it. If one carefully analyzes a host of contemporary environmental issues, problems and controversies, one would not fail to notice this approach. Take for example many 'developmental' projects in all parts of the world, where developers often do not disclose or override the concerns of the ordinary citizen. From the Qur'anic viewpoint, those who dubiously collude in order to support such pleadings are on the road, not only to ecological destruction, but to self-destruction as well, even though they may not realize it, due to arrogance and narrow desires which give rise to tunnel vision. Covering up that information which is beneficial is regarded in the Qur'an as a behavioral disease rooted in man's denial of the one and only Creator, and is denoted by the word *kafir,* meaning the one who *covers* the truth. The Qur'an stresses that truth cannot be destroyed—at most it can only be covered up, and that there is only one truth for a particular context, but a plurality of falsehoods.

Against Wastage

There are numerous Qur'anic verses and hadiths which give a good idea regarding the design of things in nature and the fact that improper usage has to do with the usage of a thing for that which it was not intended for by its very structure and related function. It can be noted that the seriousness of wastage, again is connected to the concept of purposeful usage: the Prophet said:

> While a man was riding an ox, it turned towards him and voiced [in some non-human manner] that: 'I have not been created for this purpose (i.e. carrying), I have been created for ploughing.'[100]

In this regard, the Qur'an also states:

> Eat and drink [non-intoxicants], but waste not by indulging in excesses; surely, God does not approve of the intemperate. (7:31)

100. Bukhari 3:517.

The Prophet was very concerned about wastage. In fact, one day the Prophet saw a man named Sa'd using too much water while performing ablution to wash himself for prayer and said to him:

> 'What is this wastage, O Sa'd?' Sa'd responded: 'Is there wastage even in using water for ablution?' The Prophet replied: 'Yes, even if you are by a flowing river.'[101]

The examples and teachings of the Prophet were not lost on his early followers, as they are in most cases nowadays. One of the Prophet's closest companions and nephew, Ali, instructed a man who reclaimed a piece of derelict land:

> Occupy it gladly, but you can use it only so long as you remain a benefactor, not a despoiler—a cultivator, not a destroyer.[102]

The Prophet did not even want a morsel of food to be wasted if it could be at all avoided, for he said:

> Honour the bread! God has certainly put to its service, the blessings of the universe and the Earth therein, steel, cows and human beings.[103]

Using nature in a benefactory manner was of paramount concern to the Prophet. The following hadith might sound trite, but even today, fourteen centuries later, the United Nations' findings are that:

> In 2015, 29 percent of the global population lacked safely managed drinking water supplies, and 61 percent were without safely managed sanitation services. In 2015, 892 million people continued to practise open defecation.[104]

According to a Hadith:

> The Prophet forbade that a person relieve himself in a water source, or on a path, or in a place of shade, or in a burrow of a living creature.[105]

---

101. Musnad of Ahmad ibn Hanbal. Also Ibn Majah on the authority of Abd-God ibn 'Amr.
102. Narrated by Yahya ibn Adam al-Quraish, *Kitab al-Kharaj*, on the authority of Sa'id ad-Dabbi.
103. Ibn 'Asakir, Mukasar Tarikh Dimashq, Vol. 26, p. 358.
104. UN-Water, 'Sustainable Development Goal No. 6', http://www.unwater.org/publication_categories/sdg-6-synthesis-report-2018-on-water-and-sanitation/
105. Abu Dawud. Narrated by Abu Hurairah, Mu'adh and Abd-God ibn Sarjis.

The Islamic Code for the Protection of Florae and Faunae

> Limitless in His glory is He who has created complementary pairs in
> whatever the Earth provides, out of themselves and in that of which
> they have no knowledge. (36:36)[106]

The Islamic legislation on the preservation of trees and plants, laid down
some fourteen centuries ago, covers not only forests but also wildlife. According
to these laws, certain areas are set aside as regulated sanctuaries and reserves,
called *harim* or *hima*. There were different types of *hima* for various contextually functional reasons, but most of them prohibited grazing, tree-cutting,
hunting, farming and settlement. The Prophet set up these sanctuaries and
conservation areas for the benefit of flora and fauna, and as in the case of the
first Caliph after the Prophet, that is, Abu Bakar Siddiq, a *hima* was established
for the usufruct of the poor.[107] This code of ecological legislation was based on
numerous verses of the Qur'an and the sayings of Prophet Muhammad, such
as: 'The world is green and beautiful and God has appointed you as His stewards over it. He sees how you acquit yourselves.'[108] The Qur'an states:

> Do they not look at the Earth—how many exquisite kinds [of plants]
> We have caused to grow on it? Surely, there is a sign in this: however,
> most of them do not believe... (26:7,8)

---

106. A unique aspect of the Qur'an in relation to creation in 'pairs' can be illustrated by an anecdote:
A few years ago, one of the authors, was discussing the case of a lizard (an unusual unisexual
species of whiptail lizard, *Cnemidophorous uniparens*) which does not consist of any males and
reproduces parthenogenically (i.e. only females and no males). The question which was raised
was as to how this would be in congruence with the Qur'an, which states that all living things
have been created in pairs. The discussants realized that there was more to this anomaly than met
the eye, but did not know what could tie it with the Qur'anic verse. Remember, that one could
collapse the Qur'an by showing even one contradiction in it and that the Qur'an encourages and
challenges us to see if there are any contradictions in it. We did not have a definite answer for this
question then, but several years later, an article appeared in the *Scientific American* magazine,
December 1987, by David Crews on these very lizards entitled 'Courtship in Unisexual Lizards:
A Model for Brain Evolution'. In the article it was explained that: 'Complementarity in the
ovarian cycles of *C. Uniparens* makes courtship in this species possible. During the breeding
season females will synchronize their activities so that when some individuals are preovulatory,
others are postovulatory. The females in this species reproduce by parthenogenesis, that is
reproduction without fertilization ... [but] the females in this species actively engage in lengthy
courtship behaviors that are virtually identical ... between [other "normal" sub-species that do
contain] male and female whiptail lizards.'

107. Ali, Syed Irtifaq. 'Hima—The Protected Area Concept in Islam', *Islamic Thought and Scientific
Creativity*,', p. 81. See also: Llewellyn, Othman Abd-ar-Rahman. (2003), 'The Basis for a
Discipline of Islamic Law', *Islam and Ecology: A Bestowed Trust*, pp. 200–217.

108. Muslim. Narrated by Abu Sa'id al Khudri.

With an increase in human population, the co-existence of humans and animals based on the better design and management of reserves, that involves maintaining biodiversity within the reserves, is becoming increasingly crucial.[109]

The Qur'an draws our attention repeatedly to the fact that even plants and trees are living organisms, by pointing out that they too have been created in functionally complementary pairs. And this is why in Islam, men and women are considered on a par and equivalent to each other—equal but different in various functional aspects. Like human beings and animals, they too are meant to go on reproducing to keep their species going:

> It is He who has spread out the Earth and of all fruit He produced therein are as complementary pairs. (13:3)

> We cause every exquisite [florae] to grow as complementary pairs. (31:10)

> All things We have created in complementary pairs that you may reflect. (51:49)

> It is He who spread the Earth for you as if it were like a bed; and made paths therein for you, and sent down water from the clouds. Then, We have produced diverse complementary pairs of plants. (20:53)

> Whoever plants a tree and looks after it with care, until it matures and becomes productive, will be rewarded in the Hereafter.[110]

> Even when the world is coming to an end, on Doomsday, if anyone has a seedling in hand, he should plant it...[111]

> God will reward any Muslim who plants a tree or sows a field, from which a human being, bird or animal eats.[112]

> There is a reward for whoever brings dead land to life and for whatever any creature seeking food eats from it.[113]

The Prophet forbade that one cut down, needlessly and wrongfully, any tree which provides shelter to humans or animals.[114] It is reported that, when the funeral procession passed by the Prophet he remarked: 'When a virtuous person dies, he is relieved from the trials and tribulations of

109. Margules, C.R., Pressey, R.L. (2000), 'Review Article: Systematic conservation planning', Nature, pp. 243–253.
110. Bukhari and Muslim, Narrated by Anas.
111. Musnad of Ahmad ibn Hanbal, Vol. 3, and Bukhari, al-Adab al-Mufrad, No. 479.
112. Bukhari, 3.513, Anas ibn Malik.
113. at-Tabrizi, *Mishkat al-Masabih*.
114. Abu Dawud. Abd-God ibn-Habshi.

> this world; when an unrighteous person dies, people, towns, trees and animals are relieved from him.'[115]

When the Prophet became the ruler of Mecca and Medinah, he declared the trees in and around these cities as protected, by decrees such as:

- I declare Medinah to be sacrosanct throughout the area between its two mountain paths, so that... leaves may not be beaten in it except for fodder.[116]
- The game and the large thorn trees of Wajj [territory in the neighborhood of Ta'if] are declared as sacrosanct, belonging to God.[117]
- I declare sacrosanct the territory between the lava plains of Medinah, so that its large thorn trees may not be cut down, or its game killed.[118]
- God, not men, has made Makkah sacrosanct, so that it is not permissible for a person who believes in God and in the Last Day, to shed blood, or cut a tree in it.[119]
- [Makkah's] thorn trees are not to be cut, its game is not to be molested and its fresh herbage is not to be cut.[120]

In fact, as the Prophet stated: 'Verily, Abraham declared Mecca a sanctuary...'[121] he was just re-establishing this.

These laws were enforced by a decree that the tools of a person who cuts trees shall be confiscated and shall become the property of the person who catches the violating culprit. One such case has been recorded of a man named Sa'd who confiscated the gear of a man who was cutting some trees.[122]

Early Muslims understood and respected these decrees. After the death of the Prophet, Abu Bakr succeeded him as the first Caliph in 632 C.E. Before sending off an expedition for a battle to a place named *Muta*, he gave his troops some instructions, which included the following concerning trees and animals: 'Do not cut down trees and do not kill animals except for food.'[123]

115. Bukhari, B.519. Abu Qatada bin Rib'i al-Ansari.
116. Robson, Dr. James (Translator). (1963) *Mishkat al-Masabih*, Vol. 2, p. 587.
117. Ibid. p. 590.
118. Ibid. p. 586.
119. Ibid. p. 585.
120. Ibid. p. 583.
121. Muslim, narrated by Abu Huraira.
122. Ibid. p. 590.
123. Tabri, 3, p. 123.

In later years, Muslim jurists based the Islamic legal system on such decrees and formulated similar laws covering the conservation of forests, overgrazing, water resources and animal rights, etc., among other areas of concern, which we are only now paying more attention to with greater awareness.

Chapter 4

The Use of Nature

Lessons from the Chronicles of History

The Qur'an constantly reminds man to consider the parable of history and the logical conclusion which can be drawn from it:

> Do they not see that We visit the land under their control, gradually curtailing its boundaries all around them? [i.e. from an environmental perspective, God could diminish the productive and useful land]... (13:41)

> Certainly, We let them and their forebearers enjoy the good things in life, until they outlive their prosperity. Can they not see that We visit the land gradually curtailing its boundaries all around them? Is it then, they who will prevail? (21:44)

With the misuse of sophisticated technology, especially over the last 200 years or so, we have begun to manipulate and exploit nature as never before. Indeed, in many cases, natural components cannot even regenerate fast enough to reproduce that which we are taking out of them. Furthermore, we can see that some destruction, such as the decimation of entire species, is completely irreversible. In the Qur'an, man's arrogant attitude towards nature is described, by virtue of the fact that human beings sometimes feel that they hold complete sway over everything.

> The similitude of this life is only as the water sent down by Us from the clouds, which generates all kinds of vegetation as food both for mankind and animals. As the crops grow and the Earth is adorned with the splendor and beauty, its people think that they have gained mastery over it. Our commandment occurs, by night or day, and turns their crop into rubble as if it had not flourished the day before. Thus, do We expound our signs to people who are reflective. (10:24)

> Now as for Ad, they walked arrogantly on Earth, against all right, saying, 'Who could have a power greater than ours? Were they then not

aware that God, who created them, had a power greater than theirs?'
(41:15)

A study of history reveals that ever since human beings began a sedentary lifestyle, they have always been carelessly exploiting the resources of nature to satisfy their needs and have not lived by the pillars of conduct defined by their prophets:

> Indeed, We have already sent forth our Messengers with clear evidences and sent down through them the book as well as a balance, so that humankind might behave equitably. We also sent down iron, in which there is tremendous power, as well as benefit for humanity, in order that God might mark out those who would stand up before Him and His Messengers, even though He is unseen. Verily, God is Strong, and Almighty. (57:25)

The above passage is very interesting because it sets down a basic law for societal development based on specific pillars, from which a contemporary model for ideal legislation can also be derived and hopefully, in the future, established. What is being enunciated here is that the book (the Qur'an) and the dynamic balance of nature (the Equigenic Principle) are complementary to each other. There is a symbiotic relation between the two and without basing societies' laws and policies on the realization of this fact, it is impossible to achieve a society that is highly elevated and at peace. If a society follows the laws stated or derived by these, then one can develop technology that can be both defensive and benefactory for society. One can develop technology feasibly with these two—the Qur'an and the Balance—in mind, keeping in perspective that all achievements are only a test to see who would remain in submission to the visually un-seeable Creator and to the true historical and revelatory remembrance of all the prophets who espoused pure monotheism.

Laws of History?

When human beings started to settle in larger communities in the transition from being hunter-gatherers, due to internecine and tribal conflicts, prophets were sent down to each community over thousands of years to achieve societal reformation, each optimally targeted to each local community. These prophets assisted in mitigating the collapse of societies over time, though they were decaying overall. This is because hardly any community followed the precepts of the prophets, or did so only for a short period.

The law of the rise and fall of powers was due to the injustice they meted out to humanity and nature and this became a cyclical phenomenon—that is, the 'rise' and 'fall' of particular civilizations. In most of these civilizations, the rise was not a *rise in morality in conjunction with power* as it ought to have been. Consequently, from the Qur'anic perspective, it was not a true rise of morality but only power, and therefore, fall of power was inevitable. By the time of the onset of the Dark Ages, when societies in all civilizations were being devastated by decadent imperious powers and the rise of mysticism and superstition, a major global prophet was crucially required to reform the whole world. The Muslims claim that this prophet was Muhammad, and his function was to receive the book of the Qur'an from God, the purported revelation, and to set an example by implementing it. In fact, had the Qur'an not seen light of day, global society would have totally collapsed into total barbarism, never to arise from this position till the present day. *It would have been an extended and perennial Dark Ages.* However, the Qur'an raised society to a high level globally and transformed it toward less injustice and more peace, in particular the regions where the Caliphate (imperfectly structured though it was after the Prophet and the first four successors) was established. After the Qur'an's advent, society in general, either by not accepting or (as in the case of the nominal Muslim world) not adhering to the Qur'an fully, has led to a second decline overall in both morality and power; that is, a 'New Dark Ages' as it were, has set in. Since the last two hundred years or so, despite advances in technology, with its horrendous misuses, we have reached the nadir of moral depravity. This is due to the unjust wealth distribution between the haves and the have-nots, and the destruction of the ecosystems and animals, as well as violence in all its forms and on all levels, relativism and entrenched immorality (harmful actions) and indecency and, what is worse: hypocrisy! However, with the influence of the Qur'an 'kicking in' again, society has the opportunity to rise to new heights of peace and justice for all sentient entities. To understand this, we need to look into the seemingly curious concept of 'belonging there' or 'non-dislocation' of elements in the natural domain.

The Non-dislocation of Nature's Constituents

In a verse of the Qur'an, it is stated that only those who are cognizant of the design of the heavens and the Earth, and observe the myriad signs and warnings therein are the ones who use reason and therefore do not engage in acts which are unclean. All this connects to the following, in terms of extending a particular rule in the Qur'an to a wider application: It states in the Qur'an that one should not eat swine flesh because it is unclean (*rijs*) (call this the specific rule); anything that is forbidden in the Qur'an is so because it is harmful (conclusion based on the specific rule). Extending this further (the wider rule), one can say that anything which causes harm or an imbalance or is not something which is being used appropriately, in its proper place where it fits structurally and/or functionally, and that is why it is either imbalancing or dirty. For example for a fly, a pile of refuse is not dirty, for the function of the fly is to eat that dirt and break it down further; it is indeed, a pasture of paradise for the fly, and, what is more, the fly has antibodies to cope with that 'dirt'. The fly belongs there; it is not dis-located. Similarly, the pig has its own place in nature, as akin to a vacuum cleaner; however, its meat does not belong in the human body. By extension, the Qur'an (6:145) then implies that any animals (or products) eaten that cause harm to the human body, or anything which causes disequilibrium in nature is not to be consumed and is, in effect, either *rijs,* or in a more general sense equivalent to being *rijs*, for it does not belong there (in the human body). If a particular fish is in danger of extinction, it would, by these rules become *as if it were equivalent to rijs,* for we would not, according to laws enacted by this principle, be allowed to eat that fish until the situation was rectified. In this way we see *rijs* and the concept of anti-*mizan* (imbalance) is equivalent to *zulm* (performing an unjust act). For example, smoking is an injustice to your lungs and produces harm and disequilibrium in its functionality. In the figure below, the causal nexus of this type of thinking is illustrated and its connection to the word 'Islam', where each concept leads to the next, as follows, noting the fact that the root of the word *zulm* is 'to dislocate/not put things where they belong'—normally translated as injustice:

One of the meanings of the word Islam is 'Peace' (derived from the Arabic root *s-l-m*).

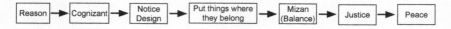

Knowledge through Observing Nature

In the context of ecology it is most significant that an important verse in the Qur'an describes knowledge in terms of the observation of nature itself and the ultimate lesson derived thereof:

Have they not observed that God causes water to descend from the
clouds and We have produced differently colored fruit. Moreover, in
the mountains are diversely colored streaks of red and white as well
as others of intense black. Human beings and the wild and domestic
animals[124] are too, comprised of various colors. Thus, only those among
His creatures who fear and have the awe of God, are truly the people of
knowledge (*ulema*). (35:27–28)

The only knowledgeable people are those who, having recognized the
multifarious signs in nature acknowledge the Creator and act in cognizance of
Him (this is the Qur'anic definition of *ulema*, meaning the knowledgeable ones).
As may be apparent from these verses and those quoted in the previous chapters,
the Qur'an has emphasized a reflection on nature a great deal. This has had a
most significant impact in the major redirection of history, the reverberations of
which are still being felt today.

The Motivational Factor

In the Middle Eastern region, around the 7th century, a truly phenomenal transformation was wrought with the advent of the Qur'an. This book inspired origin and cause seeking observations into the nature of things, in order
to discover its integrated yet diverse patterns and designs. Due to the Qur'anic
influence and the interest aroused by the Islamic laws on animals and the environment, Muslim scholars and naturalists were prompted to do research in these
fields. This transformation started to occur in the 7th century and the Qur'anic
ideas gradually spread from those regions to Europe, from the 9th to the 13th
centuries, by translations of the Arabic works and writings. As Jared Diamond,
in *Guns, Germs and Steel* reveals most accurately:

In the Middle Ages, the flow of technology was overwhelmingly from
Islam to Europe, rather than from Europe to Islam, as it is today. Only
after A.D. 1500 did the net direction of flow begin to reverse. [125]

---

124. This verse shows that some animals have been designed to be domesticated. The *domesticability*
of an animal species seems to be governed by the following factors: Diet, growth rate, problems
of capture and breeding, violent disposition, tendency to panic and social structure. Animals
possessing deficiencies in these traits or due to them tend to become poor candidates for
domestication as realized throughout the history of humankind's efforts for domestication. This
is discussed at length in the Pulitzer Prize winning book written by Jared Diamond: (1997) *Guns,
Germs, and Steel: The Fates of Human Societies*, p. 166–175.
125. Diamond, Jared. (1998), *Guns, Germs and Steel: The Fates of Human Societies*, p. 253.

The Qur'an was the main focus of attention for Muslim thinkers. Indeed, this book is profuse with statements on nature and it is not difficult to comprehend that it was this very book itself which was the prime motivational factor for the unique transformation. For example, they read the numerous verses on water, the basis of life and ecology and were influenced by its description on this. Since our planet is distinguished (so far) by being the only one in the solar system to contain an abundance of free flowing water, it is not surprising to see that the Qur'an lays so much emphasis on the importance of water. Note that the two references below describe the water-cycle, now familiar to us, but at the time, it was something not quite understood:

> Do you not see that God sends water down from the clouds and meanders it through subterranean channels; and then He causes crops of different colors to grow. However, subsequently they dry up, and you see them transform into yellow and then stubble. Verily, herein resides remembrance for those who use their minds. (39:21)

> God is the One who sets the winds in motion which raise up the clouds; We drive them to a dead land and revive the Earth after its death; ... (35:9)

The significance of water is echoed in many interesting verses in the Qur'an, which mention the uniqueness of water. One of these verses deals with the power of water as a creative and crucial substance by which all life-forms have been set in motion and have been originated, and is followed by the statement that the human's creation is a test. The mention of water in the same passage dually alludes to the usage of things in nature (including water!) as a means by which mankind will be tested on Earth, as well as the creation and ultimate evolutionary origin of man with water for the very fact that the human being comprises mainly water, and that the origin of life is connected to water:

> ...He it is who has created the universe and Earth in six periods; and His throne [of power] was on the water, in order to test you to see which of you is best in terms of the performance of deeds. (11:7)

If there were no water there would be no life and if there were no life there would be no humans and no test. Furthermore, freshwater is a scarce resource, where water management and allocation—rather than water wars—should be the main focus of the solution to water resource problems.

Knowledge Transfer from the Muslims

The notion of signs in the universe is central to the Islamic conception of nature. A great many of our terms, especially in the sciences, derive from the Arabic. A typical example is Algorithm, (from the name of the Muslim mathematician, Al-Khwarizmi, who developed *al-jabara*, which came to be known as Algebra). Words like Algebra remained and passed into European vocabulary simply because there were no concepts such as these in other languages. Curiously enough, the word 'jibberish' is derived from the name of the father of modern chemistry, the Muslim scientist Jabir, whose works in terms of comprehensibility were so unlike anything that the Europeans in the Middle Ages had ever seen before, that they were termed 'Jaberish' hence 'Gibberish',[126] jaber and jabber, words meaning incomprehensible chattering.

Before the appearance of the Qur'an, human societies both in the East and the West had plunged headlong into the 'Dark Ages'. They held strange views of nature at that time in history. In Europe, for example, it was supposed to be obvious to anyone that: the Earth was flat and that one should not venture too far afield for fear of falling off its edge; rats were reckoned to be created from garbage spontaneously, salamanders emanated likewise from fire,[127] and a dose of exorcism would cure many a dubious ailment. What was the factor that changed these errant views and metamorphized society towards an uplifting revolutionary direction?

The reality of the universe is echoed in many verses where the Creator Himself swears by the signs He Himself has created:

> By the sun and its resplendence! By the moon as it follows it! By the day, as it beams its radiance! By the night, as it enshrouds it! By the universe and He who structured it! By the Earth and He who spread it! By the consciousness of self and He who gave it order and proportion, enlightening it thereby with discernment of wrong and right. He has succeeded who purifies it, and he has failed who instills it [with corruption]. (91:1–10)
>
> ...I swear by the hiding [planets], those that sweep [celestial objects that intersect their orbit by gravity], and by the night as it departs, and the dawn as it breathes... (81:15–18)

---

126. Ewart, Neil. (1990), *Everyday Phrases: Their Origins and Meanings*, p. 65.
127. Attenborough, David. (1989), *The First Eden: Mediterranean World and Man*, pp. 124–128.

Here we see the personification of the emergent morning as if it were an entity actually 'breathing', with energies inter-flowing between plants and animals. Many verses in the Qur'an beckon man to ponder over animals and nature. They are put in a form which questions the mechanism of things with the question 'How?'. For instance, it is asked:

> ... do they not look at the camel, how it is designed? At the starry firmament, how it is raised up? At the mountains, how they are stabilized? And at the Earth, how it is spread out? (88:17–20)

Other verses in the Qur'an speak of the Earth having been created in periods,[128] not 24 hour days. The Qur'an has many verses which have pre-empted 20th century discoveries. For example, it describes the embryo evolving in stages.[129] No doubt, such revolutionary and transformative ideas had a great impact on the biological sciences, which were developed into specializations by the Muslims. As early as the 8th century, C.E., one such scholar, Al-Jahiz, wrote *The Book of Animals*. In this book he discusses animal behaviour and suggests that a change in the environment could bring about a gradual change in their physiology or form over time. There is a remarkable passage in his book relating to the transformation of species, where he states that:

> People said different things about the existence of *al-miskh* (the original form of quadrupeds). Some accepted its evolution and said that it gave

128. See for example, Qur'an, 32:5, Qur'an, 70:4 for the meaning of *yaum* as 'period of time'.

129. It is stated in the Qur'an that: 'We created man from the quintessence of clay, then We caused him to remain as a drop of fluid (sperm) in a firm lodging (womb). And then we transformed that drop of fluid into a thing which clings [i.e. the *alaqa*, which is the zygote that actually clings to the walls of the uterus], which We shaped into a chewed lump of flesh [the early stage of human development when one is the size of a pin-head].' The 'chewed lump' (*mudgha*) is appropriately termed because at this stage the embryo has teeth-like marks on it, technically called the somites. The somites, later on in development, become the backbone, as first realized by the late world renowned embryologist, Keith Moore at the University of Toronto, who was approached by Muslims (by Abdul Majeed al-Zindani) to explain the verse. Finally, in this passage it is stated that: 'In due course, We transform him into a new shape (i.e. from embryo to fetus). Blessed is God, the best of Shapers.' (23:12–14) It is important to note that prior to the 20th century, the main scientific theories in the West were preformationistic, that is, that the human being does not go through stages of development but is already formed, albeit tiny, and that all generations are present, enfolded within one another (either within the sperm or the ovary depending on the school of thought). Furthermore, one would also have required a microscope to realize the existence of the stages and the Qur'an offers a proof of being revelatory by these statements because the microscope was invented over 1,000 years later. See also: Moore, Keith L., and Persaud, T.V.N. (1998) *The Developing Human: Clinically Oriented Embryology, 6th Edition*, W.B. Saunders and Company, Philadelphia, p. 10.

existence to the dog, wolf, fox and their like. The members of this family came from this [original] form (al-miskh).[130]

It is interesting to note that Charles Darwin reached similar conclusions about 1,000 years later. It must be mentioned, however, that Neo-Darwinian and related evolutionary views are not in complete agreement with those of Al-Jahiz; for Al-Jahiz and his Muslim contemporaries and associates this evolutionary process takes place according to a well-planned pattern and a purpose set by the Creator of the Universe.[131] No record of such ideas on organic evolution being discussed existed before the advent of the Qur'an. Aristotle and Anaximander of Ancient Greece[132] had discussed the origins of various things in nature, but not the macro-biological transformations of species over time.

Sayings of Prophet Muhammad such as the instruction that we should use medicines, for God has created, in nature, a cure for every disease except old age[133] not only influenced the advancement of plant pharmacology and botany but also created respect for the value of nature. An example of a concern for animals is that of the famous Muslim jurist, Izzad-Din Ibn Abd as-Salam. As early as the 13th century he formulated a 'Bill of Rights of Animals'.[134] The jurists even formulated laws hundreds of years ago to hold in check population levels in cities—a problem which has become one of the major causes of ecological disasters these days, all over the world, due to inequities, mismanagement and corruption.

Unfortunately, early Islamic literature on such subjects dealing with nature, is widely known neither to Muslims nor non-Muslims these days. There is hardly a mention of such works in school or university textbooks. One also seldom hears about the 'Mullahs' and 'Imams' speaking on these subjects in their discourses.

130. From Al-Jahiz, *Kitab al-Hayawan*, (1909), edition, which was published in seven volumes in Cairo, Vol. 4, p. 23. See also Bayrakdar, M. (1983) *The Islamic Quarterly*, 'Al-Jahiz and the Rise of Biological Evolutionism', p. 152. As M. Bayrakdar observes, al-Damiri noted many of Al-Jahiz's statements from Al-Jahiz's *Kitab al-Hayawan* (Book of Animals). Al-Damiri's and many other Muslim scientists' book were translated into Latin by Abraham Echellensis (d. Italy 1664) published under the title *De Proprietatibus et Virtutibus Mecdicis Animalium* in Paris, 1617. This explains why the first evolutionists were from France as Muslim evolutionary ideas penetrated that region of Europe first.
131. Howard University researchers have proven that Muslim thinkers almost 1,000 years before Darwin spoke of biological evolution: Malik, Aamina H., Ziermann, Janine M., and Diogo, Rui, (2018), 'An Untold Story in Biology: The Historical Continuity of Evolutionary Ideas of Muslim Scholars from the 8th century to Darwin's Time', *Qur'anicosmos*, Volume 1, Issue 3.
132. Finley, M.I. (1970), *Early Greek Science: Thales of Aristotole*, p. 18 and p. 121.
133. Musnad of Ahmad, Narrated by Usama bin Sharik.
134. Izzad-Din Abd-as-Salaam, as quoted in *Qawa id al-Ahkam fi Masaleh al-Anam.*

A great many of them, like those before, have fallen into the non-Islamic trap of separating knowledge into 'religious' and 'non-religious'.

In most parts of the West, the Qur'an had an entirely different impact. The Qur'anic information, knowledge and ideas on nature were transferred to the Western lands by the 12th century, and greatly affected European society in two waves after the period; namely, the Renaissance and the Enlightenment. However, European society and its extensions in North and South America and the Northern areas surrounding Russia, only absorbed part of the message of the Qur'an, instead of the whole. The whole message was that one cannot make use of nature harmoniously without a deep appreciation and comprehension of the very *nature of use* itself. In Islam, it is stressed that the true nature of use—that is, the way we are supposed to use things in nature—is facilitated if we understand that the Creator of the universe is its Owner. We can reach this conclusion if we choose to see the signs of the Creator's work within nature and ourselves. This is what an early Muslim jurist, Abu al-Faraj, says:

> People do not in fact own things, for the real Owner is the Creator; they only enjoy the usufruct of things, subject to Divine Law.[135]

The use of a thing is invariably tied to economics and finance. In Chapter 7, we shall examine the Qur'anic approach to economics that helps maintain the dynamic balance of nature.

The Optimal Development of Technology

There are ways of participating with nature: we can use human technology in consonance with principles based on the Qur'an and the way nature works. The limited scope of this book will not allow us to do justice to this vast subject area. However, we shall briefly give examples of some of the principles behind ecologically sound technology from the Islamic perspective. Firstly, at the very outset, it must be emphasized that there needs to be a restructuring of our approach towards technology. From a technological perspective based on Islamic concepts, the very unidirectional use of, for example, fossil fuels, causes an imbalance, and such a system, utilized in this way, is against the teachings of Islam. What is meant by unidirectional is that there is no cyclical or re-cyclical element in the technology. Most people, nowadays, do not think in terms of cycles, processes and the interconnections between cycles and flow, though there is now a gradual increasing awareness of such concepts.

135. Al-Faraj, Abu ar-Rahman ibn Rajab, *Al-Qawa id fil—Fiqh al-Islami.*

It must be realized that when an imbalance arises because of such non-integrated technology, further harm is caused, be it biological, physiological or atmospherical—whether we know of it or not. With the development and implementation of technology based along the lines suggested by Qur'anic principles, however, we would be able to utilize nature for the benefit of not only human beings, but all other forms of life and non-life. With such technology, the form and function of things in nature would be properly deduced by reasoning, whereby technology itself would be appropriately engineered to flow with the various laws, processes and cycles in nature, rather than against them, thereby conserving the natural balance as a whole. In relation to forestry, for instance, it is of paramount importance that we study the cycles in nature and pattern our cutting of trees much the way natural processes give life and death to trees.[136] In this way, the diversity, quantity and quality of trees will not diminish while still enabling us to benefit from this replenishable natural resource and ecosystemical component.

The minimization of energy and cyclical systems in nature are the principal operational modes by which the natural non-manmade processes function. And these are the very technologies that we should be learning from directly. In the Qur'an, the Creator of the universe demands of human beings not to waste things, in words to the effect that it is tantamount to the work of Satan. Therefore, to find such wastage in nature—the very creation of this kind of a God—would be a grand contradiction. Do we find such wastage in nature though? In this universe, conservation is tied to the use of energy, wherein systems operate in such a way that there is no wastage. Nature itself has been designed in such a remarkable way that there is a conservation of energy in even the flight path of a pollinating insect. When for instance, a particular plant has been pollinated, it gives off a signal in terms of a change in colour which is in a spectral range that is invisible to the unaided human eye. The flying insect does not then approach that particular plant, because the very change in color is a signal to the insect that the plant has been pollinated, thereby saving flight energy!

In nature, the three Rs (reuse, reduce and recycle) are reduced to one R—recycling—so efficient is the system. For example, even a thing such as dung is not wasted in nature and is multi-purposive. Elephant dung in nature is used

136. Brown, Nick and Press, Malcolm. (1992), 'Logging Forest the Natural Way?' *New Scientist*, pp. 25–29.

in a variety of novel ways as a sustenance by various organisms![137] For instance, in a day, ten elephants can excrete a ton of faeces on the ground and yet none of it is wasted: butterflies and beetles feed on it; birds get seeds from it; mushrooms and fungi thrive on it; insects lay eggs on it; termites convert most of its cellulose into sugar, and vegetation thrives on it as a fertilizer. In this cycle, there is no need to reuse or reduce as the system's efficiency is 100 percent and there is zero wastage. In fact, the waste product of the elephant becomes an organic treasure for other creatures and plants. There are countless examples such as this.

In a thorough environmental analysis of wastage, by those who are environmentally friendly, there are actually *four* Rs not only three: re-use, recycle, reduce and *reject*. Some developments are not feasible at all from the Islamic perspective, which coincides with the perspective based on natural equilibrium, and such developments would thus be rejected at the very outset.

In the Qur'an, it is graphically described that humans even learned things directly, by observing animals, especially in the early part of the history of Mankind. This is a segment of the account of the murder of Abel by the jealous Cain who realized the enormity of the crime he had just committed after his observations of a bird, which depicted the means of hygienic recycling of a dead organic object:

> The consciousness of the other [Cain] drove him to self-justify the killing of his brother; he murdered him and entered the ranks of the losers. Then, God sent down a raven which started digging into the Earth to illustrate the technique by which he might cover his brother's exposed body. He felt ashamed of his conduct and thought: 'What's the matter with me? Can't I even take a cue from this raven?' And then he became regretful. (5:30–31)

Can we not take a cue from nature? We indeed owe so much to that which we are now destroying. We are literally destroying all the good ideas found in nature itself—ideas which would benefit the whole of creation on Earth! In fact, we are liquidating, at an exceedingly fast rate, that which cannot be renewed. If we still do have any sense left in us, we should fast realize that the laws of nature are based on nature's own rhythm; we must learn to cooperate

137. Isabella, Jude. (2014), 'The Natural World is an Elephant World', Nautilis, December 4 Issue. http://nautil.us/issue/101/in-our-nature/the-natural-world-is-an-elephant-world See also, Wohlleben, Peter. (2017), *The Secret Wisdom of Nature: Trees, Animals, and the Extraordinary Balance of All Living Things—Stories from Science and Observation.*

with that rhythm, if life is not only to survive, but to also flourish with the benefit of our intelligent participation.

In general, the whole approach towards technology discussed above would fall under the umbrella of the following verse in the Qur'an:

> Do not follow that of which you have no knowledge, for surely you will
> be held accountable for your hearing, vision, and mind—all of these.
> (17:36)

Such an approach towards technology would proceed with knowledge—with caution and safety, beyond profit-making—where the risk factors would be minimized. Furthermore, since the approach of the Qur'an is interconnected and non-arrogant, those individuals involved in technological development would be striving to anticipate the effects of their planned operations on the environment as well as any possible devastating biological, chemical or other detrimental causal connections. Individuals with such an outlook would not work for military-industrial complexes involved in aggressive and exploitative actions against their own people or other regions on the Earth or elsewhere. At present, in the Western nations, about fifty percent of scientists and engineers are involved in such activities. Remuneration earned by any such means in Islam that is for non-defensive war is considered to be for war, not only against innocent human beings, animals and the rest of nature, but ultimately against God. It would not take much imagination to realize who would be the ultimate loser.

The Evolution Sound Technology

As in the pure sciences, the Muslims had a great impact in the development of technology in the West, not realized by the vast majority today. It is not the scope of the book to discuss the history of Islamic technology except to mention a few pertinent factors which relate to environmental issues. Firstly, it is assumed that mechanical and hydraulic technology which led to the industrial revolution in the 19th century were developed only after the Renaissance and that during the Dark Ages which spanned hundreds of years prior to the Renaissance, nothing of much significance was achieved. However, the fact is that when we study Islamic technology from the 9th century onwards we find that nothing could be further from the truth and that it was Islamic technology which gave rise to technological developments from the 17th century onwards. In fact, in terms of technical sophistication, some of the devices which the Muslim engineers/scientists had developed were not produced until our 'modern era'. The late Donald Hill, who was a specialist in classical, European medieval and Islamic technology states that:

> This device [the trick vessel of the Banu Musa brothers who were extant in the 9th century of the Christian Era], and others like it, demonstrate an amazing skill in the use of differential pressures, and in the use of in-line valves for automatic control. Nothing like it is known to have been attempted before or since, until the advent of modern pneumatic instrumentation. Indeed, they had exhausted the subject, and it would have been impossible to emulate them in this kind of construction.[138]

Yet this technology was inspired by a rational inspection into the workings of nature, especially by the 'motions' of the planets and stars. This, in turn, led to the development of the astrolabe which was a projection of the heavenly canopy onto a plane. The observation of the heavens also led to the invention of hydraulically operated and mechanical gearing mechanisms for the operation of both astrolabes and clocks in addition to advanced forms of water raising machines, pumps, windmills and water fountains. Fountains were much admired because they were reminiscent of the Qur'anic descriptions of the beauty of nature and the appreciation of water. Extensive municipal hydraulic systems were also devised due to the need for ablution for prayers to their Creator five times a day. No doubt, these advances were built upon Hellenistic works which themselves were based on the works of earlier civilizations, which in turn were based on developments in the pre-historic age.

As in the pure sciences the Islamic scientists/engineers considered the universe to be integrated, and thereby developed integrated mechanisms as well as closed systems operating on the cyclical principle of feedback as happens in nature. In addition, the role of the concept of the balance was very significant in technological development. Examples of the principles of feedback (closed loop systems) and the balance in operation, are the devices of the Banu Musa Brothers (who developed such technology in the early 9th century A.D. and were responsible for the *Book of Ingenious Devices*, describing 100 devices) and Al-Jazari who also wrote a treatise on about 50 machines, completed in 1206 A.D. containing descriptions of wheels similar to the pelton wheel turbine used

---

138. Hill, Donald. (1984), *A History of Engineering in Classical and Medieval Times*, p. 219.

for a variety of purposes, some of which are clocks, pumps, automata and some musical instruments.[139]

The Muslim scientists/engineers never separated their so-called worldly activities with the so-called spiritual activities; their regular 'scientific' letters and discourses are replete with references to God. However, one would be hard-pressed these days to find scientists in our universities even mentioning non-mystical allusions to the 'Almighty' in their theses, papers or lectures, without being hastily expelled from such centers of learning under dubious pretexts. With respect to the great Muslim scientist Al-Biruni, historian of science, Seyyed Hossein Nasr concludes:

> The cosmos in which al-Biruni lived and breathed is the handiwork of God in which all true science leads to the Creator and possesses truth which is guaranteed only when it is sanctioned by Him.[140]

The Key to Sound Technology

As in nature, the *production cycle* must have a closed loop in the sense that the waste from any process must be transformed (and hence re-used or recycled) and/or reduced. In any analysis the analyst can rate this cycle. The key is that the so-called 'waste products' from any operation must not be seen as 'waste' products, but 'products' in and of themselves that need to be utilized elsewhere. These so-called waste products can be incorporated in present day distribution and supply-chain simulation models as raw materials to be transformed or used and databases can be established for suppliers and consumers of raw 'waste' material or transformed 'waste' material.

When manufacturing chemicals, we ought to follow two suggestions made by Dr. Michael Braungart, a German chemist and William McDonough, an American architect.[141] Their suggestions are in line with the Qur'anic approach of maintaining the balance in the ecosystem. Firstly, the production of chemicals that contain an unpredictable conglomeration of substances and do not have a well-defined chemical recipe must be restricted, and, secondly, we must not manufacture chemicals unless their disintegration process into the environment is known. To these suggestions must be added the following general

---

139. Ibid. p. 216 and p. 221.
140. Nasr, Seyyed Hossein. *An Introduction to Islamic Cosmological Doctrines*, Thames and Hudson, 1978, p.174.
141. Colborn, Theo; Dumanoski, Dianne; Myers, John Peterson. (1996) *Our Stolen Future: Are We Threatening Our Fertility, Intelligence and Survival.*

stipulation: Manufacture only those chemicals that mimic the disintegration and dispersion of natural chemicals, so as to maintain ecosystemical equilibrium as much as possible. Sim Van Der Ryn and Stuart Cowan, in their book, *Ecological Design*, elaborate on five basic design concepts which provide ecologically sensitive technology. These are: Solutions grow from the place where one is applying the solutions; cost factors for ecological processes must be accounted for at each stage; work and design with processes of nature; involve everyone in the design process; make natural processes visible.[142] Although these realizations are well in line with the Qur'anic requirements it must be pointed out that such principles in an Islamically based society would grow naturally from the foundations like trees growing from seeds planted in the ground. They would not be spokes of wood hacked into the soil from above. The foundation referred to here is the concept of ultimate ownership of the universe and the implications of that reality.

Islamic technology is based on a systems approach that would take the full lifecycle of the products being manufactured that would enable 'decision makers to see and evaluate ... trade-offs'.[143] An example of the evaluative kind of thinking that is necessary is that of a study by Opel, a division of General Motors. Opel tried to use magnesium for automotive cross beams, instead of steel, since the former metal is lighter and hence would help to reduce greenhouse gas emissions during the life of an automobile. However, with a systems analysis approach it was soon realized that magnesium does not always lower greenhouse gas emissions, since the 'cover gas' sulphur hexafluoride is used to produce volatile molten magnesium from oxygen, and, since sulphur hexafluoride is 23,900 times more powerful than carbon dioxide, its production in the manufacturing process would far outweigh any environmental gains achieved by using the lighter magnesium. However, Opel did not revert to the steel cross beams; instead they searched for a less pollutive cover gas for magnesium manufacturing.[144]

142. Ryn, Sim Van Der and Cowan, Stuart. (1996), *Ecological Design*.
143. Brady, Kevin; Noble, Duncan and Young, Steven B. (2001), *Engineering Dimensions*, 'Greenhouse gas emissions: A systems approach', p. 23. The authors of this article are with Five Winds International, an environmental management consulting firm.
144. Ibid.

Goethe's Approach to Technology

One of the striking aspects of the Qur'an is that the verses that discuss what we would consider scientific subjects cannot be categorized with one word. These verses are both artistic yet scientific, prosaic yet poetic (in the original Arabic), holistic yet breakable into parts (due to the morphological structure of the Arabic language); they possess deep complexity when delved into, yet on the surface most appear straightforward; they speak of structure yet also of process. They produce an integrated versatility beckoning both induction and deduction in a Muslim's train of thought on nature. They also elicit gratitude towards the Creator and a deep sensitivity towards nature. The Qur'an emphasizes the cycles and rhythms of nature both in content and hononymically.

The impact of German philosopher and writer, Goethe, who was intrigued by Prophet Muhammad as evinced in one of his poems, *Mohamets Gesang* of 1774,[145] has remained on the sidelines in the West in terms of science, but is now surfacing to a greater extent in suggesting a more fruitful way of apprehending nature, elements of which indeed coincide with the Qur'anic outlook towards nature. As it has been pointed out:

> Understanding a language of movement requires a reorientation in the way we observe natural phenomena. Goethe pioneered a dynamic, participatory approach to the observation of nature. To Goethe an isolated phenomenon held little value; only when it was interrelated with other forms did its significance emerge as one element of a larger progression, or 'metamorphosis', as he called it.[146]

A practical example of the value of such an outlook in discovering new technology that would enhance life is the flowform treated water. These are structures through which water is made to pass which are so designed as to create certain rhythms in the movement of water. For example, when flowform treated water was compared with a simple step-cascade through which water flowed, it was found that it produced ecologically favourable conditions for the emergence of macrofauna with an aquatic lifecycle, like that of a well-illuminated open rapids in an upstream section of a river, as opposed to the step cascade in which such macrofauna did not take residence, mimicking a eutrophic

145. Rodinson Maxime. (1974), *The Legacy of Islam*, 'The Western Image and Western Studies in Islam', pp. 43–44.
146. Riegner, Mark and Wilkes, John. (1998), *Goethe's Way of Science: A Phenomenology of Nature*, 'Flowforms and the Language of Water', pp. 234.

part of a river system. The rhythms and cycles in flowform treated water seem to produce water which is highly oxygenated. Spurred by Goethe's outlook on science, further research is being conducted in this and other areas, which, no doubt, will have many applications towards ecological engineering.[147]

The Misdirection of Technology

Together with the development of mechanisms and hydraulics—let alone various other technological sciences within the Muslim lands from the 9th to 15th centuries—there was a profound awareness of the Creator as Owner and the concept of the balance. This not only influenced the direction of the development of the type of technology as far as design went but also its proper utilization. However, in the West, the fact is that this consciousness was not realized, and the lessons learned from the Muslims with respect to the technological advances, were unfortunately misutilized in an effort to obsessively manufacture without regard to the interconnecting cyclical components, that is, the notion of dynamic equilibrium and most important of all: the awareness of a singular Creator as Ultimate Owner. It is, therefore, not hard to see that unidirectional technology, combined with consumerism and mass production, has inextricably led to the vortex of disequilibrium we are surrounded with today.

It is, in fact, very sad to see that many countries which have had Islam in their lands, are not paying attention to the Islamic engineering principles and concepts of technological development in their efforts to imitate the West in everything, to forge 'ahead' while being oblivious to the great environmental destruction which is now occurring in such countries. At the same time the West should increasingly consider organic principles that emulate the functioning of nature not only in terms of structure but especially in terms of interrelated processes. For example, solar-hydrogen coupling systems that could be developed in the 21st century must be researched and applied intensively as such a system would not pollute and be cyclical, where energy from the sun via solar farms would produce electricity which would, in turn, decompose H_2O into hydrogen and oxygen. The hydrogen would be piped/transported to cities, used in industry, homes and transportation, to provide water, electricity (via fuel cells or turbines), heating and cooling and transportation. The waste product would be water![148] Indeed, if solar cell

147. Ibid. pp. 246–247.
148. Bockris, John O'M; Veziroglu T. Nejat; Smith, Debbie. (1991), *Solar Hydrogen Energy: The Power to Save the Earth—Fuel Forever*, p. 82 and pp. 90–109. See also Fairley, Peter. (2020),

technology is improved drastically both in terms of its thickness and sensitivity to trap most colors of spectrum emanating from the sun, then it would have wide-ranging applications. Using the notion of flows and non-wastage discussed in the previous section, to resolve the problem of the variability of the sun's output of energy, during daytime, when solar cells have maximal utility, the excess electricity that is generated could be channelled through a fuel cell to yield hydrogen from water. Then during the night, the fuel cell could use the stored hydrogen to re-generate electricity.[149] If solar-hydrogen couplings are not used and the fuel cell used to produce hydrogen energy contains materials that would cause atmospheric pollution then one would not, of course, eliminate air pollution completely. This is a challenge that would need to be overcome.

From historical evidence we can see that it was the very concept of the order, design and the balance in nature under the particular singular concept of God that gave rise to modern technology, the experimental method and so on. However, globally, human societies for the most part, have been lured onto a dysfunctional tangent by a neglect of these most basic principles. We have to consequently return to the realization that the true nature of technology is the technology of nature and we must therefore learn to develop with the rhythms, structural patterns and cycles that maintain the diversity and dynamically flowing balance of nature. We can consciously use the designs of many processes and structures in nature (dubbed biomimicry) to design our human structures and processes and make them fit integrally with the natural environment. Finally, we have to remember that all 'man-made' and 'natural' technological marvels ultimately emanate from the Creator and that we must learn humility in this respect:

> O human beings! Listen to the following parable: Don't you see that those whom you invoke instead of God cannot even create a thing such as a fly, even though they were to muster all their forces towards that end! And, furthermore, if that fly did happen to snatch anything from them, they would be powerless to retrieve it from him! Weak indeed is both the seeker and the one who is sought. (22:73)

'The H_2 Solution', *Scientific American*, February Issue, Volume 322, Number 2; when fuel cells and electrolyzers that are used to create hydrogen become less expensive hydrogen power this may indeed become the initial current grid supporting energy form, as non-pollutive technology where hydrogen creates electricity and electricity creates hydrogen and as technology evolves becoming the dominant form of sustainable and green energy source for humanity. The drive toward this solution must increase.

149. Woodbury, Richard, Wosnitza, Regine. (2000) 'How to save the Earth', *Time Special Edition, Earth Day 2000*, p. 63.

...He (God) will yet create things [future modes of transportation] of which you have no knowledge now. (16:5–8)

In the next section, let us see how we can learn from nature.

Instructions from Nature

Efficiency: Workplace Environment

A legendary story of the fourteenth century Turko-Persian conqueror Tamerlane (Timur-Lung or Timur the Lame) recounts that when Timur's army was severely defeated in one of his early expansionist campaigns he was on the run. In a desperate attempt to hide from his relentless pursuers he hid in an abandoned building. As he sat there all alone, consigned to meet his inevitable and invidious fate, he noticed an ant carrying a large piece of food several times bigger than her own size. Timur watched with keen interest as the ant repeatedly tried to carry the food up and over a wall, only to have it fall down each time. The undeterred ant would pick up the food and try again and again. Timur counted ten, twenty, thirty attempts, but each time the weight of the food proved to be stronger than the little ant. It is said that finally, on the seventieth try, the tireless ant managed to push the food over the wall into the nest.

So inspired by this display of perseverance was he, that he was led to proclaim: 'If an ant can do it, so can I!' And, as history attests, he certainly did do it. He regrouped his army, redoubled his efforts and ended up routing his initially implacable foes. The point here is that apart from perseverance, patience and dedication, we humans have a lot to learn a lot from a tiny insect like ants and other species, and apply object lessons from nature to our personal lives and workplace environments, to achieve efficiency, harmony, fairness and peace.

A workplace environment is no different than the natural environment. In the natural environment the behaviour of all species is inter-connectively goal-oriented. Millions of species work on day shifts, millions of others on night shifts, while some are migrant or seasonal workers. Everyone involved plays a vital role in the interactive operation of a vigorous ecosystem that is in a natural scheme of dynamical equipoise. Everyone involved knows his or her role and submits to the perspicaciously designed laws of nature without any transgression. The complex system employed in nature always allows the best to evolve, the greatest good for the greatest number. It operates on cooperation and an overall equilibrium-maintaining competition, rather than senseless, fraudulent, greedy and exploitative competition. It allows for the maximization of productivity in a most harmonious atmosphere, the end result being increased efficiency, optimality and above all, a total elimination of wastage in the grand recycling system of nature.

The resplendent teamwork involved in daily complex operations of an ant, bee or termite colony is indeed a marvel of operational fastidiousness. Well-established division of labor with resources being shared equitably, they operate in the best interests of the group. Indeed, all members of each colony work together as a single unit. The governing laws are never subject to deviation or negotiation. Workers never go on strike or cut corners; the queen never takes advantage of workers and soldiers. The queen does not see herself as above the team and everyone else being subservient to her, but as an integral part of the team. They know full well, be it through a level of reasoning and/ or instinct, that the survival of the colony depends on efficacious teamwork. The success of this massive operation requires an effective communication system, which is achieved by releasing different pheromones, thereby passing on quick messages to one another, or to send an alarm to the entire team, as well as to warn the intruders. The interesting observation is that the best part of it is that this workplace environment is not even unionized, for there is no need for 'protection' and neither are there any lay-offs, wrongful dismissals or office politics. Just imagine a human workplace environment functioning like a termite colony. The productivity would be at its highest level. Such a workplace would indeed be so peaceful and such a joyous environment to work in. There are more than a million tiny magnetic termites that work around the clock in each colony.

Take example of this remarkable hardworking insect, have you ever considered a bee for instance? A bee must collect nectar from over 2 million flowers to make approximately one pound of honey. Bees are truly model citizens of this planet; anything a bee eats is clean, anything he drops is sweet, any branch he sits upon does not break, and that which he produces never spoils. To be like a bee in a workplace environment is: not to be jealous of co-workers, to avoid bullying, backbiting, and gossiping about fellow workers; in short, do your job effectively and go home.

Here is a further example of harmonious behaviour: anthropological studies show that predators like spotted hyenas are very adept at cooperation and problem solving in their hunting strategies. Hyenas are well-organized and follow a specific plan. The plan oversees risk assessment. Their strategic thinking is based on the existing circumstance, i.e. the type of prey and their numbers, presence of other predators, number of hyenas in the pack, etc. The pack always follows the lead of the dominant male or female. As a group they learn from trial and error and always hinge on the experiences of the older hyenas. For instance, anthropologists have learned that when a young hyena unfamiliar with the hunting task was paired with a dominant experienced one, the pack always succeeded in hunting with minimal effort. This is indeed the best model there is. This holistic model can be implemented in a workplace environment.

Likewise, lessons from the animal kingdom have been adopted in succession planning in the workplace. The idea is to build and maintain a diverse workplace environment free from unproductiveness, transgression, discrimination, harassment and stress. HR professionals argue that it is indeed essential to create a workplace environment that operates on cooperation where staff can harmoniously learn from one another. Managers are encouraged to promote teamwork and collaboration among co-workers, where both veterans and novices can be teachers to one another. An efficient and cohesive workplace is all about building the morale and productivity of employees and minimizing complaints, grievances, disruptions and legal wrangles, whereby everyone can get on with their work in a healthy and creative manner. The intrinsic feelings that motivate an employee to be creative, responsible and eager, with a sense of being part of a team would be integral factors in the formulation of an unbeatable concatenation of 'environmental attributes' that would facilitate peace, happiness, satisfaction and useful productivity, for *all* and not just 'top management'. This way of conducting work has been incipiently creeping up on capitalistic employers over the last few decades who have been, behind the façade of magnanimity to the public, ensconced in solely the 'profit motive', so oblivious to humane, humanitarian and environmental considerations. Yet, once again, even in this area, it looks like the design in nature has beaten the best human minds in optimal environmental workplace engineering, by billions of years! Perhaps one has to think like an ant to know this and if so, let's be an ant. To identify best practices we can learn far more from tiny insects than from top paid management consultants.

Conflict Resolution

Compare this human approach of conflict resolution with that of other social species, like birds. Birds use only diplomacy to resolve their differences, yet they are superfluously considered by humans as one of the dumbest creatures on earth. Thereby, derogatory terms such as 'birdbrain,' 'bird course,' 'dodo', and 'featherhead' are coined to refer to unintelligent individuals. Far from being unintelligent, birds employ the most effective form of conflict resolution in the animal kingdom that brings shame to homo-sapiens—a swift blood-free approach. When it comes to communication, birds are classy and eloquent, for they communicate with each other and to other species in magnificent style. Among most birds, singing a musical song is the weapon of choice to resolve, for instance, a territorial dispute or mating rights. A bird, by singing, first and foremost establishes his presence in the area, which alone can favorably influence the outcome of a potential situation. He likes his neighbours to know that he is rightfully in charge of his domain and that ought to be respected. Some birds have large repertoires, where each song is performed for a different purpose or performing a particular song that members of a particular species only would recognize. In their songs, birds pass on encrypted messages to their opponents, i.e. 'take a good look at my physical fitness, strength and beauty', 'go away', 'keep out', 'no trespassing', 'do not get any closer', 'back off' or 'come in', 'stay with me'. A dragged standoff only results in a prolonged musical complexity between the two challengers. Some birds can play as many as 50 different notes: in both high and low pitches. They can sing solo, duets or harmoniously with other birds in what could resemble an orchestra. The music masterfully played has structure and identifiable rhythm; indeed, they never sing out of tune.

In a highly competitive courtship pursuit, their musical performance is often accompanied by an extravagant visual display similar to a stunning fashion show and/or to a bodybuilding competition, as birds show off their beautiful vibrant feathers to exhibit their wide array of endowments and/or accomplishments. If that is not effective enough, most birds' techniques of persuasion also include extraordinary dancing rituals.

Whether birds are conscious of it or not, there is an in-depth therapeutic connection between music and peace, between beauty and peace, between art and peace. All three elements are conspicuously used in birds' diplomacy. Their life comprises of constant beautiful musical and artistic presentations, followed by a mating act in the background of a lavish green forest with a blue sky above and the constant breeze of clean refreshing air, living in a niche with plenty of renewable resources available, with the ultimate reward of raising a family. Thus, if the objective of their existence, the continuation of life, seems to be satisfyingly achievable, then why be greedy and create conflicts?

Likewise some primates such as the Siamang gibbon extant in the rainforests of Malaysia and Sumatra appeal to the same strategy—singing as opposed to entering a bloody duel. The Siamang gibbon has a large throat sac that is used to amplify sound, which can be heard from miles away. Their throat functions just like an air sac of a bagpipe. Howling melodiously is their stunning form of effective tactical communication to an intruder, in order to avoid the situation unnecessarily escalating to the use of force and aggression causing bodily harm. The message being communicated is similar to that of birds.

In the same manner, during the night, the boisterous yet rhythmic sound of many insects fills the air like a unique orchestra with cicada and crickets chirping, and the choirs of colorful frogs and toads continue to be heard until dawn, carrying the same messages to others. The loudness and frequency of each call made are indications of the male's stamina and versatility. A tiny male cricket can produce a loud sound by rubbing together certain parts of his body such as his wings. The message being broadcast is that 'I am the lord of this block!'

A tropical rainforest is indeed an acoustically noisy place like a concert hall, an opera house or a cathedral. There are always countless musical symphonies being performed by various species. Musical echoes constantly resolve conflicts, not the sound of bombs and bullets being fired and dropped. Unlike the human approach, the conflict resolution approach employed by birds and chimpanzees enhances the environment, rather than harming it. Their battlefield is nothing short of a popular musical venue in an everlasting festival of life.

In nature, there are firm rules of conduct that are well-established for all the participants and are not subject to deviation. Based on these rules, inter and intra species disputes are settled in an efficacious and expedited manner. The costs and benefits to the overall balance of the ecosystem is the sole criterion to be considered. The interesting point in any dispute is that there are no judges or juries, no mitigation or litigation, no bargaining or appeals allowed to determine the fate of a dispute. There are no enforcers to enforce the verdict either. The participants are the judges themselves. In the absence of arrogance and egoism, 'defeat' for lack of a better word, is accepted graciously. There are no cases in nature that a dispute results in the destruction of habitats or the decimation of species, quite to the contrary, it contributes to sustainability. Nature's model is all about *conflict prevention* at the root, for so-called 'Mother Nature' knows that prevention is better than cure. Nature creates conditions that are conducive to life, not to destruction. Senseless killing is not a practice of nature, not even between predators and prey. For example, zebras have no fear of a pride of lions in close proximity if they know that the lions have already had their lunch. A parasite could, but would not kill its host, since it knows that it would then have nowhere to go. *Any blood that occasionally sheds between 'adversaries' is for the maintenance of the overall equilibrium not domination of one over another.* Nothing is further from the truth than misperceiving nature, as being an ad-hoc system of manipulative domination that disrupts equilibrium; rather, nature's conflict resolution strategy has always managed to effectively keep the ratio of predator and prey in balance and the fragile ecological equilibrium at bay for the past 3.5 billion years, confirming its practical results and value. Indeed, where nature's laws rule, it is the most truly civilized and trouble-free part of the world, as all resources are guaranteed to be distributed justly to all the inhabitants.

However, there is only one area where nature's diplomacy fails, and that is when a species' interests are at odds with that of the human species. Here, for the egotistically selfish man, right is always equal to might. When humans betray their own fellow species in the quest for more profits under lies and false propaganda, which always accompanies the onset of mass violence, respect for other co-habitants of this planet is never in the picture and is consigned to the black hole of ignominy. Nature's natural way is always violated for the sake of the protection of man's interests, even if it results in the extinction and the endangerment of myriad species and habitats.

Why are there so many differences between the human and non-human approaches in the distribution of justice and consequently in their conflict resolution strategies? Can the gap ever be closed? Most probably not. Let us have no illusion here or be overly romantic. Although nature's model of conflict resolution is far superior to the best that humanity can ever construct, it will never be emulated by the self-serving man. The only way humans can implement a preventive conflict model like nature, is if resources are fairly distributed, thereby eliminating scarcity, tension and suffering. Such a model will never be emulated, as long as 40% of global assets are owned by 1% of the world's population, as long as 50% of the world's population owns only 1% of global assets, and as long as 20% of the world's population continues to consume 80% of the world's resources, the human model of conflict resolution will remain what it has been for millennia. Man can be so foolish that he gets into a conflict on conflict resolution itself. Conflicts and wars on a massive scale that could be avoided would continue to be generated under the name of spreading democracy, freedom, religion, protecting minority rights and other such obtuse and false pretexts for usurping the wealth and resources of other less militaristically powerful nations, rather than through mutual trading and co-operation, where disputes can and ought to be settled amicably for overall peace, stability and fairness. 'By way of deception, Thou Shalt Do War' is the philosophical outlook of warmongers. Conflicts and wars have deliberately become a profitable business venture for the elite nominally titled the 1%. It first and foremost sustains their power and domination. Furthermore, for corporate war profiteers, peace means recession leading to an inevitable bankruptcy.

This egocentric and criminal business model however, is symptomatic of a deeper problem: the total disconnection of reckless man from understanding the deepest and most basic principles of nature and what lessons we ought to learn from them. This is the lesson that every bird, cricket and frog keep on melodiously chirping into our ears day after day, but we are too deaf to hear it, drowned as we are by the louder reverberating sounds of the war drums, beckoning us to yet another avoidable battlefield of destruction, fostering absolute idiocy, arrogance and greed.

A bird does not have a conscious choice to resolve a conflict in any other fashion contrary to the bird's designed nature. However, the human species does have a choice—the choice and propensity to go for avoidance, tolerance, compromise, reconciliation, cooperation, sharing and love as these should all be available options on the table and are a much better alternative to war. To quote the late Rodney King: 'We can all get along together.' The choice is either to live in harmony with nature and humbly submit to its life-sustaining laws like every other species, or conversely, to walk on the earth with arrogance in pursuit of our insatiable whims and self-indulgence. Sadly, man in general has chosen the latter, to be an injurious parasite, that out of greed would rather kill and destroy its host, the whole Planet Earth, than to preserve the dynamic balance of life for an endless benefit for the present and future of the entire global family.

Chapter 5

The Islamic View on the Animal Kingdom

Ecognitions and Animal Rights

As mentioned in the preface to this book: Our attitudes toward interacting with nature in general and other creatures in particular depend upon our outlook toward life. We all live according to a set of beliefs and values; in this sense, everyone follows a particular philosophy or religion. Yet most people tend to think that religion gives guidance only in 'spiritual matters.' By contrast, the Islamic worldview, as argued by those Muslims who derive a rationalist view from the Qur'an, is integrated and global;[150] it is founded upon reason and action, infused with a consciousness of One God (God).[151] In this vein, Islam provides a comprehensive code of conduct for our worldly life, extending moral considerations toward nature as part of a truly universal ethics. The Islamic worldview and precepts, based on this viewpoint, contain absolutely no distinction between 'spiritual' and 'physical' well-being, or between 'religion' and 'secularism.'[152] In fact, Islam in this Qur'anic, source-based perspective, represents a worldview in which social and ecological systems are intervolved as a unit, where the material well-being of human beings is considered interdependent upon, and interwoven with, the well-being of the rest of nature,

---

150. Islam is both culture-free and universal: 'All praise belongs to God, the Cherisher, Sustainer and Evolver unto completion of the worlds' (Qur'an: 1:2). The Qur'an states that Prophet Muhammad was sent with a message as a mercy to the worlds (21:106–107).

151. On being conscious of God (God), the Qur'an states: 'This book is free of doubt [regarding proof of its divine origin and the truth-value of its statements] and is a guidance for those who are conscious of God.' For verses on reason, which are too numerous to cite, see, for example: 2:44, 3:190, 191; 16:90; 8:22; 4:82; 17:36; and 67:10. Perhaps if the Qur'an were ever to have been given another name, it could have been called The Book of Reason. In 67:10, for example, it is stated that one achieves salvation only through reason.

152. The Arabic word *din*, which is used for 'religion/belief system' is so comprehensive that its meaning is not capable of being captured in one word in the European languages. Essentially, *din* means 'a way of life in which one submits to one thing or another.' The great Islamic scholar Ibn Taymiyyah (1263–1328) states that '*[d]in* is the infinitive of the verb *ddna, yadinu* which means to submit and surrender' (see Abdul-Haqq Ansari, 2000, p. 316). The fact is that we all have a way of life, and we all submit to, or believe in, something or another. If we are not sure what to believe in, it is because of assumptions that lead us to uncertainty! The difference between the *din* espoused by the Qur'an and others is that the source of its knowledge and precepts (the Qur'an itself) is claimed to be without any inconsistencies, and it challenges all sentient entities to that effect (see Qur'an 4:82).

including the different kinds of life on Earth. In this age of rampant destruction of ecosystems, animal experimentation, factory farming, and other forms of cruelty and disruption, those with a strong sense of universal justice would want to intervene and defend nature and animals—who are an essential part of nature—to be advocates for the animals. But does animal advocacy exist in Islam? Is there indeed a philosophical basis in Islam for animal advocacy? If so, what value does Islam place on animals? The philosophical justification and basis for Islamic animal advocacy consists of the following principles, which recognize and uphold inherent ecological values, termed ecognition, from ecological recognition:

> **Ecognition 1:** All nonhuman animals are a trust from God.
>
> **Ecognition 2:** Equigenic rights do exist and must be maintained.
>
> **Ecognition 3:** All nonhuman animals live in communities.
>
> **Ecognition 4:** All nonhuman animals possess personhood.

Ecognition 1: *All Nonhuman Animals Are a Trust from God*

The Qur'an consistently and explicitly mentions, in numerous verses, that the entire natural world belongs to God and God alone:

> And unto God belongs the dominion over the heavens [all galactical and related intergalactical systems] and the Earth: and God has the power over all things. (3:189)
>
> Blessed... is He to whom belongs the dominion of the heavens [all galactical and related intergalactical systems], and the Earth; He who has begotten no son, nor has any partner in His dominion: for it is He who creates, designs and shapes everything, and precisely lays it out through natural laws, that determine its developmental pathway. (25:1–2)
>
> ...whatever is in the heavens [all galactical and related intergalactical systems] and whatever is on the Earth is God's; and certainly We enjoined those who were given the (revelatory) Book before you and We enjoin you too, that you should keep your duty to God. (4:131)

Humankind is given only temporary successorship/stewardship [*khilafah*] of the natural world, as a test. Therefore, humankind is responsible and accountable for any abuses of the Earth's life forms or natural resources.[153]

---

153. Qur'an 6:165.

Ecognition 2: *Equigenic Rights Do Exist and Must Be Maintained*

To establish a truly egalitarian society, our concept of rights must be re-appraised. We have become so used to thinking in terms of human rights that we tend to ignore the rights of other creatures and of nature in general. Of course, the cause of human rights is of utmost importance, but so, too, are animal rights and ecological rights. These domains are ultimately indivisible, as evinced by what we shall term the Equigenic Principle—i.e., equality or balance established through nature, as designed by God. The Equigenic Principle protects rights that are realized when human beings recognize nature's dynamic equilibrium through its structural-cum-functional design. The Equigenic Principle is based on a dynamic balance and hence, on the nature of cause and effect. Therefore, this balance is not relative or human-made; rather, it is absolute. This principle forms the foundation of individual rights and justice. The measure of the health of society is a function of how close we are to realizing this principle.[154] With the Equigenic Principle, humans, nonhumans, and the environment can attain harmonious and reinforcing interrelationships. This is succinctly and cogently captured in two Qur'anic passages:

> It is He [God] who has created the expansive universe and established the balance [*mizan*], so that you may not disrupt the balance. Therefore, weigh things in equity and do not fall short of maintaining that balance. (55:7–9)

> We have surely sent messengers with clear evidences, and sent them with the Book [the Qur'an] and the Balance [the Equigenic Principle], so that human beings may behave with equity. (57:25)

Unfortunately, in the nominal Muslim world, with the un-Qur'anic depreciation of the rational worldview since the 12th century CE, it has not been widely realized or stressed as it should have been, that two separate yet perfectly corresponding sources are referred to in this verse. The 'book' and the 'balance' refer to the book of nature (the Qur'an) and the balance of nature. In Islam, nature is the primary revelation, and the Qur'an is a perfect mirror reflecting that prime reality. This realization has immense implications for how society ought to structure itself and deal with the myriad other creatures that inhabit the Earth.

---

154. Banaei and Haque, (1995); see, in particular, chapter 2, on the Equigenic Principle itself.

Ecognition 3: *All Nonhuman Animals Live in Communities*

Muslims are responsible for animals. Islam has gone to great lengths to lay down principles on which humankind's relationship with other species ought to be based. Unfortunately, in spite of this wealth of guidance in the Qur'an and the authentic hadiths, not enough attention has been paid to the fact that the Qur'an seals the biological parity between humans and the rest of the species with passages such as the following:

> There is not a nonflying and two-winged flying [water/carbon-based] creature, but they are in communities like yourselves. (6:38)

> He [God] has appointed, precisely established and positioned the Earth [both the planet as a whole, and the Earth's crust itself] for the maintenance and development of sentient life forms [both humans and nonhumans]. (55:10)[155]

Ecognition 4: *All Nonhuman Animals Possess Personhood*

Human beings tend to regard themselves as being special because they feel they are uniquely endowed with intelligence, self-awareness, higher communication abilities, and a soul. Using these assumptions about uniqueness, humans often trample callously upon other species because they think that nonhumans either do not possess these abilities or faculties, or, if they do, that they exist in a primitive state. Indeed, humans tend to justify their actions according to these unsubstantiated assumptions. The Qur'anic—and hence Islamic—outlook reveals to us, however, that these assumptions are incongruent with reality and that if nonhuman animals' attributes are understood properly, great untapped and embracive knowledge exists that could lead to a revolution in the largely discordant relationship between humans and other species.

The Islamic perspective acknowledges animal communication in ways not yet recognized by science, though recent research is in fact shedding more light on animal communication. Fourteen centuries ago, the Qur'an mentioned numerous animals and their relationship with human beings in unique contexts:

---

155. The word *waḍa-'aha*, used in this passage from the Qur'an, means a combination of all these meanings: appoint; precisely establish and position; and maintain and develop, as a careful study of the usage of this word in the Qur'an attests.

> Solomon was David's heir, and he said: Lo! my people: We have been
> taught bird language and have been given [the abundance] of all [good]
> things—this indeed is a distinct favor on us. (27:16)

The Qur'an also describes ants communicating meaningfully with one another
as discussed on page 52.

Muslims are supposed to inculcate responsibility towards animals. Islam
has gone to great lengths to lay down the principles on which man's relationship with other species should be based. Unfortunately, in spite of the wealth
of guidance in the Qur'an and hadith in this respect, there are still some of us
who tend to shrug off animals' welfare as mere sentimental pedantry. Perhaps
such cynics will give the matter a second thought after dwelling on the subject
presented here. Lack of education is no excuse. We do not need to acquire a
post-graduate degree in 'ethics' from university to learn how to treat those
creatures that have been created and for whose care we have been entrusted.
The real reason behind our uncaring attitude in this respect is our selfishness
and indifference. Giving other species their due share according to their rights
demands some 'sacrifices' on our part—which we are not prepared to make.
Our short-sighted self-indulgence does not permit us to acknowledge the simple fact that our own well-being is intervolved with the well-being of all other
creatures on Earth as a community among communities. In fact, the Qur'anic
verse 6:38 on animals being in communities like humans, puts the seal to the
postulate of the biological parity between the human and the rest of the species
in this verse most emphatically:

> There is not a nonflying and two-winged flying [water/carbon-based]
> creature, but they are in communities like yourselves. (6:38).

One of the main reasons for the wrong impression about animals' status
is that we judge other creatures from our own misconceived standards and
values. Under this ill-conceived notion, other creatures are merely considered
as a means to an end, the end result being nothing but materialistic gain. The
Qur'an contradicts this false impression and tell us in very clear words that:
they are communities like the human community; that they are loved by God
the same as human beings are loved; that they have been created the same way
as we were created; that they are much a symbol of God's power of creation as
human beings are. Consider how the following hadith make these points clear:

> All creatures are like a family (*ayal*) of God; and He loves the most those
> who are most beneficent to his family.[156]

In addition, according to the Qur'an, besides the ant, a particular bird, the hoopoe (*hudhud* in Arabic), is mentioned, which is known by present day ornithologists to vocalize a very large repertoire of sounds. From the Qur'an we can gather that its level of syntax and semantics, as well as memory and the ability to recall, re-represent and reason within specific parameters is very high as exhibited in its communication with Solomon:

> But [the hoopoe] tarried but a short while; and [when it arrived] it said:
> 'I have encompassed something that you have never yet encompassed—
> for I have come to you from Sheba with a sure tiding! Behold! I found
> there a woman ruling over them who has been given all things, and here
> is a mighty throne. And I found her and her people adoring the sun
> instead of God; and Satan has made these doings of theirs seem goodly
> to them, and has barred them from the path, so that they cannot find
> the right way: [through this delusion they have come to believe] that
> they ought not to adore God—who brings forth all that is hidden in
> the heavens and on Earth, and knows all that you hide as well as all that
> you disclose: God, save whom no other deity exists—the Sustainer of
> the powerful throne.' (27:22–26)

From the example of the ants and the bird we can draw the following conclusions. Firstly, that animals are conscious of themselves and that animals such as those mentioned in the Qur'an have a highly sophisticated and structured language. They have what we call words and sentences. However, this does not mean that they are articulating as we do. Whatever their form of communication is, it is symbolic enough to convey sentential structures in their own modes. The ant identifies Solomon and his group and its own ant community and consciously wants to evade being killed. It is not uncommon for particular ants (in this case female) to be on the lookout when the rest are foraging. The ant, in this verse, is also aware of Solomon's awareness. The bird that has a conversation with Solomon, distinguishes the sexes ('a woman ruling over them') and has a grasp of 'God', true belief and illusions. It also judges the mental state of Solomon and his hosts when it states that: 'I have discovered something that you have not apprehended...' (27:22).

---

156. Shu'ab al-Iman. Narrated by Al-Bayhaqi. Also by Al-Khatib al-Tabrizi and *Mishkat al-Masabih*, on the authority of Anas/abd-God ibn Mas'ud.

Perhaps this all sounds a bit too far-fetched for many readers and it might come as a surprise, but the extensive research that has been done over the last few years has produced a number of startling breakthroughs. Donald R. Griffin, the pioneering cognitive ecologist in his book *Animal Minds* recounts documented studies, a small fraction of which we quote:

> An important advance was made by Todt (1975), who developed an effective training procedure called the model/rival approach. His procedure was much closer to the natural social exchanges by which birds learn their vocalizations, although with human companions than other birds ... Irene Pepperberg (1981) improved this procedure by having two trainers talk about objects in which their parrot seemed interested, one asking for one of these objects, the other withholding it according to the correctness of her verbal requests ... Using this method she succeeded in training a male African gray parrot named Alex to use imitations of several English words in an appropriate fashion. In his first 26 months of training Alex acquired a vocabulary of nine names, three colour adjectives, two phrases indicating simple shapes, and he came to use 'no' in situations where he was distressed and seemed unwilling to do what his trainers wanted, or when rejecting something offered to him.[157]

Alex went on to learn how to answer correctly more than 80 percent of the time to questions such as 'What colour?' or 'What shape?'. In further experiments he learned to say the numbers 2 to 6 plus the name of the objects when presented with sets of two to six familiar things... His responses to 'What's same?' or 'What's different?' were 82–85 percent correct when there were three options—colour, shape, or material—so that a chance score would be only 33 percent correct.[158] In addition to this, he also responded correctly 90 percent of the time when he stated that there was no difference, by saying none, when prompted 'What's different?' and 'What's same?' Irene Pepperberg's latest research regarding Alex is a conversation with the parrot:[159]

> IRENE: Okay, Alex, here's your tray. Will you tell me how many blue block?
>
> ALEX: Block.

157. Griffin, Donald, R. (1992), *Animal Minds*, pp. 171–172.
158. Ibid. pp. 157–160.
159. Pepperberg, Irene M., (1998), 'Talking with Alex: Logic and Speech in Parrots', *Scientific American Presents: Exploring Intelligence, Quarterly*, p. 63.

IRENE: That's right, block ... how many blue block?

ALEX: Four.

IRENE: That's right. Do you want the block?

ALEX: Wanna nut.

IRENE: Okay, here's a nut! (Waits while Alex eats the nut).

IRENE: Now, can you tell me how many green wool?

ALEX: Siss...[Six]

IRENE: Good boy!

Studies are also being conducted in natural settings:

> One of the clearest examples of natural animal communication that suggests conscious thinking stems from studies of the alarm calls and vocalizations of vervet monkeys.... [The tree types of calls are:] The immediate response to the leopard alarm call is to climb a tree... and the response to eagle alarm calls is to move to thick vegetation close to a tree trunk [if the monkey is already on one of the branches]... In response to the snake alarm call, the vervets simply stand on their hind legs and look at the ground. Once they can see a snake they can easily run away from it ...[160]

The vocalizations—the 'grunts and shrieks'—of such monkeys in their natural settings are also being studied and it is only now being realized by contemporary researchers that things such as the type, intensity, duration and intergroup and intragroup contextual nature of the calls is indeed very complex—a language in itself. We are only in the very early stages of our understanding of these sounds at present. Many other studies on different creatures, with different experiential settings, have been conducted. Behavioristic assumptions are indeed proving to be too narrow and prejudiced at the very outset, and many such studies are shattering some of the myths about animals as being automatons or machines with no self-awareness and self-consciousness. Such assumptions of animals as machines themselves have tended to stifle progress in this field of animal thinking/communication.

It has also now become empirically well-established that, for example, elephants get directed to remain, smell, feel and take from one place to another, the bones of dead elephants.[161] There have been noted incidents by field

160. Ibid. p. 156.
161. Kowalski, Gary. (1991), *The Souls of Animals*, p. 14.

researchers, for example, of a mother elephant trying to support an elephant shot in 1977 by poachers in front of her eyes in the wild, then trying to lift the dead elephant.[162] Finally it was observed that this particular female elephant, together with other elephants, started covering the dead body with branches and earth, then stood in vigil until dawn, when they left.[163] Such behaviour seems more human than general human behaviour! Another mother elephant was observed to have stayed with her stillborn calf for four days, one reason perhaps being to protect the carcass from lions and scavengers. It should be noted that the Prophet has spoken of animals having feelings and that the Qur'an speaks of the awareness of the hoopoe bird about God, truth and self as discussed above that resonate with the above-mentioned field observations.

Researchers appear to be approaching, but have not realized the sophistication of animal communication as outlined in the Qur'an in which certain animals have *syntactical* speech similar to humans and not just general unsyntactical sounds. For example, one researcher commenting on Irene Pepperberg's results, states skeptically:

> Such studies are extremely controversial, raising as many questions as they provide answers... If it is agreed (and it isn't), that these experimental animals are using rudimentary human language, then the question arises: Why don't they use it in nature? Or do they, and we just haven't noticed?[164]

Researchers in animal communication are now careful to factor out conditioning and the possible cueing (or telegraphing) of correct responses by animals. If such studies are conducted carefully and rigorously enough, without the fallacy of special pleading, they should reinforce our concern for the rest of the animal kingdom as feeling and thinking entities in their own right, and when seen in an overall context of the inherent animal communal rights should make us uphold those rights, primary of which are preservation, conservation and dignified treatment.

Perhaps in the not too distant future we will be able to corroborate the full extent of the communicational abilities of those animals depicted in the Qur'an, as well as animals in general. Perhaps when we develop a more advanced outlook toward nature and are also able to communicate with them

162. Ibid. pp. 14–15.
163. Ibid. pp. 15–16.
164. Morton, Eugene S. and Page, Jake. (1992), *Animal Talk*, pp. 233–234.

directly and explicitly we might even learn direct lessons from their way of submission to the Creator of the worlds! Let us just hope that we have not wiped out most of the animals on Earth if and when we do arrive at that stage in our endeavors. Could this animal-human articulate verbal intercommunication, in fact, be what the Qur'an is referring to, in chapter 27, verse 82? This is discussed further on page 171–172.

It is indeed remarkable to see that over one thousand years ago, when in Europe, there was the superstitious attitude that 'here be dragons', Muslim thinkers such as Al-Jahiz discussed animal communications to the extent that are only now being considered in this century, from an experimental and theoretical perspectives. In his *Book of Animals*, Volume 7, page 56–57, Al-Jahiz states that:

> ... Birds have a language which allows them to understand what they have to say to each other; they do not need a more highly developed tongue, and would have no use for it.
>
> ... If someone should say: That is not a language, we would reply: The Koran itself said that it was a language; poetry likewise regards it as a language, and so do the Arabs when they discuss it.[165]

He goes on to discuss the fact that we do not understand foreign tongues but are they not speech? It would, similarly, be a fallacy to conclude that animal sounds are also meaningless, simply because we cannot understand them. He then elaborates that:

> ... are not the sounds uttered by various kinds of wild and domestic birds also a language and means of expression, given that you know that they are distinctly articulated and methodically arranged, are produced by the mouth and tongue, and allow these animals to understand one another? If you can only grasp part of it, remember that these creatures can only understand part of your language. This quantity of sounds in combination represents the limit of their needs and power of expression, just as the sounds you produce represent the limit of your needs and power of expression. Besides, birds can be taught to speak [VII, 58], and they will learn, just as a man himself learns when a baby or a foreigner.[166]

165. Pellat, Charles. (1969), *The Life and Works of Jahiz: Translation of Selected Texts*, p. 180–181.
166. Ibid. p. 181.

Contemporary researchers, in this area of animal communication, would do well to pay heed to Al-Jahiz's conclusions, directed and inspired by the Qur'an.

The Interrelations Between the Four Ecognitions

The four ecognitions lay the foundation for rethinking our treatment of animals. Legislation regarding animals must be seen and assessed in light of each of these ecognitions, and in light of the interrelationships between these ecognitions. For example, what is the relationship between animal intelligence and the Equigenic Principle? With the proper Islamic view of animal personhood, would we cage animals for entertainment? If the rainforest, sustaining countless life forms, belongs to God, would we purposefully desecrate His property? If animals possess personhood and dwell in communities, how can factory farming be morally acceptable? If animals have personhood and feelings, should we taunt or make fun of them? If we perform painful experiments on animals, do we not violate all four ecognitions? Let us identify the ecognitions more specifically: from the Qur'anic definition of *'aql* (Ecognition 4), we can see that nonhuman animals have intelligence. What does this require of those who live with dogs and cats, if they follow the laws of God humbly (Ecognition 2)? If we are the trustees of our companion animals, are we fulfilling our role (Ecognition 1)? What are the psychological (Ecognition 4) and equigenic (Ecognition 2) implications of breaking up nonhuman animal communities (Ecognition 3)?

This type of deep and interconnectional thinking regarding the four ecognitions should foster a tremendous sense of awe and respect for these 'Others' and also guide us in solving our multifarious interspecies problems. This way of thinking informs us that 'they' are not just dumb brutes to be used as commodities for our own capricious whims and insatiable desires. From a rationalist reading of the Qur'anic injunctions, the optimization of animal advocacy can be achieved only through an interrelational recognition of the four ecognitions. It is with such an understanding that a universal charter of 'animal rights' can and ought to be established: one that would be imbued with *taqwa* (the One God—God, 'consciousness' and 'harm consciousness'), not just a mere list of do's and don'ts. *Taqwa* is a very deep and comprehensive word, which means in part that one is conscious of the presence of God at all times and therefore will not harm things in this life, as one will face the dire consequences for one's intentional actions in the next life. Indeed, *taqwa* serves to integrate the four ecognitions in one's thought patterns. It elevates both individual and communal responsibility for non-human sentient life forms to the very same level that human lives command. By understanding and acting upon these 'equigenic' concepts, animal advocacy becomes proactive rather than simply reactive. Those Muslims who are advocating an evidence-based view of Islam, the only legitimate type advocated by the Qur'an itself, therefore, believe that this proper Islamic belief system, based on the Qur'an, engenders appreciation and responsibility for creation, and that this naturally leads to compassion. This arises, ultimately, due to a foundation that takes into consideration the sustaining Reality behind the reality we see in front of us, where spirituality is part and parcel of rational thought, and could be called higher reasoning. Such higher reasoning would naturally lead human beings to maintain and enhance the inherent dignity of all the myriad creatures of God.

Qur'anic Verses and Hadith on Concern for Animals

In Chapter 2, some examples of inexcusable cruelties toward animals were given. In the previous section we have derived, from the Qur'an, four universal principles (ecognitions) that serve as the basis of ecological/animal welfare and advocacy. In this section we shall be exploring these issues further, using more verses from the Qur'an. There have been similar cruelties in the distant past, an example of which is given in the Qur'an. Note that the outcome proved to be most destructive for the community which practised such animal cruelty, among other injustices. The Prophet Saleh said to his people:

> 'Do you think that you would abide securely in that which you have here? Amidst your gardens and your water springs, your corn fields and palm trees, with soft and tender spathes? Or, that you would always be able to hew out your dwellings in the rocky mountains, with as great a skill as you do now? Be conscious of the one God and pay heed to me, and do not follow the ways of the extravagant—those who bring about disorder on the Earth instead of putting it in order.' The people of Thamud retorted: 'You are nothing but a deluded man; you are no better than a mortal like us. If you are one of the truthful then show us a sign to prove it!' (26:146–154)

Saleh consented to show them a sign and said:

> '... Here is a she-camel as a token sign for you. She shall have a share in water, the same as you each have on the appointed day; do her no harm, or you shall be made to pay the penalty eventually on the fateful day.'

> Yet, they hamstrung her to death and, though they were remorseful later, the chastisement overtook them. Verily! There is a sign in this—but most people would not believe in it. Verily, your Sustainer is Almighty, most Merciful. (26:155,156)

In our age, one could go on giving countless examples of the inhumanity of human beings. In fact, the more one studies the relationship between man and animals, the more one will be affected by the growing realization of the fact that man cannot rise above the status of the animals unless he kills the beast within himself, before it starts gnawing away at his soul.

In stark contrast to the many socio-environmentally dysfunctional societies that have emerged over history, the degree of kindness, shown by the Prophets of God who were in peaceful submission to His will, such as Solomon and David is highly exemplary. Such kindness emanates from being grateful to God:

> Behold, He [Solomon] would always turn to Us [God] in penitence: Whenever well-bred and light-footed steeds were brought before Solomon at the close of the day, he would exclaim: 'I am steeped in the love of all good things, because they remind me of the glory of my Lord'—and he would go on saying such things until they were out of sight behind a curtain. Or, he would order them to be brought to him and caressed them on their shanks and necks. (38:30–33)

> We caused the mountains to join with David [no doubt in some special acoustic manner] in magnifying Our limitless glory, and the birds too. (21:79)

What a vast gulf of difference stands between such truly caring behaviour and that which is exhibited by the gratuitous among humankind today! There are four hadiths among a great many, which make this point very abundantly clear:

> Whoever is kind to the creatures of God, is kind to himself.[167]

> A man came before the Prophet with a carpet and said, 'O Messenger [of God]! I passed through a wood, and heard the voices of young birds.

---

167. Amin, Mohammed. (1965), *Wisdom of the Prophet Muhammad*, p. 200.

I took and put them into my carpet. Their mother came fluttering around my head, whereby I uncovered the young. Then I wrapped them up in my carpet. Here are the young which I have!' The Prophet then said, 'Put them down!' And when he did so, their mother joined them and Muhammad said, 'Do you wonder at the affection of the mother towards her young? I swear by Him who has sent me, verily God is more loving to His creatures than is the mother to these young birds. Return them to the place from which you took them, and let their mother be with them!'[168]

The Prophet told of a prostitute who, on a hot day saw a thirsty dog hovering around a well, lolling its tongue. She lowered her shoe down the well and all her sins were forgiven [for this one act of kindness].[169]

The Prophet told his companion that a prophet in the old days was stung by an ant and he ordered the whole of the ants' nest to be burned. At this point, God reprimanded this prophet in these words:

Because one ant stung you, you burned a whole community from among the communities which sings My glory?[170]

Some of the companions of the Prophet snatched the young ones from the nest of a bird called in Arabic *hammara*. When the Prophet saw the mother bird hovering above in grief, he asked as to who has hurt the feelings of this bird by taking her young. He then ordered them to return the fledglings to the nest.[171]

God's power of creation, sustenance and instruction to animals is exhibited in many verses, a few of which are given here:

Do you not see that it is God whose praises are celebrated in the Universe and on Earth, even by the birds as they spread out their wings? Each creature knows its prayer to and glorification of God—and so does God know what they are doing. For God's is the dominion over the universe and the Earth, and with God is all journey's end. (24:41)

Do they not observe the birds above them—spreading their wings out and closing them? None but the Merciful God can uphold them there for verily, He keeps all in sight. (67:19)

---

168. Abu Dawud, Sunun, Ibn al-Kathir, al Jami, Vol. 4, pp. 529–530, hadith 2634.
169. Muslim, Narrated by Abu Huraira.
170. Bukhari and Muslim, Narrated by Abu Huraira. In Sahih Muslim, Vol. 4, Hadith, English translation by Abdul Hamid Siddiqi; Sh. Muhammad Ashraf, Lahore, Pakistan; 1976; Vol. 4, hadith no. 5567; p. 1215, narrated by Nafi as reported from Abdullah.
171, Narrated by Abdul Rahman bin Abdullah bin Masud. In Sahih Muslim.

The story of Noah's Ark is well-known. The Qur'an tells it in Chapter 11, Verses 36–38: When the deluge came and the flooding of the whole area[172] was imminent, there was the danger that some species of animals and birds might get exterminated. Even at such a time, God showed His concern to save at least one pair of each species, along with the faithful followers of Noah, by giving him the following instructions: '…load in the Ark two of all species—one male and one female of each kind …' This approach to nurturing, safety, preparation and guidance is a far cry from the present-day buccaneering approach to nature, in which the ark of life has been raided and pillaged.

God's knowledge encompasses all the activities of His creatures including those of animals:

> God knows what female bears and by how much the wombs may fall short [of gestation], and how much they may increase—for with Him everything is in due measure and proportion. (13:8)

It is interesting to note that from the Qur'anic verse 24:42, the domain of the Earth belongs to God, not man, and that He knows everything that is regarding His property.

Animal Intelligence

From a historical perspective, prior to the 19th century, intelligence was erroneously seen as being connected to verbal communication, and animals in general were held in contempt, mostly because they cannot talk just like humans. Lacking the power of speech is seen as an indication of mindlessness. This had given the wrong impression that they not only have no intellect, but also have no feelings and that they therefore do not deserve the same treatment that we accord to our fellow human beings. Animals have also been denied the quality of intelligence by such thinkers as Descartes, because they equated intelligence with volition and free-will, and there is the assumption that animals do not possess such capacities. Some others associate intelligence with morality, creativity, abstract reasoning and aesthetic appreciation. Such philosophers usually take a narrow and biased definition of intelligence which is too peripheral in scope, shallow in depth and somewhat subjective. In assessing children's IQ, many developmental and educational psychologists are expanding the above notion of intelligence, to go beyond its definition as epitomized

172. It was a localized massive flood, not a global one according to the Qur'an, because Noah was a local Prophet and only his tribe was destroyed for not paying heed to the Creator.

by the middle and upper-middle class white man as being the intelligent entity. The notion of intelligence is being entirely redefined from what it was in the 19th century A.D. and in the early 20th century A.D.

The conception of intelligence must be comprehensive enough to deal with all that which we know is occurring on the Earth—a planet full of various interacting creatures. This definition of intelligence is not a relative one; rather, it is an objective measure of the degree of balance maintained by any particular sentient organism with even a rudimentary nervous system as it interacts in nature. To realize this point, one must analyze what is meant by 'intelligence' from first principles. Intelligence is the ability to organize, interconnect, and then utilize information, which can be obtained by senses from the surrounding environment. Interconnection, organization and utilization of data is an indication that both the mind and senses exist.

This process is in a context that has spatial and time components. The time component means that the animal is pursuing a particular goal, and therefore, interconnects things to achieve this goal as related to its structure. From this definition, an organism which manifests this, is indeed a self-conscious and intelligent being. However, quantitatively and qualitatively intelligence may differ in degrees from one organism to another. Having defined intelligence as such would allow to differentiate between mere thoughtless conditioned behaviour and intelligent behaviour. The problem is that the notion of intelligence is often defined from a subjective specio-centric, and at times from an ethno-centric point of view that would only include a particular group and exclude the rest of the world. Such a narrow notion of intelligence is a green light for committing atrocities upon 'sub-standard class, culture and beings', be they from the human or non-human community, where no intelligence, as defined, usually means no rights. It becomes a justification for tyrannical subjugation.

From the Qur'an we can gather that intelligence is connected to reason. The Arabic word for reason in the Qur'an is 'aql from the root aqala, which means to 'bind' and hence 'to secure something' and from this we can say that to interconnect integrally is securing something. Reason, therefore, is the natural interconnection of information that corresponds with concrete reality. Natural interconnection means that the items being connected fit integrally— for example, it is unnatural to try to fit a square peg into a round hole, but natural to fit a square peg in a square hole—this is what is meant by 'natural interconnection'. Intelligence is therefore the utilization of reason as defined above by any animal in its particular domain or context. From the Islamic perspective, animals are intelligent and conscious of their own selves and environment. We know all creatures interconnect things through their senses. The key issue here is the notion of interconnectivity to maintain the equilibrium, be it instinctual or reasoned out. As indicated, the context has a spatial and a temporal component. The spatial component refers to the organism being able to relate to its surroundings. All animals are able to relate to their surroundings. The temporal component refers to the organism being able to pursue a particular goal or end and thus interconnect things to reach this goal. The goal at the outset, is explicitly related to the organism's structure and it can be achieved by trials and errors. Therefore, intelligence is the utilization of reason, as defined above, by any natural organism in a particular context. For example, animals behave in a certain way to survive in nature, by reacting adaptively to their environment—receiving and integrating information in a beneficent manner. Some such examples, which the reader could study are: hibernation; home-building; dam building by beavers; the conscious use of camouflage; and ingenious methods for catching prey, etc.[173] They all conduct themselves in a manner which is useful, by interconnecting things to pursue goals. This is a general contextual definition of 'intelligence', as it should be logically defined. Yet there is a general consensus that has developed among some ethnologists, animal psychologists and biologists, particularly those who adhere to behaviorism, that all that animals possess is instinct, and that this being the case, they are not conscious of self, the way humans are. What is given less weight in this debate is that if one acts on instinct it does not mean that one is not aware of what one is doing. When an animal, for example, uses its camouflage to evade a predator, it is both conscious of its self, a threatening environment, and possesses the notion of self-preservation. The animal acts on either learned or automatic instinctual impulses or the combination of both. Such an intelligent behaviour only goes to prove that there is the consciousness of self, and that instinct is seamlessly structured with reasoning as an organic whole. The consciously intelligent instinctual behaviour also appears in human beings in various areas such as in the area of the mother-child relationship.

173. Morris, Desmond. (1990), *Animal Watching: A Field Guide to Animal Behaviour*. Von Frisch, Karl. (1974), *Animal Architecture*.

The Status of Animals in Islam[174]

A study of history reveals that ever since they began a sedentary lifestyle, humans have been carelessly exploiting the resources of nature to satisfy their needs. Other species also use the resources of nature but they use them in a sustainable way—that is, in such a way that nature can replenish them. Unlike humans, animals always naturally conform to the Laws of Nature and are perfectly adapted to their environment; in this sense they are 'Muslims'— literally 'ones who fit into the flow of things the way they have been designed, thereby naturally submitting to the cosmic Designer, concomitantly following His natural laws':

> Have they, then, never considered any of the things that God has created? Their shadows incline to the right and left, in prostration to God, whilst being humble. It is unto God whatsoever that is in the Universe and on Earth prostrates—including solid-bodied creatures and angels. They do not bear themselves with false pride. They all revere their Sustainer above them, and obey His commands. (16:48,49)

> Do you not see that unto God prostrate all things that are in the universe and on Earth—the sun, the moon, the stars, the mountains, the trees, the animals, and a large number among mankind? However, there are many who deserve chastisement... (22:18)

> There is not an animal but He [God] has grasp [control] of its forelock [region behind which exist the frontal lobes in the brain where higher thinking occurs]. Verily, my Sustainer is on the straight path. (11:56)

The Servitude of Animals

Almost all religions allow the use of animals for necessary human needs. man has always used them and their labor just as human beings take each other in service. There seems to be nothing wrong in this arrangement, except that the animals are not capable of protecting their rights as the human labor unions can do. The protection of animal rights is left mainly to human conscience, social censure and government legislation, though the last does not count much, as the legislation always follows the trends of public opinion. Most political leaders and most reformers are two different species.

---

174. Pages 128 to 149 have been reprinted with modifications from Al-Hafiz Masri's book *Animals in Islam*, by the kind permission of Compassion in World Farming (CIWF).

All religions have tried to regulate the use of animals humanely and with equity and justice. There are many laws in the Scriptures, which cover specific cases; but the problem is that human needs and social conditions are constantly ringing the changes. The modern scientific and technological revolutions; the current interlacing of global cultures; the international and politico-economic pressures; and numerous other influences are demanding modulation in our respective lifestyles. Our social and moral values are changing so fast that an average man is no longer sure how to act. In this section the following subjects will be discussed, from the Islamic point of view: Medical and other experiments on animals; modern practices of intensive and battery farming; use of animals for pleasure; hunting and fishing for sport; animal fights; beasts of burden and other similar controversial fields of inquiry.

The Islamic Juristic Rules

Most of the above mentioned issues did not exist about fourteen centuries ago and, therefore, there was no occasion to pass any specific laws about them. It was felt sufficient to lay down the general principles as guidelines. In cases like these, Islamic Jurisprudence *(fiqh)* has left it to the Muslim Jurists *(fuqahaa)* to use their judgment by inference and analogy. The first source of the Islamic law *(shariah)* is the Qur'an. The second source is the historical records of the Prophet's sayings and doings *(hadith)*. The third is inference by analogy, called *ijtihad*. Since the law by analogy or *ijtihad* will be quoted in many cases below, a brief explanatory note is called for here.

With the expansion of Islam into vast regions grew the need for law and justice by inference and analogy in cases which were not mentioned specifically in the Statutory Law of the Qur'an and hadith. During the early period of this development, the Muslim jurists were greatly influenced by the Latin terms: *jurisconsults* or *prudentes* were named in Arabic: *fuqahaa* (plural of *faqih*): the *responsa prudentium,* meaning, answers to legal questions were named *qiyas* in the sense of 'legal opinions' based on analogical deductions from the Qur'an and hadith. Some such 'opinions' by the accredited jurists came to be accepted as 'canons' *(fatawah,* plural of *fatwah)*—very much similar to that known in the Roman law as *Jurisprudentia* or *Responsa* or 'case law' in the West. The Roman freedom of 'opinion' based on Equity, in spite of the rescript of Hadrian, had originated from secular concepts and did not meet the requirements of Islam. It was, therefore, found necessary to codify Islamic law by speculation *(qiyas)* into a reliable system which would be more in line with the spirit and intention of the Qur'anic and the hadith law. This system is known in Islam as law by *ijtihad;* which literally means to try hard to do or achieve something.

The Islamic law by inference and analogy has since long been a controversial issue among the Muslims. This controversy is mainly due to the fear that the admissibility of the *ijtihad* law could be used by some unconscientious theologians to take liberties with the spirit and intention of the law of *shariah* to suit their convenience and transitory exigencies. Others, however, feel strongly that a total rejection of analogy would close the doors for Muslims to make the necessary adaptations according to the changing conditions of life. This whole disputation can be resolved without much fuss if a fundamental principle of Islamic jurisprudence were to be understood. It is that: the law by analogy and inference is subordinate to the intrinsic spirit and intention of the laws of the Qur'an and Hadith—just as the hadith is subordinate to the Qur'an. In fact, the jurists of the early Islamic era followed this principle and built up a juridical miscellanea which we have been using for centuries and called them case law or 'Juristic Rules' *(qwaidatul fiqhiya).*

Any juristic opinion which does not conform to the *shariah* law, or even if it does not conform to its spirit and intention, would be rejected on the grounds of the above stated principle. An example of such a case is the suggestion made by a Turkish leftist newspaper, *Cumhuriyet,* to the effect that the Islamic prohibition of pork consumption be rescinded in modern Turkey.[175]

Experiments on Animals

To kill animals to satisfy the human thirst for the unessential is a contradiction in terms within the Islamic tradition. Think of the millions of animals killed, in the name of commercial enterprises, in order to supply a complacent public with trinkets and products they do not really need. And why? Because we are too lazy or too self-indulgent to find substitutes, or to do without. It will take more than religious, moral, or ethical sermons to quell the avidity and greed of some multibillion dollar corporations and their willing customers.

Many of the experiments that are being done in the name of research and education are not really necessary. Animals are being cut to pieces, organ by organ and often without anaesthetics, just for the students to look at their anatomical structures. This kind of knowledge could easily be imparted by

175. *Arabia—The Islamic World Review*, Vol. 4, No. 49, September 1985; Slough, England, p. 11.

using charts, pictures, photographs, dummies or the corpses of animals that have died their natural death. In other spheres animals are poisoned, starved, blinded, subjected to electric shocks, or similarly abused in the alleged interests of science. Some scientists generally scoff at the religionists as sticklers for convention. Are such scientists themselves doing any better by sticking to their primitive practices even when there are so many alternatives available now?

Some research on animals may yet be justified, given the principles of the Qur'an. Basic and applied research in the biological and social sciences, for example, will be allowed, if the laboratory animals are not caused pain or disfigured, psychologically traumatized or kept in horrid conditions and if human beings or other animals would benefit because of such research. The most important of all considerations is to decide whether the experiment is really necessary and that there is no alternative to it. The basic point to understand about using animals in science is that the same moral, ethical and legal codes should apply to the treatment of animals as are being applied to humans. According to Islam, all life is sacrosanct and has a right to protection and preservation. Prophet Muhammad laid so much emphasis on this point that he declared:

> He who takes pity [even] on a sparrow and spares its life, God will be merciful on him on the Day of Judgment.[176]

Like all other laws of Islam, its laws on the treatment of animals have been left open to exceptions and are based on the criterion: 'Actions shall be judged according to intention.' Any kind of medical treatment of animals and experiments on them becomes ethical and legal or unethical and illegal according to the intention of the person who does it. If the life of an animal can be saved only by the amputation of a part of its body, it will be a meritorious act in the eyes of God to do so. Any code of law, including religious law, which is so rigid as not to leave a scope for exceptional circumstances, results in suffering and breeds hypocrisy.

Take, for example, a high security jail where cut-throats, murderers, rapists, serial killers and other hardened criminals are imprisoned but well taken care of, and compare it with a so-called research laboratory where innocent and helpless animals are cooped up in cages. By what stretch of imagination can we justify the difference in the living standards of these two places? What moral or ethical justification is there for the difference in their treatment? In the case

176. Narrated by Abu Umama. Transmitted by 'Al-Tabarani'.

of human prisoners you are not allowed even to prick a pin in their flesh; while animal captives are allowed to be lacerated and hacked by surgical knives, in the name of science and research, most of which is for futile commercial purposes. These and many other such disparities are being allowed in our human and so-called humane societies only because of the double standards of our moral and ethical values. The real and ideal approach to this problem would be if we could set forth for ourselves the criterion that any kind of medical or scientific research that is unlawful on humans is unlawful on animals.

Human Needs and Interests (al-Masaleh)

It has been mentioned earlier that certain kinds of cruelties, which are being inflicted on animals these days, did not exist at the time of the Prophet Muhammad and, therefore, they were not specifically cited in the law *(Shariah)*. Commercially motivated scientific experiments are one of such cases. We have to seek guidance on such issues by analogy and inference which is the third source of law, i.e. the Juristic Rules, based on *ijtihad*. One of the main excuses for all kinds of artful cruelties to animals is selfish interest or human needs. Let us see how the Juristic Rules define 'needs' and 'interests' and judge these cases according to those definitions. The basic Juristic Rule *(qdidatul fiqhiya)* that would apply to pecuniary experiments is: 'One's interest or need does not annul other's right' *(Alizteraro yabtul haqqal ghair)*. The question arises that there are certain needs that deserve to be regarded as realistic and that the use of animals to fulfill such needs should be legitimate and justifiable. The Juristic Rules are well-defined for such cases. To begin with, needs are classified as follows:

1. The necessities *(al-Masaleh zaruriyah);* i.e. the essential needs or interests without which life could not be sustained.

2. The requisites *(al-Masaleh hajiyah);* needs or interests that are required for comfort and easement from pain or any kind of distress, or for improving the quality of life.

3. The luxuries *(al-Masaleh tahsiniyah);* needs or interests that are desirable for exuberance, enjoyment, or even for self-indulgence.

It should be kept in mind that each of the above categories differs in degree, according to circumstances. These Juristic Rules can be applied to various situations of life; but, for the present, they concern us only in relation to the use of animals in science or otherwise.

Under category (1) come the experiments which are absolutely essential for the commonweal of both the humans and the animals and are done genuinely for medical research. The basic principles under which such experiments could be made permissible are the following Juristic Rules:

1. 'That without which a necessity cannot be fulfilled is itself a necessity.' This rule only states an exception, and underlines the importance of making sure that the experiment is really a necessity *(wajib)*. However, after leaving the door open for the unavoidable necessary cases, all sorts of restrictive and prohibitive conditions have been imposed by the following Juristic Rules (2–9).

2. 'What allures to the forbidden, is itself forbidden.' This rule implies that material gains, including food, obtained by wrongful acts, such as unnecessary experiments on animals, becomes unlawful (haram). The following verse of the Qur'an supports this stance when it condemns those who fulfill their needs by illicit means, in these words:

   Why do not their learned men and doctors of law prohibit them from saying sinful things and from eating things forbidden? Certainly, it is evil what they do. (5:63).

3. 'If two evils conflict, choose the lesser evil to prevent the bigger evil.' According to this rule, even genuine experiments on animals are allowed as an exception and as a lesser evil and not as a right.

4. 'Prevention of damage takes preference over the achievement of interests or fulfillment of needs.' This rule lays down the principle that the advantages and the disadvantages of an experiment should be weighed from all angles.

5. 'No damage can be put right by a similar or a greater damage.' When we damage our health and other interests by our own follies, we have no right to make the animals pay for it by inflicting similar or greater damage on them, such as by doing unnecessary experiments to find remedies for our self-induced ailments.

6. 'Resort to alternatives, when the original becomes undesirable.' This rule has a great bearing on the current controversy about the use of alternatives for animals in experiments, such as tissue culture and other substitutes. Muslim experimentalists should take this Juristic Rule seriously. It places a great moral responsibility on them, as well as on the Muslim medical students, to find alternatives.

7. 'That which was made permissible for a reason, becomes impermissible by the absence of that reason.'

8. 'All false excuses leading to damage should be repudiated.'

The above last two rules leave no excuse for Muslims to remain complacent about the current killing of animals in their millions for their furs, tusks, oils and various other commodities. The excuse that such things are essential for human needs is no longer valid. Modern technology has produced all these things in synthetic materials and they are easily available all over the world, in some cases at a cheaper price. In the distant past, for example, furs and skins were a necessity. Even the Qur'an mentions the animals as a source of warm clothing (16:5). However, this refers only to the skins and furs of the domesticated cattle which either die their natural death or are slaughtered for food. There are thousands of wild animals which are still being killed these days commercially just for their furs and skins, while their carcasses are left to rot. Fourteen centuries ago Islam realized the absurdity of this wasteful and cruel practice and passed laws to stop it in the following hadiths summarized below:

Prophet Muhammad prohibited the use of skins of wild animals.[177]

The Prophet forbade the skins of wild animals being used as floor coverings.[178]

The Prophet(s) said: 'Do not ride on saddles made of silk or leopard skins.'[179]

It is important to note that the first hadith covers all wild animals. The reason why leopard skins have been mentioned specifically could, perhaps, be that the Prophet might have seen someone using a saddle of leopard skin. Similarly, the specific mention of floor coverings and saddles does not mean that they could be used for other purposes.

According to the spirit and the overall teachings of Islam, causing avoidable pain and suffering to the defenceless and innocent creatures of God is not justifiable under any circumstances. No advantages and no urgency of human needs would justify the kind of calculated violence, which is being done these days against animals, especially through international trade of livestock and

177. Narrated by Abu Malik on the the authority of his father. 'Abu Dawud' and 'Tirmidhi' as recorded in 'Garden of the Righteous—Riyad as-Salihin' of Imam Nawawi; translated by M. Z. Khan; Curzon Press, London, 1975; (hereafter referred to 'Riyad'); hadith No. 815, p. 160.
178. Ibid.
179. Narrated b Mu'awiah. 'Abu Dawud'; (see 'Riyad', Ref. No. 202); hadith No. 814, p. 160.

meat. One of the sayings of the Prophet Muhammad tells us: 'If you must kill [animals], kill without torture.' While pronouncing this dictum, he did not name any animal as an exception—not even any noxious or venomous creature, such as scorpions and snakes. You are allowed to kill them if they become a threat to your life or limb; and that, too, without torture.

There are more recorded sayings of the Prophet on this issue. During the pre-Islamic period, certain pagan superstitions and polytheistic practices involving acts of torture and general cruelties to animals used to be common in Arabia. All such practices were condemned and stopped by Islam. The following few sayings of the Prophet will illustrate this point: 'Jabir told that God's Messenger(s) forbade striking the face or branding on the face of animals.'[180] The same companion of the Prophet reported him as saying, when a donkey which had been branded on its face passed him by: 'God curse the one who branded it.'[181] This hadith is concerned with causing pain to the animal on the sensitive parts of its body, as well as with the disfigurement of its appearance.

When the Prophet migrated from Mecca to Medinah in 622 A.D., people there used to cut off camels' humps and the fat tails of sheep, The Prophet ordered this barbaric practice to be stopped. The temptation for the people to perform this sort of vivisection on the animals was that the juicy humps and fatty tails could be eaten while the animal remained alive for future use. To remove this avidity, he declared: 'Whatever is cut off an animal, while it is still alive, is carrion and is unlawful (haram) to eat.'[182]

To make sure that no injury was inflicted on the animal while there was even a flicker of life in it, it was forbidden by the Prophet to molest the carcass in any way, such as: by breaking its neck, skinning, or slicing off any of its parts, until the body is dead cold. One of his sayings on this theme is: 'Do not deal hastily with a "being" before it is stone dead.'[183] Umar ibn alKhattab used to instruct repeatedly: 'Give time to the slaughtered "being" till it is dead cold.'[184]

---

180. Narrated by Jabir ibn Abdullah. Sahih Muslim. Ref. 5281.
181. Narrated by Jabir ibn Abdullah. 'Muslim', Vol. 3, hadith No. 2116. Also 'Awn al-Ma'bud Sharh Abu Dawud'(hereafter referred to as 'Awn'); 7:232, hadith No. 2547. Also 'The Lawful and Unlawful in Islam' (in Arabic); Yusuf el-Kardawi; Mektebe Vahba, Cairo; 1977; p. 293. Also 'Robson', p. 872.
182. Narrated by Abu Waqid al-Laithi. 'Tirmidhi'; hadith No. 1480, Chapt. On 'Al-At'imah. Also Robson (Ref. No. 200); p. 874.
183. 'Kitab al-Maqanna', 3:542. Also 'Al-Mahli', 7:457; Ibn Hazm; (both in Arabic).
184. 'Al-Mahli', 7:457; Ibn Hazm; (both in Arabic). 'Umar ibn al-Khattab was a close companion of the Prophet Muhammad and second Caliph (634–644 A.D. = 12–22 A.H.).

Many other Muslim authorities have also given juristic opinions *(fatawah)* to the effect that, after slaughter, time should be given for the *rigor mortis* to set in before cutting up the carcass.[185] Another malpractice in Arabia in those days which caused pain and discomfort to the animals was stopped by the Prophet in these words: 'Do not store milk in the dug (udders) of animals, and whoever buys such animals, has the option to keep them or return them.'[186] Storing of milk in the dug was perhaps done to preserve milk longer or to beguile the prospective buyers.

Not only physical but also emotional care of animals was so much emphasized upon by the Prophet that he once reprimanded his wife, Aishah, for treating a camel a bit offhandedly. Aishah herself narrates: 'I was riding a restive camel and turned it rather roughly. The Prophet said to me: "it behoves you to treat the animals gently."'[187] The Prophet himself was once reprimanded by God for neglecting his horse, as the following hadith tells us:

> The Prophet was seen wiping the face of his horse with his gown *(jullabiyah)*. When asked why he was doing that, he replied: 'Last night I had a reprimand from God regarding my horse for having neglected him.'[188]

The following hadith forbids the disfiguration of the body of an animal:

> The Prophet said: Do not clip the forelock of a horse, for a decency is attached to its forelock; nor its mane, for it protects it; nor its tail, for it is its flyflap.[189]

There are many hadiths forbidding blood sports and the use of animals as targets, some of which are as follows:

> The Prophet (s) condemned those people who take up anything alive as a mere sport.[190]

---

185. Kitab al-Nil wa Shifa' al-Alib, 4:460; (in Arabic).

186. Muslim and Bukhari. Also 'Holy Traditions'; 1st Edition; Vol. 1; Muhammad Manzur Ilahi; Ripon Press, Lahore, Pakistan; 1932; p. 149.

187. Narrated by Aishah. Muslim, Vol. 4, hadith No. 2593. Also Awn, 7:155, hadith No. 2461; (Ref. No. 205).

188. Narrated by Yahya bin Said. Malik bin Anas al-Ashabiy. Also 'Al-Muwatta', (in English); Divan Press, Norwich, England; 1982; p. 205.

189. Narrated by 'Utba bin Abdul Salamiy. 'Abu Dawud'. Also Awn, 7:216, 217, hadith No. 2525; (Ref. No. 205).

190. Narrated by Abdullah bin 'Umar. 'Muslim', Vol. 3, hadith No. 1958.

The Prophet forbade blood sports, like the Bedouin. [191]

The Prophet said: 'Do not set up living creatures as a target.'[192]

The Prophet condemned those who use a living creature as a target.[193]

The Prophet forbade an animal being made a target.[194]

The Prophet was reported as saying: 'Do not make anything having life a target.[195]

Ibn Omar happened to pass by a party of men who had tied a hen and were shooting arrows at it. When they saw Ibn Omar coming, they scampered off. Ibn Omar angrily remarked: 'Who has done this? Verily! God's Messenger has invoked a curse upon one who does this kind of thing'.[196]

The Prophet passed by some children who were shooting arrows at a ram. He told them off, saying: 'Do not maim the poor beast.'[197]

The fact that these hadith repeat the same sayings of the Prophet in slightly varying wordings shows that he took the matter very seriously and repeated them again and again on different occasions in the presence of different people. Another significant point to note in this respect is that, to stop the use of animals as targets or in blood sport, the Prophet did the same as he did in the case of camel humps and sheep tails, quoted above. He declared their meat as *Mujaththema* and unlawful *(haram)* for consumption, according to the following hadith:

> God's Messenger (s) forbade eating a *mujaththema* (carrion) of a bird or animal set up and shot at as a target for shooting.[198]

One might also appeal to the Islamic law *(Shariah)* to oppose using animals in military research in general and in the so-called wound laboratories in particular. The above quoted hadiths, as well as the Juristic Rules, would seem

191. Narrated by Abdulla Ibn Abbas. Awn, (Ref. No. 205); 8:15, hadith No. 2803. Also 'Robson'; p. 876. (Ref. No. 200, but does not mention 'Bedouins').
192. Narrated by Abdullah bin Abbas. Muslim, Vol. 3, hadith No. 1957. Also 'Robson'; p. 872; (Ref. No. 200)
193. Narrated by Abdullah bin Umar. Bukhari and Muslim. Also 'Robson'; p. 872. (Ref. No. 200).
194. Narrated by Anas. Recorded by 'Riyad' (Ref. No. 202); hadith No. 1606; p. 272.
195. Narrated by Ibn Abbas. Sahih Muslim—Kitab-us-Said Wa'dh-Dabaha'ih; Chapt. DCCCXXII, Vol. III; Sh. Muhammad Ashraf, Lahore, Pakistan, 1976; hadith No. 4813; p. 1079; (hereafter referred to as 'Kitab-us-Said').
196. Ibid. Narrated by Said bin Jubair.
197. Narrated by Abdullah bin Ja'ffar. *An-Nasai*, 7:238.
198. Narrated by Waqid al-Laithi. Abu-al-Darda. Tirmidhi, hadith No. 1473, Chapt. Al-At'imah. Also 'Robson' (Ref. No. 200); p. 874.

to support the view that our wars are our own problems and that we have no right to make the animals suffer for them.

There is no doubt that the Islamic prohibition against the cutting or injuring of live animals, especially when it results in pain and suffering, does apply to modern vivisection in science. We are able to support this interpretation of the Islamic teachings by referring not only to the above quoted representative Hadith, but also to the Qur'an. In the verses quoted below, we find expressed the principle that any interference with the body of a live animal, which causes pain or disfigurement, is contrary to the Islamic precepts. These verses were revealed in condemnation of the pagan superstitious custom that the she-camels, ewes or nanny goats which had brought forth a certain number of young ones in a certain order should have their ears slit, let loose and dedicated to idols. Such customs were declared by the Qur'an as devilish acts, in these words:

> It was not God who instituted the practice of a slit-ear she-camel, or a she-camel let loose for free pasture, or a nanny-goat let loose … (5:103).

> God cursed him [Satan] for having said: 'I shall entice a number of your servants, and lead them astray, and I shall arouse in them vain desires; and I shall instruct them to slit the ears of cattle; and, most certainly, I shall bid them so that they will corrupt God's creation.' Indeed! He who chooses the Satan rather than God as his patron, ruins himself manifestly. (4:118, 119).

Animal fights, such as bull and cock fighting, is another kind of vivisection. The only difference is that, in this case, man does not do it himself—he makes the animals tear each other apart to provide amusement for him. Those who seek entertainment in such scenes of violence and if the sight of blood warms their own blood, would do better by watching different 'sports'. All kinds of animal fights are strictly forbidden in Islam. Out of the numerous such injunctions, one would suffice here: 'God's Messenger forbade inciting animals to fight each other.'[199]

It is interesting to note that, like the camel humps, fat tails of sheep and target animals *(mujaththema)* as stated above, the meat of animals which die as a result of fights is also declared in Islam as unlawful to eat *(haram)*. For example, the Spaniards hold fiestas on special occasions to eat the bull killed by a matador. There is no room here to give the gruesome details of such

---

199. Narrated by Abdullah bin Abbas. Bukhari, Muslim, Tirmidhi, Abu al-Darda, recorded in 'Riyad' (Ref. No. 202); hadith No. 1606; p. 271. Also 'Robson'); p. 876.

bullfights. Suffice it to say that the meat of such animals is *harám* (forbidden) for the Muslims. Some very revoltingly cruel dogfights have been brought to light recently, some of which have resulted in prosecutions. Lastly, we ought to quote a particularly strong hadith against animal mutilation:

> Whoever mutilates a living creature and then does not repent, God will mutilate him on the Day of Judgment.[200]

Factory Farming

Man's exploitation of animals and the resources of nature is spreading like an epidemic. The contagious influence of the West, in this respect, has started affecting the character and destiny of the economically underdeveloped countries. Formerly, in those countries, cruelty to animals used to be inflicted mostly through individual ignorance and lack of veterinary facilities. Now it is becoming a mammonish creed of rapacious grabbing by fair means or foul. The agrarian mismanagement, referred to above, is particularly of concern to the environmentalists because of the change in our attitude to nature which has characterized the last fifty years or so. This concern for nature becomes deeper when it applies to farm animals and wildlife, whose dependence on ecology is absolute. Those economically underdeveloped countries which have started copying the current methods of agriculture and animal husbandry should try to learn from the mistakes of the West.

Ever since the enclosure of commonly owned land, an ecologically sound system of farming had been developed in the West, based on the beneficial interaction between the animal and the soil. Thus, in the simplest rotation called the Norfolk four course rotation, a quarter of the farm would be down to root crops such as the cattle food called mangolds or mangels and swedes or turnips; a quarter to barley; a quarter to clover grass mixture and a quarter to wheat. Each year the fields would be rotated, so that the exhausting and the restorative crops would alternate for the benefit of fertility. As a field never had the same crop growing on it for two years in succession, crop weeds and pests, as well as fungus diseases, were prevented from building up.

Sheep, not without cause called the golden hoof, grazed over at least half the farm each year and enriched the soil. Flocks would graze the barley and wheat stubbles as well as the clover leys after the hay crop had been taken. They were also to be seen arable folded during the winter time on the turnips. All the

200. Transmitted by Ahmad, narrated by Ibn Umar.

crop by-products, such as straw, manure, etc. were jealously conserved and had to be returned to the soil. A tenant farmer could be dispossessed if he burned even a small amount of straw or sold hay off the farm. In the rotational mixed farming system, animals were related to the land—and to the benefit of both. The 'rules of good husbandry' were written into every tenancy agreement and no one considered breaking them.

Today this cyclic system has been displaced by a straight-line system on many farms in the Western so-called developed countries, and the costs are only now being realized, with a consequent trend to reintroduce many of the old techniques. Let us look at what happened. Increasingly, the animals were taken off the land and reared intensively, tightly packed together in window-less houses of the factory farms. They were not allowed straw to lie on be-cause this would mean extra labor and would in any case block the pumps that deal with the effluent slurry. The fields, devoid of livestock, were brought back into large hundred acre blocks by the removal of hedges and trees and the filling in of ditches. Instead of a variety of cropping, the most profitable crop—barley—was grown continuously and each year an embarrassing bulk of straw burned in the field where the combine harvesters had left it. The soil structure started to deteriorate, and fertility could only be maintained by ever increasing doses of artificial high nitrogen fertilizers until the soil, devoid of the micro life, became addicted to chemicals. Plant diseases and pests prolifer-ated like the plagues of ancient Egypt and could only be controlled by recourse to the agricultural chemist's skill in devising toxic sprays. Weeds also were able to pose a challenge to the spray manufacturers. The weeds of old that the harvester knew—poppies, charlock and thistles—used to be kept in check by through-cultivation methods. Herbicides quickly eliminated these weeds and a new spectrum of more troublesome weeds arose, such as Shepherd's Purse, Pierts Parsley and the like. The wildlife disappeared from the cultivated areas, retreating to woodlands and motorway banks.

Now a host of new troubles are being studied. There is a link between some of the diseases of modern life, particularly cancer, with forced growth crops and forced growth animals. In some parts of the country the water supply has been so contaminated with nitrogen runoff from fields that it is considered unsafe for life in general and for babies in particular. Rivers and streams have become septic where no aquatic life can survive. Straw burning is an increasing cause for complaint and is thought to cause salmonella outbreaks. Concern about the deterioration in wildlife, especially insects, such as bees, is making itself felt in the same way as the deterioration of frogs in some of the developing countries. Added to this catalogue of concerns is the growing pressure on politicians and the economists from the scientists and the lay public about the welfare and protection of animals. The religious institutions are starting to murmur that the 'Covenant' was not made with man alone, but with the non-human species also.

The politicians and the economists of so-called Islamic countries that have started following blindfold in the footsteps of the Western model should ask themselves a few pertinent questions at this stage—before they get their countries entangled inextricably in the Western system of farming and animal husbandry. Do these animals, upon which man has always depended for his food, have certain basic rights? For instance, the right to the companionship of their own kind, the right to an appropriate diet to keep them in health, and the right to a natural life and a painless death? If their Divine Creator gave them legs, is it not a blasphemy to shut them in crates where they are unable to walk? Are we perhaps forcing them back upon their own evolution by taking them from the fields and the hills and putting them in rows, unmoving like rows of vegetables? In so doing, are we perhaps reversing our own evolution and becoming more bestial ourselves, unable to know right from wrong? Let us look at some of these areas of concern.

The patient dairy cow is now forced by genetics and nutritional science to yield many times more milk than her forebears did only ten years ago, and to such an extent as to shorten her productive life to about three years. Her calves which bring her into milk with their birth, are taken from her at two or three days old, artificially fed and then put into the market, probably to be bought by veal farmers. Such is the stress and trauma of the market that some 70 percent of calves pick up enteric diseases during this stage and so need medication with antibiotics on the receiving farm.

Some veal farmers rear the calves in communal pens on beds of straw, but there are still others who put the calves into narrow crates as soon as they are brought onto the farm. There they stay unable to walk, gambol or even turn round until they are ready for slaughter at about 16 weeks old. Although calves are highly social animals, they cannot touch one another and can scarcely see each other in their restrictive crates. They lie on bare wooden slats so that the dung and urine can be cleared away mechanically as slurry. Although ruminant and having a strong urge to chew the cud, they are denied any sort of roughage and so pluck the hair from their own shoulders and flanks to satisfy their appetites. Any slaughter-man will tell you that the stomachs of these calves contain indigestible hairballs.

Chickens kept for egg production are packed tightly into wire cages and kept there all their productive lives crouching on a sloping wire floor. The sole purpose of their existence is supposed to be to lay eggs and they are denied any other inherited behaviour. They cannot stretch their wings out. Indeed the wingspan of a battery hen is 30 inches or thereabouts, yet five or sometimes even six are crowded into a 20 inch wide cage. They cannot scratch the ground, searching for seeds or grub; they cannot dust bathe; they cannot even flee from a more aggressive cage mate.

Perhaps the most offensive aspect of all this is the contempt for life, which is bred into the modern farmer. Even cattle are no longer individuals but numbers in a herd. Poultry flocks are not numbered in hundreds these days but in tens of thousands. Will this contempt affect our sensibilities and eventually be extended to others of our own species? Even from the spiritual point of view, meat of such animals is unhealthy to eat. Our dieticians do not lay enough stress on the point, but history of nations bears the fact out that there is a strong ethological link between diet and character formation. Animals reared under unnatural and inhumane conditions become frustrated, morose and cantankerous. Such characteristics are passed on to those who eat their meat, though it may take many generations to show. The biological laws of nature are the same for the human species as for the rest of animals. Their diet, environment and the general living conditions affect all of them alike. Like human beings, animals too have a sense of individuality. Even chickens are individuals, and if given the chance, will demonstrate their own characters peculiar to the individual. However, many hens that are relieved from factory farms are unable to perch, and may stare vacantly at the new experience called 'grass'. It was something out of this world for them, until taught by other freer cousins the joys of free-range.

The basic moral question is: how right is it to deny these creatures of God their natural instincts of living their natural lives so that we may eat the end product? For the Muslims these questions pose the additional question of a fundamental moral pertinence. Prophet Muhammad's overwhelming concern for animal rights and their general welfare would certainly have condemned *(laana)* those who practice such methods, in the same way as he condemned similar other cruelties in his days. He would have declared that there is no grace or blessing *(barakah)*—neither in the consumption of such food nor in the profits from such trades. These are not just hypothetical questions. The cruel and inhumane methods of intensive farming are being practised in most of the Islamic countries these days, even in countries where indigence is no excuse.

For some years the developing countries, including the countries nominally labeled as Islamic, have been importing high technology farming systems and the trend is growing fast. According to the figures published in the 'World Poultry' gazette for October 1984, European firms have developed special projects of high technology farming units for the Middle East. One of their laying houses in Egypt was producing 25 million eggs per year. Another project, under construction there, was for 60 million eggs per year. According to the same gazette, similar projects have been installed in Saudi Arabia, Libya, Morocco, Tunisia, Oman and other Middle Eastern states. Pakistan, Indonesia and countries are following suit. Under the intensive farming system, a hen lays on average about 250 eggs a year. One can imagine from the above figures how many millions of hens are being subjected to the un-Islamic methods of food production in all these countries put together. Most of such un-Islamic businesses are flourishing there due to the ignorance of the consumer public. People do not know how the chickens are being reared and how they are being fed on chemical nutrients to fatten fast and to produce more and more eggs. Fowls and other food animals are no longer creatures of God; they are numbers in their computers. After all, computers can give the breeders up to the minute figures of profit and loss at the touch of a button, while God's reckoning is a long way off in the Hereafter.

If only the average, simple and God-fearing Muslim consumers of such food animals knew of the gruesome details about the Westernized meat industry in their own countries, they would be dismayed at what they are really consuming. The least that the Muslim *Ulama* can do is to inform the lay public how their food is being produced, so that people can, with knowledge, decide what to do about it. Some may decide that the product of intensive factory farms are not suitable, both from the compassionate and the health points of view, and seek more naturally produced eggs and meat; or give up eating meat altogether. In April 2004, The Canadian Food Inspection Agency had to come to grips with an avian influenza breakout that occurred in the province of British Columbia. As Bruce Passmore of the Vancouver Humane Society and member of the Canadian Coalition of Farm Animals has pointed out most astutely, organic poultry operations have mostly been free of infections whereas their factory farming cousins have been severely affected by the virus. This has led to the decision to cull millions of infected birds. He states that:

> The Canadian Food Inspection Agency's investigation into the cause and spread of avian flu should include the role played by the welfare conditions of the poultry affected, including their health, housing and stock densities.[201]

General Reforms of Islam

The Islamic teachings have gone to great lengths to instill a sense of love, respect and compassion for animals. As already mentioned, some of the cruelties to animals which used to be practised during and before the time of the Prophet were stopped by him. However, we come across many cruel practices these days which, though not mentioned in Islamic law, are obviously against the very spirit of the teachings of Islam. It is sad to see that most of such cruelties are taking place in the so-called civilized Western countries. Nonetheless, it is encouraging to see that the protest of the Western Animal Welfarists against all kinds of cruel exploitation of animals is well-organized and, hopefully, will prevail.

From the Islamic point of view, however, the concern is that the economically developing countries have started emulating their Western preceptors in practices such as: intensive farming methods; use of insecticides which are harmful to human and animal health and do more damage to the environment than good to crops; export of animals in millions for exotic foods or for profit motivated experiments to manufacture cosmetics and other such luxuries, etc. Better and quicker returns, plus the feeling that Western industrialized societies have given their tacit approval to these and many other cruel methods of making money, are corroding the moral ethos of the economically underdeveloped as well as the affluent nations of the East. Islam's directive teachings in cases like this are very helpful and educational, as the few examples given below will show.

---

201. *Big Poultry at risk over Avian flu?* Bruce Passmore, April 13, 2004, Toronto Star.

The Moral Appeal of Islam

Most of the sermons from our pulpits are admonitions against sin. If someone were inclined to choose a subject pertaining to animal welfare, there is enough material in every scripture to choose from. For example, here are two sayings of the Prophet Muhammad which could make very appropriate themes for such sermons. In the following sayings the Prophet has placed the killing of animals without a justifiable reason as one of the major sins:

> Avoid the seven obnoxious things [deadly sins]: polytheism; magic; the killing of breathing beings which God has forbidden except for rightful reason ... [202]

> The baneful [sinful] things are: polytheism; disobedience to parents; the killing of breathing beings.[203]

As indicated earlier the Arabic word for 'breathing beings' is *nafs*. Until recently it used to be taken as meaning 'human beings' only. All the Arabic dictionaries give the meaning of *nafs* as *ruh* (soul), and since they are breathing creatures, there seems to be no reason why the Qur'anic verses 6:152 and 15:33 should not comprehend all 'breathing beings', i.e. all species of animals. These verses should be read in conjunction with other verses of the Qur'an and numerous Hadiths which speak of the sanctity of life as a whole.

The Prophet has even tried the 'punishment and reward' approach, in the following statements:

> A woman was punished because she had kept a cat tied until it died, and she was thrown into Hell. She had not provided it with food, or drink, and had not freed her so that she could eat the insects on the ground.[204] (This hadith has been recorded by almost all the authentic books of Hadith).

> 'On Judgment day, God will question anyone who kills a bird without justification.' The congregation asked him [the Prophet Muhammad]:

202. Narrated by Abu Huraira. 'Sahih Muslim—Kitab al-Iman.'; Chapter. 39, Vol. I; Sh. Muhammad Ashraf, Kashmiri Bazar, Lahore, 1976, p. 52. Also Bukhari, 4:23 and in addition in Awn al-Ma'bud Sharh Abu Dawud, hadith No. 2857.

203. Ibid. Narrated by Abdullah bin 'Amru.

204. Sahih Muslim, Vol. 4, Hadith, English translation by Abdul Hamid Siddiqi; Sh. Muhammad Ashraf, Lahore, Pakistan; 1976; Vol. 4, hadith No. 5570; p. 1215, narrated by Nafi as reported from Abdullah. According to this English translation, this hadith was also narrated by Abu Huraira, see hadith No. 5573, p. 1215. The translation of hadith No. 5570 has been edited for idiomatic expression by the authors.

'How could it be justified?' He replied: 'To be killed for food, not simply for decapitating its head and throwing it away.'[205]

The Prophet said, 'One of the rights of a female camel is that it should be milked at a place of water.'[206]

A person suffered from intense thirst while on a journey, when he found a well. He climbed down into it and drank [water] and then came out and saw a dog lolling its tongue on account of thirst and eating the moistened Earth. The person said: this dog has suffered from thirst as I had suffered from it. He climbed down into the well, filled the shoe with water, then caught it in his mouth until he climbed out and made the dog drink it. God appreciated this act and forgave him. Then [the Companions around him] said: 'God's Messenger, is there a reward for [serving] even such animals?' He [the Prophet] replied: 'Yes, there is a reward for service to every living animal.'[207]

Physical Cruelty

The following sayings of the Prophet Muhammad lay down the principles that the animals in the service of man should be used only when necessary and for the purpose for which they are meant, and that their comfort should not be neglected:

The Prophet once saw a man sitting on the back of his camel in a market-place, addressing people. He said to him: 'Do not use the backs of your beasts as pulpits, for God has made them subject to you so that they may take you to places you could not otherwise reach without great fatigue.'[208]

The Prophet once passed by a lean camel whose belly had shrunk to its back. 'Fear God,' he said to the owner of the camel, 'in these dumb animals and ride them only when they are fit to be ridden, and let them go free when it is required that they should rest.' [209]

About taking care of animals during traveling, the Prophet used to give the following advice: 'When you journey through a verdant land, allow

205. Ad-Darimi, *Sunan*, Vol. 2, p. 84. suffered from it.
206. Narrated by Abu Huraira. Al-Bukhari hadith 3.565.
207. Sahih Muslim, Volume 4, English translation by Abdul Hamid Siddiqi, (1976) hadith No. 5577, Sh. Muhammad Ashraf, Kashmiri Bazar, Lahore. p. 1216.
208. Narrated by Abu Huraira. Awn (Ref. No. 205); 7:235; hadith No. 2550. Also *Traditions of Islam*; Alfred Guillaume; Khayats Oriental Reprinters, Beirut, Lebanon; 1966, pp. 106, 107. (hereinafter referred to as 'Guillaume').
209. Narrated by Abdullah bin Ja'ffar. *Awn* (Ref. No. 205); 7:221; hadith No. 2532.

your camels their portion of it, but when you are traveling through barren land, where vegetation is scarce, quicken your pace [lest hunger should enfeeble the animals]. Do not pitch your tents for the night on the beaten tracks, for they are the pathways of noxious nocturnal creatures.'[210]

Saying daily prayers (*salat*) is one of the five most important obligations in Islam. In the following Hadith, one of his companions tells us that the Prophet and his fellow travelers used to delay even saying their prayers until they had first given their riding and pack animals fodder and had attended to their needs:

When we stopped at a halt, we did not say our prayers until we had taken the burdens off our camels' backs and attended to their needs.'[211]

Ali's general advice about pack animals is: 'Be kind to pack animals; do not hurt them; and do not load them more than their ability to bear.' [212]

It is related from Ibn Abbas that the Messenger of God, forbade inciting animals to fight one another.[213]

Mental Cruelty

Islam's concern for animals goes beyond the prevention of physical cruelty to them, which, logically, is a negative proposition. It enjoins on the human species to take over the responsibility of all creatures in the spirit of positive philosophy of life and be their active protectors. Prevention of physical cruelty is not enough; mental cruelty is equally important. In this age of scientific research and knowledge, it should not be difficult to comprehend that these so-called 'dumb animals', too, have feelings and emotional responses. Dogs, cats and various other animals that have become part of human society as pets, were originally untamed brutish animals. It was only love and care that won their confidence in man; and it is only their ill treatment and neglect by man that brings back the beast in them.

---

210. Narrated by Abu Huraira. Sahih Muslim—Kitab al-Iman (Ref. No. 53); Vol. III; Chpt. DCCCVII; hadith No. 4723; pp. 1062, 1063.
211. Narrated by Anas. Awn (Ref. No. 205); 7:223; hadith No. 5234. Also 'Guillaume' (Ref No. 240); pp. 106–107.
212. Maxims of Ali; translated by A. Halal from *Nahj-ul-Balagha* (in Arabic); Sh. Muhammad Ashraf, Lahore, Pakistan; p. 436. (Hereafter referred to as 'Maxims'. Ali bin Abi Talib was the son-in-law of the Prophet Muhammad, and the fourth Caliph (644–656 A.D. = 22–34 A.H.).
213. Narrated by Ibn Abbas, Abu Dawud and al-Tirmidhi.

The incidents of the Prophet Muhammad's personal grooming of his horse; his wife Aisha's rough handling of her camel; the Prophet's prohibition of cutting forelocks, the mane or tail.[214] The condemnation of striking and branding on the face or ears—all these and many other such hadiths show that this great man, Muhammad, had realized even fourteen centuries ago that animals have a sense of adornment and sensitivity. In the following incident, a bird's emotional distress has been understood as well as any physical injury:

> We were on a journey with the Apostle of God, and he left us for a while. During his absence, we saw a bird called *hummara* with its two young and we took the young ones. The mother bird was fluttering above us in the air, beating its wings in grief, when the Prophet came back and said: 'Who has hurt the feelings of this bird by taking its young? Return them to her.'[215]

> It is reported that: A man once robbed some eggs from the nest of a bird. The Prophet had them restored to the nest.[216]

Slaughter of Animals for Food[217]

Islam has allowed the slaughter of animals for food. Let us see what instructions it gives us to ensure humane slaughter, with as little pain to the victim as possible. The following hadiths are self-explanatory:

> God's Messenger was reported as saying: 'God who is Blessed and Exalted, has prescribed benevolence towards everything [and has ordained that everything be done in a good way]; so, when you must kill a living thing, do it in the best manner and, when you slaughter an animal, you should [use the best method and] sharpen your knife so as to cause the animal as little pain as possible.' [218]

214. The hadith states that: 'Do not clip the forelocks of horses or their manes or their tails. Their tails are their fly-traps, their manes are their warmth, and their forelocks have a blessing in them.' (Narrated by Utba ibn Abd al-Sulami, transmitted by Abu Dawud).

215. Narrated by Abdul Rahman bin Abdullah bin Mas'ud. Muslim. Also Awn (Ref. No. 205) hadith No. 2658. Also 'Guillaume' (Re. No. 232); p. 106 Bukhari. Also Muslim; Vol. 2; Ch. 11; Section on Slaying; 10:739; verse 152. Also 'Robson' (Ref. No. 200); p. 872.

216. Ibid. (Ref. No. 219); hadith No. 4817; p. 1079.

217. On the issue of vegetarianism and Islam, readers are encouraged to delve into Al-Hafiz Masri's book *Animals in Islam*, Richard C. Foltz's book: *Animals in the Islamic Tradition and Muslim Cultures*; the paper by Nadeem Haque in the *Journal of Agricultural and Environmental Ethics*, and the chapter by Nadeem Haque and Mehran Banaei in *Africa and Her Animals* (as referenced in the Bibliography).

218. Narrated by Shaddad bin Aus. Muslim; Vol. 2; Chpt. 11; Section on 'Slaying'; 10:739, verse 151. Also 'Robson' (ref. No. 200); p. 872. Also recorded in 'Riyad' (Ref. No. 202); hadith No. 643; p. 131.

The Messenger of God was heard forbidding to keep waiting a quadruped or any other animal for slaughter.'[219]

The Prophet forbade all living creatures to be slaughtered while tied up and bound.[220]

The Prophet said to a man who was sharpening his knife in the presence of the animal: 'Do you intend inflicting death on the animal twice—once by sharpening the knife within its sight, and once by cutting its throat?'[221]

Ali says: 'Do not slaughter sheep in the presence of other sheep, or any animal in the presence of other animals.'[222]

Umar once saw a man denying a sheep, which he was going to slaughter, a satiating measure of water to drink. He gave the man a beating with his lash and told him: 'Go, water it properly at the time of its death, you knave!'[223]

It is reported about Umar that he once saw a man sharpening his knife to slaughter a sheep, while he was holding the cast sheep down, with his foot placed on the snout of its face. Umar started lashing the man until he took to his heels. The sheep, meanwhile, had scampered off.[224]

It is related from Abu Waqid al-Laythi that when the Prophet came to Medinah, the people used to like [eating] the humps of camels and would cut off the fat tails of sheep. He said, 'Whatever is cut off from an animal while it is alive is carrion and is unlawful to eat.'[225]

Domestication of Pigs

As we have attempted to show in this book, everything has a proper place in the scheme of existence designed by the Creator to serve a particular purpose in space and over time. As an example of misplacement, in this book we have shown cases where the misplacement of animals causes a disruption in the natural dynamic equilibrium in nature. There is an interesting case of this misplacement which highlights this very approach. The case has to do with

219. Bukhari. Also Muslim; Vol. 2; Chapt. 11; Section on Slaying; 10:739; verse 152. Also 'Robson' (Ref. No. 200); p. 872.
220. Ibid. (for Ali see Ref,. No. 4).
221. In Arabic: Al-frou Min-al-Kafi Lil-Kulini; 6:230.
222. Ibid. (for Ali see Ref. No. 244).
223. Reported by Ibn Sirin about 'Umar and recorded in 'Badae al-Sanae' (in Arabic); 6:2811.
224. Ibid. 6:2811.
225. Timirdhi; hadith No. 1480, Chapter on al-At'imah. Also 'Robson', p. 874.

the pig. Our main thesis is that: The domestication of the pig has caused the spread of the deadlier strains of influenza among humans and if pigs had been left in the wilderness—for which they were intended—they would have served their optimal function as vacuum cleaners, breaking down waste, as part of the grand organic recycling machine of nature, and would not have caused such contagious harm.

If this thesis eventually turns out to be proven, through further research, then the domestication of swine will have proven to be one of the greatest unsuspected and unrealized ecological disasters. If the world population accepted and followed the Qur'anic and Judaeic injunctions not to eat swine flesh (for dietetic reasons) then all those tens of millions of people who have been unnecessarily killed by influenza over the ages would not have succumbed to such premature fates and suffering, not to mention the suffering of pigs themselves.

Let us examine the theory of the pig as the transmitter of deadly flu viruses to humans given what we now know. In 1918 more people died of Swine Influenza or the Spanish Flu than did during the whole of World War I—30 million.[226] The likely cause of this was the pig, but there is still some debate about this conclusion. However, recently there is a theory that:

> Pigs on farms in Asia (where both the 1957 and 1968 pandemics originated) are often kept close to ducks and chickens. And pigs have receptors on their snouts not just for their own virus but for bird and human viruses as well. So, potentially, a pig could snort up a bird virus in infected droppings or water, inhale a human virus spread by a coughing farmer, and become a mixing vessel for the two. The viral progeny might then infect humans nearby… This might explain the deadly 1918, 1957 and 1968 pandemics… [It must be noted] that every fall since 1918, pigs in the United States have come down with the classic swine flu, a gift of the virus H1N1, which is a relative of the 1918 human virus. (The Flu classification system numbers flu strains by variation in their hemagglutinin and nearaminidese genes). The Hong

226. Here it is being taken for granted that viruses exist. If they do not, and there is a gross misinterpretation, as former virologist Dr. Stefan Lanka has pointed out in his vitally important research, then the above analysis does not hold. Note that in Germany, based on Lanka's case concerning the causation of measles, it was judged that it was not provable that viruses cause measles, by the highest court in the land. This decision has major implications, but is only slowly spreading through the media. We are, however, retaining this analysis of viral existence and transmission just in case it is correct that viruses do exist. An in-depth discussion is out of scope in this publication, but one of the authors will engage in this ontological debate in a future specialized publication.

Kong flu of 1968, however, had a hemagglutinin related to one not found in pigs, but in birds… There had already been evidence that the 1957 and 1968 flu pandemics were caused by human viruses that had substituted avian genes—probably from waterfowl for some of their own. Yet catching flu from pigs seemed more likely. While humans don't carry receptors for bird flu on their cells, pigs do. The going theory was that flu viruses might resort more easily, and become more compatible with humans, if they mixed in an intermediate host like a pig.[227]

If pigs do sometimes serve this function [of being mixing vessels], their involvement might help explain why pandemics commonly originate in China: millions of birds, pigs and people live closely there.[228]

If pigs were displaced from the environment where they were serving as part of the natural hierarchy for the staged decomposition of waste, then if they were taken out of that environment and placed in a human environment, they would not only create a problem by their *presence* in the human domain, but by their *absence* in their natural domain. If one were to conduct research in this area, there is no doubt that, by force of logic, they have contributed to upsetting some aspects of nature's balance by being removed from their natural setting. What biological, ecological or pathogenic harm this has caused is, at the present time anybody's guess, and would require extensive, interdisciplinary research.

227. Gadsby, Patricia. (1999), *Discover Magazine*, 'Fear of Flu', January 1999, Vol. 20, Number 1, p. 82–88.
228. Laver, Graeme W., Bischofberger, Norbert, Webster, Robert G. (1999), *Scientific American*, 'Disarming Flu Viruses', Volume 280, Number 1, p. 82.

Chapter 6

Animal Afterlife

The scriptures of the revealed religions have been drawing our attention to the fact that all sentient beings possess souls right from the very beginning. In spite of this, most of the commentators and exegetes, while expounding their respective Scriptures, have been persistently transfusing the sense that the term 'soul' used in the context of animals means nothing more than a kind of subliminal self, i.e. a conscious state of mind not sufficiently developed to enforce recognition. Such exponents did the same in the case of the theological concept of slavery. In order to give their moral and ethical sanction to the slave trade, they went on for centuries to try to prove from the Bible that the 'Negroid Races' were some sort of a lower stratum of humanity. The same has been the case in respect of the status of women. The early European scholastic renderings of the Scriptures are full of interpretations purporting the male chauvinistic predominance over the female. It took conscientious objectors a very long time to convince such clerics that their scriptural interpretations were wrong.

This objectification has not been confined to segments of humanity but has extended to animals as well, through the denigration of animal psyche, that impinges on the concept of the 'soul'. This chapter explores whether the soul exists or not, whether animals possess it, and whether the animal soul continues to exist in an afterlife. We shall be looking into the Transfocation Model of Consciousness, developed by one of the authors (Haque), Qur'anic verses on animal afterlife and anecdotal claims/evidence. The question of animal souls has great bearing on the crucial question of theodicy in relation with God's purported justice and compassion and our treatment of them. Indeed, the very logic of natural as well as of moral philosophy of animal-human relationship has to be based on and infused with the postulate that all living beings have been endowed with *nafs* and *ruh*, without which they would remain agricultural products and commercial commodities, and man would go on treating them as such.

Animals and Theodicy

Most individuals who have pets, that are lost, killed or die of natural death, are often naturally led to ask and wonder about this important and intriguing question of animal afterlife at some point and, in this chapter, it will be shown that it is a question that *does* have a definitive answer through the Qur'an. Tom Cartwright, an animal rights promoter who had been active in animal welfare for many years, expressed the sentiment to one of the authors (Masri) that he had been a nominal Christian who had never practised his faith (Catholicism) since he could never reconcile to the teaching that only human beings have immortal souls while animals do not. He felt that this would mean that the most pernicious human being would have a hope of eternal life while the most abused creature of the so-called 'lower orders' would not. This seemed to him to defy logic if one is to believe in a loving God. It had, therefore, been the cause of his latent disenchantment with the church.[229] In this respect, many individuals have been seriously questioning the issue of *theodicy*—a term which refers to the defence of God's goodness in view of the existence of evil and suffering, and in this case, pertaining to the consideration as to whether what happens to animals is unjust, if an afterlife does not exist for them. If all manner of evil people will eventually be forgiven by God after suffering some punishment, what about the animals? Indeed, what does happen to animals after death; after all, they are always in submission to God, according to the Islamic view? Do they end up in oblivious non-existence? Is there any justice? Indeed, such questions of theodicy make us wonder about what happens to animals after they die; what happens to their consciousness, their 'soul', or their inner being, if they do possess it, or, indeed, if such a thing even exists for any sentient creature in the first place? Many cats, for instance, are aware of the demise of a human being so much so that they are used in old-age nursing homes and are never wrong (more on this later). It is hard to believe that such a creature that knows of the death of someone, will be devoid of an afterlife!

But other than speculation, can we know for certain that an afterlife exists for our beloved pets and all other creatures? Is it just wishful thinking for the sadly dispossessed? Let us first examine the history of the reception of the soul's ontological status in connection with animals, and then we will examine a new model that tackles the 'hard problem' of consciousness in a totally radical way. We will then apply this model to assist us in solving this problem of animal

229. May 24, 1992—Tom Cartwright's letter to Al-Hafiz B.A. Masri.

afterlife. Following this we will see if the Qur'an sheds any light on this subject, and whether it corresponds with logical analysis for the existence of the 'soul' in general, and animal souls in particular.

Historical Attitudes Towards Animal Souls

We have come a very long way from our mental attitude in respect of our Planet Earth and the rest of the creatures inhabiting it. It was not too long ago that we used to consider ourselves as the chosen species, created by God to wield the sceptre over the world. Our nescience of the deep and sacred secrets of life on Earth made us look down upon everything and everyone, other than ourselves, with the egotistical assumption that the human being alone was the 'final cause' of this elaborate process of cosmic scheme. Unfortunately, the very foundation of animal-human relationship was laid, right from the very beginning, on this paralogistic premise. Normally, the relationship between two parties is dictated by their estimation and appraisal of each other's worth and quality—resulting either in mutual esteem and respect or otherwise. However, it is not always just a simple psychological process of influence of a theory on belief. Factors, such as prejudices and pragmatic considerations, often blur the distinction between empirical and metaphysical ontology. After all, speciesism is but a hypertrophic growth of the social tumors of parochialism, sexism, regionalism, tribalism and racialism. Any psychological approach to our relationship with other species should engender a positive viewpoint, based on the logic of facts, and not on primordial hypotheses based on man's egotistic claim of being the centre of interest in the universe.

Animal Souls in the Ancient Period

The question of animal souls has always been open to controversy. The primordial concept of ancestral spirits being migrated into animals and trees was brushed aside by philosophers as superstitious fetishism of the savages. Even the Pharaonic theory that animals and birds were endowed with 'Spirit', more or less analogous with the soul of man, was taken as mere zoolatry or animal worship. The Egyptians, more than 4,000 years ago, had the discernment of making a distinction between the soul and other aspects of the human consciousness, believing that the soul had a divine origin and that the decision about its life in Amenti (the celestial abode) would be made in the Hall of Osiris by the divinely appointed 42 Assessors. It does not seem to be

159

an isochronal coincidence that various sages, mystics, philosophers and even theurgists, started disseminating similar views more or less during the same era of history, about the interrelation between the human and animal souls by way of metempsychosis.[230] The ancient Hindu Vedas[231] promulgated the doctrine of mutual interchange of the souls among humans and animals. Belief in the transmigration of soul through reincarnation is still one of the fundamental tenets of Hinduism, Buddhism and Jainism. The Pharaonic concept, as discussed above, coincides with the same era. The Pythagorean school of philosophy too, believed in the transmigration of soul, whether human or animal. This school had its following in Greece and Southern Italy in and around the 4th century B.C. During the same period of ancient history, we come across a mystical concept which also bears a semblance to metempsychosis. Orpheus, according to mythological legend, was a Thracian (part of ancient Balkan) and son of Apollo, the famous Olympian god. It is believed that the music of Orpheus could charm animals and trees. His doctrine too, known as the Orphic Mysteries, bears upon the Egyptian concept of interrelation between human and animal souls, along the lines elucidated in the 'Book of the Dead.'[232] The above-mentioned Pythagoras declared, about 2,500 years ago, that animals possess souls in these words: 'Animals share with us the privilege of having souls.'[233]

Animal Souls in the Modern Period

Moving into the more recent period in the West, the primordial concept of our relationship with animals was based on certain postulates which have now been proven to be, to say the least, wishfully partial in favour of the human species. For example, animals were not supposed to have a capacity for emotional states or feelings and, hence, were denied consciousness—which according to Minot,[234] is one of the fundamental phenomena of at least animal life, if not, as it is quite possible, all life. The most that our naturalists had been, and in some cases are, conceding to animals is 'instinct', in the sense of natural impulses and involuntary or unconscious promptings to action. Many

230. The doctrine of metempsychosis was laid down by the founder of this creed, Pythagoras, the Greek philosopher (582–aft. 507 B.C.).
231. Vedas, cir. 1,500–1,^9^9^9. B.C.
232. cf. *The Book of the Dead*. It is supposed to have been written by the god Thoth, while in reality its composition spread through many centuries.
233. Pythagoras, as quoted by Ovid, the Roman poet (43 B.C.–17 A.D.).
234. Charles Sedgwick Minot, American histologist and embryologist (1852–1914).

philosophers had tried to define instinct and, most of them became confused in their definitions of 'instinct', 'impulse', 'consciousness', 'intelligence', etc. Paley[235] calls instinct a propensity prior to experience, and independent of instruction. According to Whatley,[236] instinct is a blind tendency to some mode of action, independent of any consideration on the part of the agent. The fact is that our classical philosophers, scholars and naturalists considered animal psychology beyond the province of their research, including Charles Darwin.[237] Even the later psycholinguists such as Sigmund Freud,[238] C.G. Jung,[239] Alfred Adler,[240] could not shake out of their systems the pre-19th century notion that psychology was a branch only of the human soul and mind and not concerned with research in animals' psyche. A.H. Keane,[241] however, seems to be one of the odd men out among scholars who believed that anthropology need not be confined to the psychosocial organism of man only, but should also embrace all the other species. The underlying reason for this attitude has been that, since animals do not possess souls, they have no mind with rational faculties and therefore are outside the pale of the super-sensible in the transphysical sense, the term as used by Albertus Magnus,[242] or as explained by Andronicus of Rhodes,[243] the editor of Aristotle's[244] works.

The Transfocation Model of Consciousness

Atheists hold that even man has no 'soul' let alone animals, and hence that animals are not secure by any 'religious' sanction against outrage. Indeed, the soul is seen as a superstitious unscientific informed as is the existence of a Creator. The interesting fact is that: Consciousness is either there, or not, in an organism; it is not *how* much consciousness one has. It is to have it or not to have it—to be or not to be, if we borrow from Hamlet! Take the following

235. William Paley. English Theologian, 'Evidences of Christianity' (1743–1805).
236. Richard Whatley, English rhetorician, logician, economist, academic and theologian, who also served as Archbishop of Dublin and scholar (1787–1863).
237. Charles Robert Darwin, English naturalist (1809–1882).
238. Sigmund Freud, Austrian neurologist, founder of psychoanalysis (1856–1939).
239. Carl Gustav Jung, Swiss psychiatrist and psychoanalyst, founder of analytical psychology (1875–1961).
240. Alfred Adler, Austrian psychotherapist and pioneering psychologist (1870–1837).
241. A. H. Keane. Augustus Henry Keane (1833–1912), Irish Roman Catholic journalist, linguist, and ethnologist.
242. Albertus Magnus, (c. 1193–November 15, 1280), was German Catholic Dominican friar and bishop.
243. Andronicus of Rhodes, Greek philosopher (fl. C. 60 B.C.).
244. Aristotle, Greek philosopher (384 B.C.–322 B.C.).

analogy: If someone was infected by the Ebola virus and a nurse said: 'She is more infected by it than he [not more *affected* by it]' would that not be a ridiculous statement? Either you are infected or not. Furthermore, one must not confuse the degree of intelligence with consciousness. Whether a creature has more or less intelligence to navigate nature is a matter of the functions of its nervous system and its concomitant physical structure, not whether it is conscious or not. This 'thread' actually gives us a clue as to what consciousness is, and if it had been followed properly it would have led to the whole rope. According to an analysis on what consciousness is, animals also possess consciousness drawn from the Consciousness of God, as explained by the *Transfocation Model of Consciousness*.[245] In developing the Transfocation Model of Consciousness, Muslim and Haque show that it is the critical configuration of the biological entity (in terms of the *specific pathways* of photons and not only electrons) that allows the entity to become conscious—that is, to possess a soul. This 'accessing' consciousness from the Consciousness of God, whose objectless infinite space we are in, is akin to 'possessing a soul', and is the core explanation of *transfocation*; however, the Transfocation Model is not dualistic, emergent, pantheistic or based on panpsychism. Non-human animals, therefore, also possess consciousness drawn from the Consciousness of God, as a natural outcome of the Transfocation Model of Consciousness.

The Qur'anic Concepts of *Ruh* and *Nafs*

What is surprising is that the Transfocation Model, arrived at through logic and empirical evidence, coincides with the Qur'anic view of consciousness. Much to the chagrin and consternation of fundamentalist Christian missionaries (not introspective and analytical Christians) of the sort who are inimical to Islam, 'evangelical atheists', and, in general, other hyper-emotional agitators against Islam, the Qur'an has been remarkably accurate and prescient about various 'scientific matters' such as the Big Bang, the Expanding Universe, and Embryology, pre-emptively. Again, here, there is over-abundant evidence and information about this topic.[246] Given the accuracy of the Qur'an about these

245. Haque, Nadeem & Muslim, M. (2007). *From Microbits to Everything: Universe of the Imaginator: Volume 2: The Philosophical Implications,* Optagon Publications Ltd., Toronto. pp. 163–265.

246. Haque, Nadeem, and Banaei, Mehran, 'Bridge between Science and Religion', *Scientific GOD Journal,* November 2011, Vol. 2, Issue 8, pp. 756–762. Accessible at: http://scigod.com/index. php/sgj/article/view/143/170. The Big Bang was described in the Qur'an, about 1,400 years ago, in the following verses, literally translated: 'Do those who cover the truth not see that the entire universe, including the Earth, was joined together as one piece, which We [God] suddenly ripped

scientific matters it becomes intriguing to further explore what the Qur'an has to say about the 'soul' and merits serious consideration. The Qur'anic concept of the mind or 'soul' is comprehensively encapsulated by the notions of *ruh*.[247]

This is what the Qur'an has to say about the *ruh*:

> And they will ask you about the ruh. Say: 'This ruh is by my Sustainer's command, and you have been granted but a small portion [of the body of] knowledge [needed to know its exact nature]'. (17:85)

Ruh is brought into existence by a creative commandment of God and is a word that means consciousness, in modern parlance.[248]

The other word in the Qur'an used for self in relation to human beings, that is, *nafs*, or the self, also extends to animals. For example, the Qur'anic verses 6:151 and 17:33 forbid the killing of any 'breathing beings' except for a justifiable reason, and declare it as one of the most abominable of misdeeds as in a complementary hadith, the Prophet stated that one must not kill a *nafs* which God has made sacrosanct, except for a justifiable reason.[249] The Arabic word used here is *nafs* which applies to any creature which breathes (i.e. has some form of respiration to put it generically), is conscious and therefore has a self. Prophet Muhammad used these very verses (that is 6:151 and 17:33) as references in support of his declaration that:

> If any person kills a sparrow or anything smaller without justification, God will question him about it.[250]

But how are the words *ruh* and *nafs* related? If one were to draw analogies between *ruh* and *nafs*, one could say that *ruh* is like the software in a computer, whereas *nafs* is the self-developmental aspect that impinges due to the empowered *ruh*: the build-up of data. Animals have a high level of consciousness[251]—of

apart/split, and made every [carbon-based] life form out of water? Will they [even] then not believe?' (21:30).

247. See also Qur'an 2:87, 4:171, 15:29, 32:9, 58:22 for more instances of this word.
248. In *From Microbits to Everything: Universe of the Imaginator, Volume 2: The Philosophical Implications*, Haque and Muslim offer a detailed examination of the *ruh*—the mind and consciousness.
249. Narrated by Abu Huraira. *Sahih Muslim—Kitab al-Iman.;* Chapt. XXXIX, Vol. I; p. 52. *Bukhari,* 4:23. Also Awn al-M'bud Sharh Abu Dawud, hadith No. 2857.
250. Narrated by Ibn 'Umar and by Abdullah bin Al-As. 'Nasai', 7:206, 239, Beirut. Also recorded by *Musnad* and by *Musnad al-Jami—Ad-Darimi*; Delhi, 1337. Also *Mishkat al-Masabih*; English translation by James Robson, in four volumes; Sh. Muhammad Ashraf, Lahore, Pakistan; 1963 (hereafter referred to as 'Robson').
251. Haque, Nadeem and Masri, Al-Hafiz Basheer Ahmad. (2011), 'The Principles of Animal Advocacy in Islam: Four Integrated Ecognitions', *Society and Animals*, 19, pp. 270–290. https://www.animalsandsociety.org/wp-content/uploads/2016/05/haque.pdf

individuality, community, intelligence and communication, and that spark of life that is instantiated at their beginning of life is also a *ruh*, since if they possess *nafs* they must also possess *ruh*. The *ruh* is the plenum consciousness as accessed continually from the Consciousness of God and the *ruh* is the self or *nafs*: the personality and memories that naturally accrue. The presumption that humans, *jinn* or alien human-like entities and alien *jinn*-like entities on other planets are the *only* ones who will gather before God is shown to be false on the basis of the Transfocation Model that takes into account the primary source of relation between *ruh/nafs* and God, as a universal law (set by the Creator), on the basis of a grander physics,[252] for want of a better description: Particles structured spatially in a particular way in space access consciousness *automatically*. It is, consequentially, not only humans who have this feature of particle configuration that allows access to consciousness like a key opening a lock, but the countless myriad other creatures that are teeming throughout the Universe according to the Qur'an.[253]

According to the transfocation model of consciousness, just as electronic apparatus accesses radio signal from space, so do our bodies 'capture' consciousness from absolute, object-less space. Indeed, with the evolution of human knowledge we can now talk of accessing consciousness and computer/radio analogies (a laptop accessing WiFi); however, in the distant past, no one would have been able to understand wireless technology. But remember that at the basis or source of this consciousness is the only real or absolute consciousness: God. Unfortunately, the term 'soul' has led to either pantheism or dualism, none of which accords with reality according to both the Qur'an and logical analysis.

If animals possess a consciousness (the *ruh/nafs* complex) that exists after their death, then this helps us solve the theodicy problem in connection with whether animals get their just deserts in an afterlife. In the context of 'gathering together' on Resurrection Day, in the Qur'an there are two passages pertaining to animal afterlife:

> There is nobody in the rest of the Universe [that is, human-like or non human-like alien or any other creature] or on Earth, but shall come to

252. Muslim, M. and Haque, Nadeem. (2001), *From Microbits to Everything: A New Unified View of Physics and Cosmology, Volume 1: The Cosmological Implications*. https://www.scribd.com/document/47770990/Microbits-Vol1-v-2

253. Haque, Nadeem and Shahbaz, Zeshan. (2015), 'Extraterrestrials in Islam', *Nexus*, Vol 22, No. 5 (August–September).

God the Beneficent as a servant; He has included all of them in His reckoning, and assigned a number to each of them individually; they shall appear before Him on the Day of Resurrection all alone. (19:93–95)

There is no ground-based animal or two-winged flying creature that does not live in communities like your [human] community, and to their Lord/Sustainer will they all be gathered. (6:38)

Having armed ourselves with some foundational concepts we can now formulate three arguments that show that animals exist after death in some form.

Cogent Arguments for Animal Afterlife

Here are the three arguments for afterlife based on an analysis of the Qur'anic outlook:

1. Animals will not be brought to God for judgment because they are all in submission to God and cannot therefore commit 'sin' or transgressions. But if this is the case, why would they be brought to the Day of Judgment in the first place? It does not make any sense whatsoever to presuppose that animals will be gathered on the Day of Judgment and then after being gathered will cease to exist through instant annihilation by God! That would indeed be a pointless exercise, but we know that God does not do pointless things. The gathering of animals unto God must therefore be, at least to firstly, show all creatures that God is the Sole and Supreme Power, and secondly, to admit them into some type of peaceful life we have no idea about and in forms they will continue to exist that we cannot imagine, where those in paradise could interact with them in a meaningful manner that we, likewise, cannot even imagine right now! Here, it is being taken for granted that God exists; for proofs on this subject, please refer to the publications cited.[254]

2. The Qur'an emphasizes that all the injustices and imbalances caused by mankind will be redressed on the Day of Judgment or Accountability and that God is not unjust to His creatures.[255] This accountability would also redress the wrongs done by humans to animals and the environment. Indeed, the suffering endured on Earth of not even one of the creatures of God will be neglected. According to the Islamic concept, after death, each human will be

---

254. Haque, Nadeem and Muslim, M. (2007), *From Microbits to Everything: Universe of the Imaginator: Volume 2: The Philosophical Implications*. Banaei, Mehran and Haque, Nadeem. (1995), *From Facts to Values: Certainty, Order, Balance and their Universal Implications*.
255. Qur'an 22:10.

held individually accountable for all individual actions, where the treatment by human beings of animals and nature will be judged on par with the treatment of our fellow human beings. Note that equality of treatment suggested between man and beast in the following hadith pertaining to the issue of animals: It has been concluded in the *Mishkat Al-Masabih,* which contains the Prophet Muhammad's hadith from Bukhari and Muslim that: 'A good deed done to an animal is as good as doing good to a human being; while an act of cruelty to a beast is as bad as an act of cruelty to a human being.'[256] In consonance with the assertion made above regarding the continuance of the existence of the *nafs* (self, personality, consciousness that develops as we interact in our bodies) or *ruh* (the identity of self-consciousness bringing about the *nafs*), the Qur'an declares that animals will be gathered unto their Creator after death, because the Creator wills everything to be conserved or stored.

However, animals would not merely be brought back to life on Judgment Day simply to testify against humans, because trillions of animals over time never had any contact with humans but *all* are being raised up (resurrected) according to the Qur'an in 6:38. Besides, if the reason for raising animals after death was simply *only* to testify against humans, then there would be no need to do so, as there is a book that records all deeds and does not leave a single thing out[257] and their resurrection would be a redundant act, were it just for the purpose of testification. God does not perform redundant acts.

3.   God is not unjust to His creatures but having no afterlife would be unjust, as they would have suffered in this life and not have been compensated for in the next. God Himself asks us to follow the balance and establish justice; if this be true, why would He then have double standards and not apply this to Himself and to the trajectory of His created universe and all the diverse entities in it?

A view that bars animals in the afterlife is highly problematic with respect to the nature of God for it devalues the rest of sentient creation and casts a negative aspersion. Indeed, it sets a very narrow existential scope, diminishing the magnanimity and judiciousness of God—i.e. the glory of God is tarnished in the eyes of mortals; however, the term 'glory be to God' which in Arabic is *subhan-Allah* means: *not ascribing that which is unbefitting to the majesty of the One God.* With an afterlife, justice would be provided for all animals who have suffered and died. After all, they were created in a universe

256. *Mishkat al-Masabih,* Book 6, Chapter 7, 8:178.
257. Qur'an, 99:6–8.

simply for the reason that this whole scheme of testing humans, other highly intelligent humanoid carbon-based lifeforms scattered throughout the countless galaxies, *jinn* and other similar *jinn*-like entities scattered throughout the universe, could be fulfilled. In this respect, non-human animals have certainly played an integral role, and for that alone, non-human animals deserve a place in the afterlife, rather than being discarded into oblivion as insipid nonentities after using them, as it were.

Anecdotal Evidence of Animal Afterlife

There is documented evidence compiled by the veterinary bioethicist Michael W. Fox of deceased animals manifesting themselves in various ways to their human companions, which provides phenomenological support of life after life. This is what Fox has to say on the subject:[258]

> The after-death physical manifestations of dogs and cats to their human companions point to other realities beyond this mortal plane. Such manifestations, documented in my two new books *Dog Body, Dog Mind,* and *Cat Body, Cat Mind,* (The Lyons Press), are sometimes visual, either as an aura of light or even a clear image of the animal, or are often purely auditory or tactile, as when the deceased animal's footsteps are heard, a cold nose is felt on one's leg, or the deceased cat is felt jumping onto the bed. These phenomena suggest that there is more to the states of life and death than we fully comprehend. There is some form of being, not non-being, after physical death, possibly in a transitional form or state for some time after separation of the physical body from the supra or metaphysical, that some call spirit or soul. This phenomenology of life after life is significant to me because I believe that it is an antidote to the prevailing materialism and ultimate nihilism of these difficult times. The sad state of the natural world that mirrors the human condition that is responsible for so much violence, destruction, and animal suffering, are in large part attributable to a nihilistic attitude that has no regard for the sacred; for the sanctity of life. Materialism and nihilism essentially deny the spirit, the existence of realities other than the purely physical. 'You live, then you die, and that's it. There is simply being and nothingness, so make the most of it, and take all you can, because you can't take it with you,' are typical nihilistic statements. I also document another dimension of the great

258. Fox, Michael W. (2011), *Animals & Nature First: Creating New Covenants with Animals & Nature.* See also accounts compiled in: 'Is There Life After Life?' posted on www.drfoxvet.net.

mystery that I term the empathosphere, a realm of feeling and awareness that cats and dogs are clearly connected with, while most of we humans are not. A typical example is that of Bay, a mutt dog from St. Paul MN who knew when one of his beloved family members, the grandfather of the house, had died in hospital. Bay had kept a vigil by the old man's chair, day and night, for five days, but quit and resumed his normal activities the morning the grandfather had passed on. During his vigil he took no food, and refused to go outside, being carried out to go to the bathroom. The recent account of the cat Oscar, the feline resident of a nursing home in Rhode Island who has predicted the passing on of 25 in-patients, jumping on to their beds and staying close during the in-patients' release from terminal dementia. On the basis of Oscar's behavior, the doctors and nurses know when one of their patients is dying. But as I detail in these two new books, cats and dogs do not have to be present to know when their loved one is dying and has passed on.

How does Fox's narrative square with the Qur'anic view? The Qur'anic view is that after death, the individual's consciousness transfers into another lighter body, totally invisible to the 'living' (made of *smaller* particles that do not interact with 'normal' particles). It is *almost* instantaneously created for us and is similar in form to our old bodies (a *simulacrum*), when we die the earthly death, but not the same, discussed in great depth in one of Haque's books.[259] As has been illustrated above, animals also possess *ruh* or *nafs* and therefore this law of continuance of consciousness applies to them too. From our analysis of the Qur'an, it seems that the Islamic concept of the soul is neither substance-dualistic, nor materialistic. For want of a better word, the 'soul' does *not eternally* pre-exist for the animal or human *before* birth, according to the Qur'an, nor do Muslims believe in the existence of ghosts, be they animal or human—since there is a 'barrier' (*barzakh*) between the living and the dead. It is to be noted that the living and dead are totally cognitively and physically disconnected due to the *barzakh*. There is a great misunderstanding among Muslims world-over that needs to be cleared up: The *barzakh* is not a place, but a barrier due to a density difference between the particles that constitute the carbon-based body and the 'new body' (you can call it an energy barrier of sorts in absolute three-space, *tantamount* to being in another dimension but not actually). Recall that in the Qur'an it speaks of two saltwater seas

---

259. Ibid. *From Microbits to Everything: Universe of the Imaginator: Volume 2: The Philosophical Implication*, pp. 231–232.

not mixing and that there is a barrier (*barzakh*) between them[260] as well as freshwater and seawater;[261] spectacular examples of these exist on Earth (they are called *haloclines*), as for example, the Mediterranean Sea and the Atlantic Ocean near Gibraltar.[262] The barrier, therefore, is a density barrier. According to this view, there can be no interaction between the living and the dead, unless exceptions are made by the will of God. Are the examples that Fox depicts merely exceptions then? This is something intriguing to reflect upon, and is left to the readers for further research. However, it is simply the will of God to decide whether or not to continue the consciousness of an animal in another form and realm in the *next* life, as He does with human beings: the nature of the universe, logic and the Qur'an do lead us inexorably to this.

Further Questions Resolved

The scientist Rupert Sheldrake who has been very critical of dogmatic and narrow mindedness associated with materialism. In a personal communication with one of us, concerning the contents of this chapter which are from an essay, Sheldrake raises some very interesting points.[263] He states:

> What's important is that your essay leaves the question open, and also gives a rightful impression of God as embracing all possibilities, and including everything, rather than as a dogmatist and legalist. In medieval Christian theology, St Thomas Aquinas developed Aristotle's idea of the soul, but did not very clearly address the questions you are discussing. For him, all plants animals and humans had a vegetative soul that gave them their form and maintained their bodies. This is rather like what I call the 'morphogenetic field'. In addition, animals had an animal soul, concerned with behaviour, instincts, emotions, sensations and so on.In the classical world, animals were assumed by everyone to have souls, which is why the word animal itself comes from the Latin word for soul, anima. In addition to vegetative and animal souls, humans had a spiritual soul, concerned with reason and language, and this was open to the spirit of God. But as far as I know he left open the question of survival of animal souls, and confined his discussion to humans. Anyway, your essay raises as many questions as it

260. Qur'an 55:19–21.

261. Qur'an 25:53.

262. Banaei, Mehran. (2013), 'A Desert Dweller with Pre-emptive Knowledge of Haloclines'. https://mehranbanaei.wordpress.com/2013/06/20/a-desert-dweller-with-halocline-foresight/

263. Personnel communication via email with Nadeem Haque, November 8th, 2018.

answers and the nature of animal souls in an afterlife is clearly a matter for speculation. Do predators go on being predators? And how would this work? And if they and other animals enter a kind of beatific state beyond predation, how does this influence present day living animals of the same species? Are their lives open to a spiritual dimension? As far as I know, in Christianity all these questions are open, and if they're also open in Islam, that gives us great freedom. Since God's mind contains all possibilities, it is the ultimate arena of freedom, in which by God's grace we share to our very limited capacities. Anyway, thank you for such a stimulating essay.

My response to Sheldrake's comments:

1. On Predation

In the next life there will be no predation; predation only exists in this universe because it is necessary to maintain the balance (al-mizan); so animals will not have to suffer (neither will there be work animals) for there's no such toiling in the next life. There is no entropy in the next universe as it is based on a wholly different set of laws.

2. On Animal Spiritual Life

Animals such as the *hudhud* bird (the Hoopoe) for example is very spiritual as it knows of God and converses with Prophet Solomon about God (in the Qur'an) and the rejection of God by the people.[264] Prophet Solomon and others with him were taught the speech of some animals (it states this in the Qur'an in reference to birds, but he also understood ant communication).[265] So it is not a stretch to generalize and state that animals in the Qur'an would have their own varying degrees of understanding of a Creator depending on their level of cognition (from worm to dolphin). In the Qur'an, it further states that in the unspecified future, God is going to raise a creature that is aware of the signs of God with certainty. This is in the chapter of the ant (al-Naml, Chapter 27) where it states in verse 82 the converse about human beings:

> We [God] will bring forth for them an animal/creature from the Earth who will tell them that they had no certainty concerning [God's] signs.

This 'creature' from the Earth (the word for creature or animal is *dabbatan* and its form is an accusative feminine indefinite noun) interestingly appears

264. Qur'an 27:22.
265. Qur'an 27:16 and for ant communication see Qur'an 27:19.

in chapter 27, that recounts articulate animal communication extensively. Also all animal examples are concerned with certainty in this chapter: Prophet Solomon's scouting bird bringing back truth about the neighboring civilization (certainty of what is happening elsewhere: in fact the word 'certainty' is used here),[266] the scouting ant warning the others to get out of the way lest Solomon's army crushes them unawares etc. (certainty of being crushed).[267] Interestingly, in chapter 34, verse 14 the term *dabbatu-l-ardi* (*dabbatu* being in the nominative feminine form) is also used to describe the tiny creature that ate Prophet Solomon's staff. Prophet Solomon had died and was still sitting on his throne when this had transpired. His staff supported his body to be upright and the *jinn* prisoners who were serving him never realized he had died, for otherwise they would have fled. So here again we have a so-called lowly creature showing certainty. In the Qur'an in chapter 6, verse 38, the word *dabbatin fi-l-ardi* is also used to depict carbon-based ground creatures. This lends credence to the supposition that the creature is connected to human and animal intercommunication, and that it will be a ground-based (not flying) carbon-based creature. I believe it is an animal that we will be able to communicate with, as we are now beginning to understand animal language (through sonogram studies, for example)[268] and that this information will be broadcasted widely so that everyone on Earth will realize and reflect which category they fall into, as far as certainty goes.

One of the themes of this chapter is animal communication, and even though the verses on animal communication are disparately placed in Chapter 27, they are nonetheless in the same chapter. There is, in fact, another example, where similar themes occur in the same chapter. For example, the Qur'an's Big Crunch verse (appearing in the Qur'an in chapter 21, verse 104), occurs in the same chapter as the Big Bang verse (21:30). This only goes to strengthen the case that the *dabbatan min al-ardi* is referring to future human and animal meaningfully articulated communication, where both syntax and semantics are involved, where the animals even understand and comment on the mental state and thoughts of humans (such as the ant and the hoopoe bird)!

Most Muslims, however, think of *dabbatan min al-ardi* as some juggernaut of a strange-looking hybrid creature that will go about the Earth as a

---

266. Qur'an 27:22–23.
267. Qur'an 27:18.
268. Jad Abumrad and Robert Krulwich, January 20, 2011, 'New Language Discovered: Prairiedogese' https://www.npr.org/2011/01/20/132650631/new-language-discovered-prairiedogese, NPR.LIS

romper-stomper, confronting people in an odd manner, separating believers from non-believers, by physically marking them as believers and infidels! Indeed, such strange descriptions of 'the beast' have cropped up about this in the hadith, that are taken without question to be his authentic sayings; however, one can easily see that the Qur'anic verse on *dabbat-al ard* is very different than these fanciful hadith. It is to be noted that the Qur'an takes precedence of hadith and Muslims are supposed to reject hadith that contradict the Qur'anic information or facts, as being either fake, inaccurate or apocryphal.

The very fact that all animals will be brought before God on Judgment Day, ensures their eternal continuance in some form that will offer them eternal dignity and peace, which we can hopefully witness someday, if we too, end up on the right side! Is not giving dignity to all deserving creatures of God, above all things?

Chapter 7

Equi-nomics: The optimally balanced economic system for humanity and nature

The best economic system that maximizes justice and peace should be *the* optimal system for *both* humanity and nature. In this chapter, it will be illustrated, in a brief but hopefully concise manner, that what we are terming *Equi-nomics* is that optimal system, because it is the only one that has the ability to foster the crucial four Ecognitions (ecological recognitions) which comprehensively embrace *both* nature and humanity and lead to the ultimate sought after justice and peace. These Ecognitions, which have also been discussed in Chapter 5 in connection with Animal Rights/Welfare can be modified to cover Economics as well, by extending Ecognitions 3 and 4:

- **Ecognition 1:** Everything ultimately belongs to a single non-anthropomorphic creator.
- **Ecognition 2:** The Equigenic Principle must be upheld (based on *al-mizan*—the balances in nature: equi (equal/balance); genic (origin).
- **Ecognition 3:** Community rights must be upheld for all humans and animals as they all live in communities.
- **Ecognition 4:** Personhood rights exist and are to be upheld for all humans and animals.

Note that each ecognition works in concert with the others and there is a hierarchy among them, the most foundational one being Ecognition 1. To understand the relationship between these ecognitions, take Ecognition 3, for example; it is necessary for Ecognition 2 (equilibrium): Since animal communities operate with dynamic equilibrium, Ecognition 2 is maintained. But Ecognition 2, recursively creates Ecognition 3!

In an optimally healthful society, all these ecognitions would be upheld, and, like 'Newton's' three laws, these four Ecognitions have the ability to define the totality of the socio-environmental ethical policies for this, and any other planet in the universe, where carbon-based life abounds, according to the Qur'an. In failing to understand this concept and to continue to base our economics on the 'interest-based', monopolistic and plutocratic economic systems, is like basing an understanding of the solar system on geocentrism. In addition, trying to fix such a faulty system would be like adding epicycles to geocentric orbits, only compounding the ever-growing problem. We *must* go back, or rather, move forward to these four principles of ecognition if we are to extricate ourselves from the maze of confusion and destruction. Indeed, we have no choice if we are to avert the decay of civilization, a madness which humans have brought upon both themselves and nature, as irresponsible novice 'managers of nature'. Everything flows from these ecognitions. The breakage or non- fulfillment of any one of them inevitably causes a disruption in the natural flow towards justice and peace. Analogously speaking, these 'geocentric' economic systems that we have been plagued with have arisen because of various socio-political developments several hundred years ago, of which we are, most of us at least, hapless victims. Let us now dig into this assertion to gain further insights through history to see the proximate cause of our victim-hood.

Hapless Historical Victims

The current economic system is primarily based on the present banking system which has caused a great strain on humans and the environment, because the creation of money has been transferred to the private banks. It should be realized that it is not merely a problem of interest bearing loans, but the very banking structure itself which compounds the problem, in that, the central banks make interest payments to the chartered banks; however, it was the central banks who gave the chartered banks money creation rights in the first place.

What is the basic banking mechanism for money creation and how did we inherit such a detrimental structure? Why is the current banking system 'unjust'? Here is a brief summary: The origin of the modern banking system is from England, where the monarchy had usurped the gold and silver that the rich had deposited in the Tower of London. These rich, therefore, decided to keep such precious items with goldsmiths, who had strong boxes already, for their own valuables. These goldsmiths gave the depositors receipts for their deposits and convinced them that the goldsmiths ought to be able to lend the money to their friends at a rate which was higher than 5%, the rate which the goldsmiths would pay the depositors. The depositors then saw the advantage in using the receipts from the goldsmiths to pay their bills instead of actually withdrawing their gold. In addition, the goldsmiths realized that they could make more loans than the amount of gold kept at hand, especially since not everyone demanded back their gold at the same time. Thus evolved the modern banking system which was given a boost when the government became a partner to this unscrupulous system, after chartering the Bank of England. Gold reserves in the U.S. which used to be 25% in the early 20th century, meant money could be loaned four times over; the reserves' requirement was reduced over the years. Cash reserves in the U.S. are currently 3% for current accounts and 0% for savings accounts. In Canada, cash reserves have been 0%, since the 1991 Bank Act amendments.

Money is created every time you take a loan from the chartered bank, with you providing a collateral. You then repay with interest. In Canada, for example, over 90% of the taxes go into making interest payments to the chartered banks. However, if money creation returns to the hands of the central government, then the central government would have the sole power to create and direct the money for schemes that would benefit all peoples, including social and educational programs, healthcare, ecological clean-ups, environmental initiatives and innovations, etc. A new vision for banking, along these lines, is desperately needed, as perhaps a first step, which can then evolve into a transactional system that is radically different and does not involve the banking system that arose in the Middle Ages, but a whole new type of system based on trading in 'representational tangibles' (i.e. gold and silver, through modern transactional exchange means and mechanisms at our disposal). [269]

Within the general plutocratic framework of most societies, there have been periods in the history of many nations, where more inclusive policies have been enacted. In Canada, for example, in 1939, when war broke out, the Bank of Canada was engaged in money creation when: The government sold their bonds to the Bank of Canada. The interest due on these bonds was canceled by the Bank of Canada issuing dividends to the government, effectively making the net exchange an interest free loan. This money creation led to the positive development of Canada, through the central bank's self-generating money for such developmental schemes. Since 1974, this mechanism for money creation

---

269. *Do You Know Where Money Comes From?* (2002): A Publication of the Canada Action Party. See also: www.comer.org (The Committee on Monetary and Economic Reform). The way in which the modern banking system is structured is as if one owns a grocery store, but then forsakes it and purchases goods that one needs from a neighboring grocery store, owned by a competitor. Such behaviour would be considered the height of insanity. Yet this is exactly what is currently being done by the West's Central Banks. Even the Federal Reserve Bank of the U.S.A. is a private corporation; it is not Federal and has no reserves either!

has been abandoned, helping to lead to a decline in social services development and the many interconnected environmental issues. Indeed, with many of the politicians worldwide, having become subservient to corporations, it is difficult to pass proper social and eco-sensitive legislation. The central banks of the Western Nations after 1974 were bamboozled into passing the money creation facilities onto this private bank-corporation complex. The elites who hold the reins of these corporations are not really concerned with the environment or social welfare, but only with their short-term gains. Tragically, it is not recognized by them, that they are part of the system, where the social and atmospheric system will adversely affect themselves, in both this life and the next. In this callous atmosphere of unconcern, propelled by greed and selfishness, anything and everything can be bought or expertly marketed to serve the narrow interests of the elite.

A totally rational reform that benefits humanity and nature would be to revert to the just transactional system focused on trading, and if the world does *freely and peacefully*, without any coercion, come to their senses and become united or federated in the future, it would apply socially and ecologically sound policies, wherein the purse-strings are controlled directly by such a just world system which legislates according to socio-sensitive and eco-sensitive principles that most of the public would adhere to by rational choice[270] and without compulsion. It cannot be overstressed that if sane social and environmental policies are to be bolstered, the modern banking system must be transformed to a radically alternative one as the one in vogue right now violates the ecognitions through both its overall intentions, mechanisms and goals.

Equi-nomics: An All-embracive Economic System

The ecognitions, (discussed in Chapter 5) form Equi-nomics, for they take into consideration the fact that all levels are interlocked together in the transient chain of existence constituting all life and non-life. In contrast to such an approach, the present notions of 'GNP' are completely inadequate for such an integrated realization of reality. This shortcoming only serves to create an illusion of progress as to what constitutes development. In fact, it is becoming ever so blatantly obvious that, as we erode our resources, the 'costs' will eventually

---

270. Hellyer, Paul. (2001), *Goodbye Canada*. This view which is collinear with Islamic principles, in fact, has been advocated as one of the main platforms for the reform of the economy for every nation state, starting out with Canada, by the Canadian Action Party, in the 2004 Canadian federal elections, as initially propounded by its founder Paul Hellyer.

end up showing even in our present very limited economic measures such as GNP or GDP. For example, when contaminants are leaked into the environment, they travel up the food chain causing health problems among human beings. This results in an increase in health costs and the reduction of productivity and these are not captured by such measurements and indices.

The equation of balance (*al-mizan* in Arabic)—which is the paramount concern in Islam—includes the effects of human interactions upon the existing balances in nature (Ecognition 2). Not only must all of these natural resources be dealt with as if they were assets, but the notion of assets must itself be re-assessed as being encapsulated by the foundational understanding that these assets ultimately belong to the Creator of the balance and not to specific families, corporations and governments (Ecognition 1). These balancing components and entities deserve proper treatment because it is their natural and not synthetic or artificial right. Such rights are not man-made, but are inherent rights realized from the fact that if we do not maintain the balance, then disorder will ensue (via the concept of the violation of *Equigenic Rights*).

In an economic system operating along the lines of the Qur'an, there would tend to be a minimization or elimination of the consumption and demand for harmful products, both for human beings and nature. But how can we help to direct consumption? Economist Omer Chapra, in his illuminating book, *Islam and the Economic Challenge*, succinctly discusses how such a consumption pattern can be brought into being:

> The relative scarcity of resources compared with unlimited claims on them necessitates a filtering device. All claims on resources must pass through this filter...[271]

From the Islamic perspective, this natural filtering device is the,

> ...system, which influences the inner consciousness of the individual, makes him aware of the trust nature of resources and provides the criteria needed for their efficient and equitable allocation and distribution.[272]

Market prices and governmental regulation would be gauged according to the scarcity of resources, keeping in mind the balance in nature. These would, in fact, be the secondary filtering mechanism both flowing out from and supporting that first natural filtering mechanism (of the behavioural pattern emerging

---

271. Chapra, M. U. (1992), *Islam and the Economic Challenge*, p. 214.
272. Ibid. p. 348.

from a consciousness of a Creator (*taqwa*) and the balance). In such a system, it would become easier to evaluate and appreciate the natural resources on Earth, both for ourselves and for the other creatures that depend on them. This would be so, due to the fact that the pricing of resources itself would be fair and just, and not skewed, inflationary or exploitative as it is today; indeed, our financial assessments would be based on a reflection of a deeper understanding of nature, due to the realization of the pricelessness of the balances in creation.

A truly socio-environmentally friendly financial governing system has the filter of the consciousness of God as sovereign through the constitution of the Qur'an, the corroboration of facts, and the structuring of policies and legislation through the evidence, all of which espouses socio-ecological equilibrium via the Equigenic Principle. This filter, filters out harm by rational and objective sieving, that is, by capturing and discarding anything that causes disequilibrium in the causal nexus, be it in the environmental, social or biological realm. This concomitantly leads to local and universal peace and justice. Conversely, it becomes apparent that capitalistic systems possess contaminated filters, as the concepts of God as the Sovereign and respect for the created balance are either not present, are distorted or are minimalized, leading to injustice and socio-environmental destruction. If greed, corruption and mismanagement were eliminated one could mend both environmental and sociological problems simultaneously, one without the expense of the other. Needless to say, we cannot even begin to have such a system that resolves our problems globally and in many cases locally, unless the Creator is seen as the Owner and Inheritor of the universe, a view which would lead humans to deal with property, with respect to God, in all senses of the word 'respect'.

The New Mathematical Equations of Equi-nomics

It is a fact that measurement can produce awareness, and awareness can lead to change. In Equi-nomics, the primary concern would be the socio-environmental deficit, that is the measure of how far away from the balance we are. What needs to be taken into account is a socio-techno-ecological equation and concept—a new measure of deficit. The following generic equations whose parameters could be quantified, show the various relationships between some of the major concepts being discussed here:

- **Socio-environmental Deficit** = Cost of what you displace from nature that destroys a natural cycle + cost incurred by the misapplication of purpose-designed objects or entities in nature.
- **Socio-environmental Deficit** = Amount of deviation from the Equigenic Principle.
- **Health of Society** = 1-Socioenvironmental Deficit (where 1 is the optimum, i.e. 100%): you can call this the Equigenic Index (EI).
- **Equigenic Principle** = Qur'anic Principles.

All of the above would form the Equigenic Index (EI) that can then be multiplied with GDP or the Human Development Index, thereby reducing their values (because EI will always be less than 1), so that we can understand where societies really stand in relation to their well-being/health.

Sanctity as Part of Equi-nomics

It is certainly a noteworthy distinction that a creature such as man, from among things in nature, has been given the trust associated with being able to choose to a wider degree, an ability not commensurate or structured for any other type of carbon-based corporeal or inanimate thing on Earth:

> Assuredly, We did offer the trust to the celestial systems, the Earth and the mountains: but they all refused to bear it because they were cautiously afraid. Yet man took it up—verily, he was unjust and ignorant. (33:72–73)

According to the Qur'an, due to our ungratefulness we have forgotten that we are not ultimately the creators of anything. We only use things and transform them. The simple truth, is that whatever we make with our own hands, is in the ultimate sense, made by God, because it is God who has created and designed humans:

> Do you worship that which you have carved (idols), even though it is God who has created you and all your handiwork? (37:95–96)

He is the ultimate creator in the sense that He has given us the ability to develop things. However, God is not the creator of that which is harmful since God wants man to utilize his limited choice mechanism to do good and avoid indulging in harmful practices:

> Whatever good happens to you is from God; and whatever evil befalls
> you is from your own self. (4:79)
>
> God does not wrong anyone by as much as an atom's weight. (4:40)

In the following context, note the reference to 'ships' which is juxtaposi-
tioned with natural phenomena that God has made, reminding us exactly who
their Ultimate Creator is:

> … He it is who has engendered opposite sexes; and who has made for
> you ships, as well as beasts on which you ride, that you may mount
> firmly on their backs and, while so poised, may recall to mind the favors
> of your Sustainer and say: 'Glory be to Him who has put these in our
> service, for we could never have accomplished this.' (43:12–14)

With the development of such an inter-connective outlook and thinking pattern, the sanctity of the totality of creation is realized without dichotomies,
where the Earth, society, nature, worship, work, rest and play would be seen as
a means to a higher end. As the Prophet Muhammad said, 'The whole Earth
has been made a mosque for me, pure and clean.'[273]

The Concept of *Zulm*: Dislocation

Zulm in Arabic means: the placement of an entity or object where it does
not belong or fit, or conversely, the removal of something from its natural setting where it does fit by the nature of its design: in other words, a misallocation
or dislocation. The highest dislocation is ascribing a partner with God or *shirk*
as it is denoted in Arabic in the Qur'an. In fact, in his advice to his son, *zulm*
of such an ascription is at the top of the list of ten pieces of advice the pious
personality Luqman gives to his son:

> My son, ascribe no partners with the One God; certainly, such ascription
> is a great injustice (*zulm*). (3:13)

This universe is based on cause and effect and each of the components fit
in a specific way by their structure and function that ensures balance, functional harmony and justice. Now since the human being has the ability to
misplace and misuse things without regard to their actual intended usage due
to the structure and function, this causes the converse, that is, harm. By following the ecognitions, everything is put in its rightful place and there is no

---

273. Narrated by Jabir ibn Abd-God and others. Bukhari, Muslim, Tirmidhi.

dislocation, or *zulm*. The Creator Himself is not unjust (*zulman*) to His creation (see Qur'an: 3:108, 109), but we humans are and can be.

Riba: Exploitation Compounded

Monopolistic systems are governed by the Arabic word *riba*[274] which means the increase in the wealth of a party or parties by unjust means that are based on *zulm* if we take the Qur'anic root meaning of the word *riba* and its uses in the Qur'an and Hadith. *Riba* disrupts the flow of things in nature and leads to a lack of balance because the natural transformation efforts that are made to the elements of nature for human use are not given a value that is based on natural needs that regulate supply and demand, in turn based on fair competition, efficiency and co-operation. This creates a disruption in the natural flow of things and diverts funds to a small group thereby sabotaging the proper distribution of wealth. Therefore, although trade in things that maintain socio-environmental balance can be deemed as part of nature, *riba* transactions go against the grain of nature by creating a primarily one-way vortex of exchange, as if, to draw an analogy of a vital form of exchange in the rest of nature, humans exchanged carbon dioxide but never received oxygen from the plants. Rather money should be seen as a two-way form of exchange for overall stability, just as the mutual carbon dioxide and oxygen exchange between plants and animals is a beneficial cycle. In other words, in Islam, the meaning of *riba* covers, monopoly, charging interest and so on, that is, anything that causes this financial imbalance, hence socio-economic imbalance and resulting environmental imbalance. There is no room in the ecognitions for any *riba*.

One of the main problems with the interest-based economy is the way loans are made for business ventures. The Islamic model bases exchange on co-operation where the borrowers and lenders (and any intermediaries, such as any radically restructured lending institutions along Islamic lines) are in the same boat, being involved in ventures on the same scheme as official partners, where all parties have an interest in keeping the boat afloat, not to blast it to smithereens by torpedo, if the boat met high seas and was in jeopardy, as would do radical capitalistic institutions at present and have been doing so for centuries, in one form or another. In fact, all parties would also then be concerned about the type of enterprise they may be getting involved in, in terms of environmental soundness, especially if, that is, the government was applying

274. 2:275, 276, 278; 3:130; 4:161; 30:29.

Qur'anic legislation to uphold the balances in nature. True Islamic loans are 'brotherly' whereas interest based loans are 'otherly'.

Under the present scheme there is the urge among various institutions to fund projects, be they detrimental to the receiving countries, because interest can be charged, this monetary goal being the be-all and end-all of the true goals of such international money-lending institutions. Here, there is no real concern for the welfare of nature or the indigenous populations, from the controllers of such organizations, despite hypocritical consolations to the contrary. The other crucial aspect, from an Islamic point of view, is that the printing of money (electronically or otherwise) would be taken out of the hands of corporations such as private banks,[275] where it has come to reside in Western countries; whatever solid monetary system then evolves from the ecognition principles outlined would be under the full control of a government upholding these principles, as opposed to the current financial system that is the root cause of financial instability and income distribution inequalities that feed into ecological pressure, which is an exploitative system that is so grossly sub-optimal. Tragically, currently most nations in the world that consider themselves as being free after independence from the colonial powers, are, in fact, quite the opposite, because of the impositions of international banking lending schemes that dictate severely onerous terms to them. This is a mutation of old-style colonialism, for it is colonialism by remote control or proxy, by which such poor nations find themselves entrapped and enslaved, their peoples and animals suffering, leading to the current mess we find ourselves in globally. Economist and historian Robert Sidelsky, in his book *Money and Government: A Challenge to Mainstream Economics* states a truth that remains cloaked, which is that 'Ideology is highly influenced by the structure of power, as well as helping to bring about a structure of power favourable to it' and that '…the dominant ideas of any epoch are those of its ruling class.'[276] Be it current domestic or foreign policy, such controls rule across the globe, creating much suffering by bringing about economic hardships.

Given all these considerations, it is high time that we should take a stand and demand a better future for all life-forms. This basic change towards the sustenance of true wealth will not occur unless we, in sufficient numbers,

---

275. This parallel view, in fact, has been advocated as one of the main platforms for the reform of the economy for every nation state, starting out with Canada, by the Canadian Action Party, in the 2004 Canadian federal elections, as initially propounded by its founder Paul Hellyer.

276. Sidelsky, Robert. (2018), *Money and Government: A Challenge to Mainstream Economics.*

recognize and act upon the fact that we are trustees of the natural dynamic balance, under God and for His creation based on the correct type of transactional system whose foundational mechanism is solid representational tangible modes of exchange tied to the ecognitions (such as gold and silver coins) under the rubric of modern day transactional conveyance modes and not vaporous monetary instruments that do not really exist. Economics will then serve *us*, rather than *us* serving economics, and this will be the best solution and outcome for *all* humanity and nature, and not just the proverbial one percent of the human population.

It is hoped that a better system along the lines being espoused here will eventually develop. However, given the dominating reach and mindset of capitalistically ingrained mentalities, it will be a long struggle and humanity will have to, it seems, pass through many unpleasant phases, where injustice and exploitation will be the order of the day. It does not have to be that way, but this projected outcome is due to the fact that rebelliousness against the Prime Originator is a dominant feature of the human race, and that sad predisposition has the tendency to override humanity's true innate, pure nature.

Chapter 8

The Overpopulation Myth

Population Growth

Aside from technology, or the misuse of it, it has been contended by some environmentalists and politicians that the rate of increase in human population is one of the main causes of environmental destruction. In fact, this group believes that the burgeoning of the human population is one of the main root causes of the problems we are facing. For instance, environmentalist, film-producer and author Michael Tobias states that:

> The global population by the year 2100 [will] potentially [be] surpassing 20 billion. Such futuristic numbers are woven with mathematical paradox ... the possibility that we will be unable to effect planetary remediation.[277]

Tobias's general stance is that the population explosion is one of the cardinal causes of our dilemmas and he believes that the solution lies in establishing a universal Total Fertility Rate of either 1 or zero, that is, trying to 'skip a generation of youth as much as possible.' Similarly, environmentalist Jonathon Porritt states that:

> ... reducing the rate of growth in human numbers is the single most important goal to be found in this or any other book about the state of the Earth.[278]

The concern of such environmentalists, is that people will not be able to feed themselves, the environment will be drained of resources and that overpopulation will end up destroying nature. How valid is this assertion? While it is certainly logical and true that the pressures on the ecosystems will be tremendous with the population surge, especially if our role and place in the world is not properly understood, and that more people with less understanding in terms of dealing with themselves and the environment will create even

---

277. Tobias, Michael. (1994), *World War III: Population and the Biosphere at the End of the Millennium*, p. xxxiii.
278. Porrit, Jonathon (Ed.) (1991), *Save the Earth*, 'Population: Crunching Numbers,' p. 117.

more pressures on it, is it really true that the population problem is singularly at the root of our environmental dilemmas or one of its main causes?

Population in Perspective

The views expressed above could be true, if the ecosystem was static and not dynamic, resilient, compensatory and adaptable to keep the supply up with demand.[279] More to the point, we know for a fact that the resources of nature have a huge capacity for self-renewability on their own, not to mention the benefit of the proper use of technology, in sensibly increasing food production. Nature as a whole does not totally collapse as a result of the so-called overpopulation. Some experts believe that the problem of food shortage does lie in mismanagement, not in overpopulation. More bluntly, the problem lies in the inequality of income distribution and unjust distribution of resources. This is the root cause of hunger, not population growth. By existing standards, there are many highly populated countries like the United States and Japan where there are no food shortages at all. Conversely, there are underpopulated regions in East Africa where there are serious shortages of food; if it is claimed that overpopulation is a primary modern Cassandra[280] then there is something wrong with this line of thinking. John Scott states:

> [Food Shortage] is manifestation of man's mismanagement of his environment rather than of any preordainment and irrevocable imbalance between his number and his resources. The Earth has everything necessary to grow and synthesize enough food to feed us all… The task lies in utilizing resources in an orderly manner to produce food and distribute it where needed. It is a problem of management— world economic management.[281]

Frances Moore Lappe and Joseph Collins argue that the notion of overpopulation used to explain food scarcity is mythical (which they designate as Myth No. 3 out of twelve myths about the causes for food shortages).[282]

---

279. Brown, James H., Whitham, Thomas G., Ernest, S.K. Morgan and Gehring, Catherine A. (2001), *Ecology Through Time: Complex Species Interactions and the Dynamics of Ecological Systems: Long Term Experiments*, pp. 648–649. (In part, this paper discusses the remarkable flexibility of similar species in responding to human-caused perturbations to maintain a homeostatic condition in particular niches, thereby offering resilience, though *within limits*).
280. Cassandra or Kassandra was a Trojan priestess of Apollo in Greek mythology cursed to utter true prophecies, but never to be believed.
281. Scott, John. (1969), *Hunger: Man's Struggle to Feed Himself*, p. xiii.
282. Lappe, Frances Moore and Collins, Joseph. (1986), *World Hunger: The Twelve Myths*, pp. 23–32.

In addition, the notion of overpopulation itself is very ambiguous and highly problematic in this context. 'Overpopulation' is a relative concept, its meaning and implication depend entirely on a point of reference. The point of reference is arbitrary. What do we consider as the optimal population and how do we come to such a figure, compared to which anything above or beyond or below, is designated as being overpopulated or underpopulated?

In discussions on the resolution of the population problem, it is more often than not, forgotten that the Earth and our usage of technology in the proper way can support a population many times larger than the existing population. Many agricultural experts would bear the fact out that this planet is capable of sustaining at least several times more people than the present population. For instance, Christopher Hallowell, reports that: 'Even though the world's population surged by 105% between 1955 and 1995, to 5.7 billion people, the global grain harvest grew by an even faster 124% during that span, thanks to a Green Revolution that relied on hybrid seeds and increased use of fertilizers, pesticides and irrigation.'[283] Furthermore, while human population is on the rise, so are milk and dairy products.[284] The success in yield increase comes only if we would manage agricultural and husbandry projects diligently and more sensibly by changing our outlook towards things in nature, from which our myriad problems arise. Many demographic experts, as well, would agree that the Earth can support many times the present population, even with the present technology. What is not clear is the exact number or the exact carrying capacity of the Earth because of the many variables that would have to be known to calculate this figure.[285] However, we believe that with proper distribution, management and proper technology it is only logical that the carrying capacity of the Earth would be extremely high. In 1976, when Earth's population was 3.5 billion, Paul Ehrlich, a renowned leader of the environmental movement created uncalled for panic among the existing population, by claiming apocalyptically, that feeding 6 billion people would be completely impossible in reality. However, technological advances have increased yields over time; it is equitable distribution that remains the main problem.

If so-called mother nature fails to cope with its children's dietary demands, it is all because this poor mother nature has lost its health, agility and vitality. Analogously, like any sick mother, breast milk would be inadequate. Therefore,

283. Hallowell, Christopher. (1997), 'Will the World Go Hungry?'
284. Grant, Wyn. (1991), *The Dairy Industry: An international Comparison*, Ch. 2.
285. Cohen, Joel E. (1996), *How Many People Can the Earth Support?*, pp. 161–211.

if saving mother nature for its own sake is not a good enough reason for her self-centered egotistic dependents, then for her dependent's very own survival, it is wise to keep mother healthy. Besides, if the threat is serious enough, one could use formula milk. Similarly, mother nature, if devastated by man, can still benefit from the wise use of technology, to concentrate more on food production, than harmfully produced luxury goods.

Islam has a lot to offer by way of guidance on the issue of population control. There are no objections on the usage of proper birth control methods for keeping the number of children at a desirable level, so long as it brings no harm to either couple.

Human Effort

In the Qur'an, it is abundantly clear that it is the Creator who provides sustenance for all creatures on Earth. However, there is one point in this respect which must be discussed here, concerning certain attitudes towards sustenance. It is generally argued that God has promised to provide sustenance for every mouth He creates. Verses of the Qur'an, such as those quoted below, are recited in support of this argument:

> He is the Sustainer of the universe and the Earth, and all that lies between them—if you could but grasp it with certainty. (44:7)

> With Him alone lies the power of the keys in the universe and the Earth. He augments or circumscribes the means of sustenance to whomsoever He wills—for He is cognizant of everything. (42:12)

God is indeed the Ultimate Sustainer. However, in the fervor of their notion of God the Provider, people tend to forget that the very same God and in the same book lays down that man shall have to earn by the sweat of his brow and that his share shall be in proportion to his labor; and that God knows best as to who deserves how much. These verses could apply equally to individuals and nations:

> He placed on it stabilizers (mountains), and He blessed it (the Earth),[286] and measured sustenance therein in equitable proportion, in four periods, in accordance with the needs of those who seek. (41:10)

---

286. Is it not significant that God has bestowed blessings on the Earth? And how can we humans then despoil that which is blessed by the Most High!

What these and other similar verses on this theme are trying to tell us is that God, no doubt, is the Sustainer—but not in a sense that He pushes morsels of food down our throats. He is the Sustainer in the sense that He has equipped this planet with all the necessary ingredients to sustain life; and that it is up to us to produce and distribute food in a sensible way. It is only then that God has promised to give us our share in proportion to what we have earned through our labor, according to our needs. Are we doing that in a sensible way?

The use of agricultural land by the late 1980s, for example, had become wholly inefficient. More than 80 to 90 percent, or four-fifths, of the Earth's arable land was, by then, being used for producing fodder for cattle. We needed 100 acres of fertile land to pasture enough animals to feed 20 people. The same 100 acres could produce enough maize to feed 100 people; or wheat to feed 240 people; or beans to feed 610 people. In the same time period in the United Kingdom, for example, they consumed about 450 million animals every year. To feed these animals, they imported cereal from the same economically underdeveloped regions of the world where people are constantly undernourished and even dying of starvation. To date the situation has not improved: clearly a more balanced approach is required in respect of how much and what we eat—especially given the recent advances in the nutritional sciences.

To re-iterate: A careful examination of the statistics and facts will show that the root problem is corruption and mismanagement—the maldistribution of wealth and the internecine strife which puts undue agricultural, industrial and human populational pressures on the land. For example:

> India ranks near the top among third world agricultural exporters. While as many as 300 million Indians go hungry, the country exports everything from wheat to beef and government officials agonize over how to get rid of mounting 'surpluses' of wheat and rice—24 million tons in 1985, more than double the entire world's annual food aid shipments in a typical year.[287]

In conclusion, it is apparent that the basic problem is a philosophical one from which attitudes have arisen, leading to exploitative behaviour. 'Overpopulation' is not the real problem. Indeed, we must go much deeper to the philosophical underpinnings—to mechanisms of elite group control over the masses through the concoction of irrational justification systems. This misplacement of food, people and resources causes pressure on the environment, but this misplacement

287. Lappe, Frances Moore and Collins, Joseph. (1986), *World Hunger: Twelve Myths*, p. 11.

is a result of our individual and collective thinking patterns, from which all un-equigenical policies have originated. To illustrate analogically, it is the building's foundation which has to be stabilized, since it is that which is causing the pressure in the walls. It is not an overpopulation of wall cracks which is the cause of the problem. Such cracks, here and there, can be temporarily sealed to avoid critical situations that have arisen because of the faulty foundation. Rather, for a complete solution, we must reinstate a solid foundation to eliminate the defects that have arisen in the wall itself. We need a new consistent system, that is, a worldview founded on nature. But is such a system attainable?

Chapter 9

A Worldview Founded on Nature

Mankind's New Beginning as Part of Nature

In a published volume, *Islam and Ecology*, Kaveh Afrasiabi's critical essay[288] sees Islam as being dominated by anthropocentrism and utilitarianism that imposes a great reformist challenge ahead, to bridge 'the gap between theology and ecology', in terms of the competing interests of ecology and man. But how valid is such a charge? As would be obvious to readers by now, we believe that through a completely objective and careful study of the Qur'an, one would realize the Equigenic Principle that the Qur'an itself recursively links to. The Equigenic Principle is not a matter of interpretation, a mere graft to bridge the chasm between ecology and theology. Rather, such concepts are in the Qur'an itself and are infused in such a way that we cannot separate ecology and theology. To really understand this point, it requires reading and understanding the *whole* of the Qur'anic message, which has been neglected or not emphasized because, firstly, over the last several centuries, the environment was not facing the critical dangers it has been over the last century; secondly, social emancipation from the yoke of colonialism was the priority; thirdly, due to the witting or unwitting partial and/or decontextualized analysis of the Qur'an by Muslims and non-Muslims alike, or due to flippant prejudicial statements based on Islamophobia, that have no bearing on Islam based on its prime textual source—the Qur'an.

A factor which must be understood about the nature of the Qur'an is that it is a multidimensional mirror of the universe. In the 20th/21st century, we have come to realize the critical situation in which the planet has floundered both ecologically and biospherically, and we have, as a whole, become focused on the dynamical balance, conservation, etc. In a parallel development, so too is it being realized that a plethora of Qur'anic verses and words exist on this matter, which were not paid attention to, due to the nature of our focus. The Qur'an has many verses and words that describe the dynamical balances, the

---

288. Foltz, Richard C., Denny, Frederick M. and Baharuddin, Azizan. (2003), Editors, *Islam and Ecology: A Bestowed Trust*, Foltz, Richard C. 'Toward an Islamic Ecotheology', p. 290–291.

191

sensitivity of the Earth to our actions, as well as the interrelated way in which it has been designed, that we have endeavored to explain in previous chapters.

The problem with the Qur'an or Islam then, lies not with the Qur'an or Islam *per se*, in terms of any inherent deficiency, or of the need to bend the scripture in order to suit the vicissitudes of time; rather it pertains to the fact that the explicit and implicit instructions that it exudes have not been read at all, or read properly. It is as if we were to open up a box to assemble a complicated piece of furniture and start mis-assembling hastily without reading the instructions, or by skipping parts of the instructions. The reality is that both the furniture and the instructions correspond to, or mirror, each other perfectly, in terms of consistency. It is likewise with the Qur'an. If what we are claiming is true, and indeed it is falsifiable and verifiable, it would make the 'eco-friendly' version of Islam *the* one true version of Islam, the version that Richard Foltz sees only as an *option* to be opportunely seized and implemented:

> As I have stated in my earlier writings on the subject, my own opinion is that we need not be overly concerned with which of the many interpretations ... of Islam or any religion is historically or originally 'the correct one', but rather, we should acknowledge that among all possible interpretations available to us, it is the eco-friendly, nonhierarchical ones that we desperately need to articulate and put into practice.[289]

It is argued, based on what has been discussed in depth in the previous chapters, that it is not an option, but part and parcel of the essence of Islam and mandatory (in Arabic, *fard*)! Such a practice would not be a choice, but a demand thrust upon those who call themselves Muslims and others who want a viable foundational solution, as it is not simply a version, but the directive imposed by the Creator and by inescapable logicality. In this final chapter then, we shall be tying together the various concepts discussed in previous chapters to see how everything ought to inter-fit, so that we obtain *Ecolibrium*, that is, the balanced dwelling place (from *oikas*—house and *librium*—balance), as required by this directive.

Concepts espoused by the Qur'an which we have distilled such as Ecognition 4, the concept of Personhood in relation to consciousness and creative evolution produces what can be referred to as 'Affinity': affinity is a much

---

289. Foltz, Richard C., Denny, Frederick M. and Baharuddin, Azizan. (2003), Editors, *Islam and Ecology: A Bestowed Trust*, Foltz, Richard C., 'Islamic Environmentalism: A Matter of Interpretation', p.249.

deeper and more all-encompassing than the concept of 'brotherhood' which Muslims usually speak about. It also incorporates the concept of brotherhood, as a subset, based on a solid linkage of our interconnections as living beings. This emerging New Synthesis is what is exhibited by modern research into nature and animals and documents such as the Qur'an; these sources of knowledge provide the motivation and methodology that can lead to Affinity. How so? Firstly, from the Qur'an, it can be shown that all life evolved from constituents in clay and water.[290] Furthermore, all consciousness in creatures has its origin from One Creator (as the claimed solution to the mind-body problem) according to Qur'anic analysis.[291] Remarkably, one word in the Qur'an captures the concept of evolution and a common source for consciousness. This word is *Rabb*, which means Sustainer, that is, one who creates and sustains all consciousness and creation. *Rabb* also means:

> The Evolver/Developer unto completion of nature and its constituents, and the entire universe, or the Evolver/Developer of something from one stage to another until it reaches perfection or completion.[292] The consequences of such a concept are shown in Fig. 1.

Most people in both East and West, Muslims and non-Muslims, are not aware that the Qur'an not only espouses creative evolution, but that the origin of evolutionary theory in the West (though now divorced from God) in mainstream science has its origin in the Qur'an and the very early Islamic thinkers.[293] For example, the word *yaum* in Arabic does not mean day only, but it can be used to mean periods, as per Qur'anic usage. The Earth was created in six periods and God did not need to rest or go on a vacation after that to a divine Bahamas! These ideas were taken up by the first French Evolutionists during the Enlightenment and then passed on to Darwin (who was learning Arabic). The conclusion is that: the origin of all animals (including humans) is one: therefore, individuality is from the same source:

290. Haque, Nadeem. (2009), *From Microbits to Everything: Beyond Darwinism and Creationism, Volume 3: The evolutionary implications.* Toronto: Optagon Publications Ltd.

291. Haque, Nadeem and Muslim, M. (2007), *From Microbits to Everything: Universe of the Imaginator: Volume 2: The Philosophical Implications,* (Toronto: Optagon Publications Ltd., 2007) 163–277.

292. As explained by the 11th to 12th century (C.E.) Arabic linguist and Qur'anic commentator Al-Raghib al-Isfahani, who wrote *al-Mufridat al-Gharibi-l-Qur'an.*

293. Bayrakdar, Mehmet, 'Al-Jahiz and the Rise of Biological Evolutionism', *The Islamic Quarterly,* Third Quarter, 1983.

> Do those who cover the truth not see that the rest of the Universe and the Earth were one piece and We [God] suddenly ripped them apart, and made every living thing (*dabbat*—carbon-based animal) from water. (21:30)

The *causal nexus of peace* is described by the following formula in Fig. 1:

Affinity is further reinforced for a Muslim by the following consideration: What does it mean that: 'All non-human animals prostrate to God', according to the Qur'an? As was astutely pointed out by Masri: 'The Qur'an (24:41) further tells us that nonhuman animals, who offer their obeisance to God in every movement, know what they are doing. This verse makes it abundantly clear that they are capable of consciously performing such acts, and, being Muslim (*always* in total submission to God—one of the complementary meanings of Islam), they coexist with their environs in constant, natural genuflection.'[294] In this sense, they submit to God (the prime meaning of Islam):

> Do you not see that unto God prostrate all things that are in the universe and on Earth: the sun, the moon, the stars, the mountains, the trees, the animals, and a large number among mankind? However, there are many who deserve chastisement... (22:18)

294. Haque, N. and Masri. B.A. (2011), 'Principles of Animal Advocacy in Islam: Four Integrated Ecognitions', *Society & Animals* 19, p. 284.

The Islamic system is not theocracy, democracy, capitalism, communism, socialism and any others besides. The Islamic system of governance, politics and socio-economics is utterly unique. Currently, there is no nation on Earth following the system as specified in the Qur'an in its entirety. We can, however, understand the true Islamic system by analyzing the humble bee, which is depicted in the Qur'an and has been honoured by a whole chapter named after it—*Al-Nahl*. How can the ideal and realizable socio-political human structure or society be realized from this tiny creature? Recently, it has been discovered that bees choose the new hives in a complicated procedure[295] which involves an elaborate dance that conveys the distance, direction and quality of their favorite finds:

> To report this food source, a bee runs through a figure-eight pattern on a vertical comb. ...As she passes through the central portion of the dance, she performs the waggle run, vibrating her body laterally, and the angle of the run indicates the direction to the food source. The duration of the waggle run relates to the distance to the food source. ... [The difference is that] When waggle dancing refers to nest sites, it occurs on the surface of a swarm rather than on the combs inside a hive.[296]

The longer the dance the better is deemed the potential site in terms of more waggle dance circuits that are performed. When a scout returns from a favorite hive and dances in support of it, to convey the information to the other bees, the other scouts do not simply buy that news at face value, but also go to the source, that is, the celebrated hive itself; in other words, they reconfirm it. Once there is a quorum of bees to be seen at a particular hive, the critical number which is 15 at any given time during the hive selection process, or 150 bees in total having visited that site, the swarm then, en masse, moves to this new hive which has been given the best rating, based on this threshold number.

This whole process has also been succinctly captured in the Qur'an, in the following verses, about fourteen hundred years ago:

> And your Lord inspired to the bee: Choose for yourself hives among the mountains, trees and that which they [human-beings] build. (16:68)

295. Seeley, Thomas D., Visscher, P. Kirk, and Passino, Kevin M., (2006), *American Scientist*, May–June 2006, 'Group Decision Making in Honey Bee Swarms', p. 223.
296. Ibid. pp. 220–229.

The word in the Qur'an used for 'choose', in this passage, is *ittakhathee*, which has been used extensively in the Qur'an to denote what one chooses (see, for example Qur'an 9:107 and 18:15). This word, although it also has the meaning of 'taking', has been applied in several other verses as meaning taking something selectively. For example, if I have six identical apples and I ask you to take one, the choice function does not enter into the equation. However, if I have various fruits in a bowl and ask you to take a fruit, you will choose one, in most cases, and not be indifferent. Here, the taking includes the choosing. In addition, the same word *wahi* in the form of *ahwaa* in the sentence is used in connection with guidance to the bees, as has been used in connection with human guidance through written revelation. In other words, such revelation conveys the best for humanity, it being thereby fostered, just as *wahi* for bees is the best guidance for helping the colony of bees to flourish. The choice function is derived from the general inbuilt instructions that the bees receive (the *wahi*). In a similar manner, one has to use one's reason (via the Equigenic Principle) to determine the best for human beings and the environment *as a whole*, given various options, just as the bees use their decision-making process that involves finding out the optimal or close to optimal location for a new hive, by going to the source. There is therefore an interplay between *revelation* and choosing, where the choosing is within the limits and direction placed by the *wahi* (revelatory guidance). Similarly, the choosing for human beings must also be circumscribed by the basic principles of the Qur'an, where the *wahi* for human beings, involves verification and proof from the original source of the information, rather than hearsay or speculation.

What are some of the best options that we can make so that we may live in the best type of dwelling, that is, what is the best type of home we can make on Earth? The decision-making procedure would involve following clear-cut injunctions of the Qur'an. Where an issue would be unclear, research would be conducted so as to see how one could arrive at a solution based on Qur'anic principles, including the Equigenic Principle, which corresponds directly to the Qur'anic Principles. This would be presented to the legislators and legislation would be passed based on the best solution, among a variety, which would be closest to the Qur'anic principle, if an ideal equigenic solution was not available due to the current situation. Legislation, in other words, would not be based on frivolous whims and desires, on a dictator's neurosis, on majority vote, on a plutocratic agenda, for lobby groups with narrow interests, but on the best rational, equigenically based solution, that, by the very nature of the term *equigenic*, has been verified to be so. The Islamic society would be governed by these thought patterns which are indeed like a formula for achieving peace and justice. Now if the variables in this formula are removed or are implemented in the wrong order the goal will not be achieved.

We have seen from preceding discussions that Islam, by its very linguistic definition, is not a label but the very description of nature itself, in the sense that, this description embraces all non-human creatures and universal systems as submitting to the One Originator, through natural laws. Like the rest of nature, every human being is ideally supposed to submit to this Originator, by realizing the existence and attributes of this Singular Creator, by pondering on the universe—on existence, origins, purpose, transformations and ends. This is, in fact, the prime directive naturally imposed by the very structure of the human being's reasoning and questioning mind. The expansive organic theatre of nature itself provides ample proofs for the existence, oneness and nature of God.

In the Qur'an, it is clearly stated that Prophet Abraham attained certainty when he realized who the Creator and Possessor of the kingdom of the universe and the Earth really was. He achieved this by employing his mind, eliminating that which did not make sense, by exercising reason. In the Qur'an, it is depicted that, Abraham, for example, shed incertitude by rejecting that which did not make sense. He refused to mix that which was proven to be true with its antithesis. In essence, this is how he freely entered into submission (Islam) and thereby aligned himself in complete unison with the rest of nature towards his Creator. Anyone who realizes that the structure of nature is actually pointing to the Originator, cannot possibly abuse nature, for it is the prime reality of nature that inexorably serves to prove the presence of One God who has no intermediaries, mystical incarnates, demi-gods or any other humans or non-humans as associates. Certainly, anyone, anywhere, anytime, who is behaviorally conscious of this state is, in a definitional and practical sense a 'Muslim'. In fact, whether he or she has even heard of the Qur'an or the term 'Muslim', is completely immaterial and irrelevant in this context, for it is the process of realization and resultant action which ultimately counts.

It was through such thinking that Abraham attained certainty. Certainty is the outcome of conclusive evidence. It has implications on one's behaviour in relation to one's surroundings: it is the primary and foundational motivation behind how we deal with all forms of life on Earth. The 'certainty' being referred to here is the certainty of reality—the certainty of beginnings and ends, of change and permanence, of the finite and the Infinite, and of the created and the real Creator. It is the certainty of these things, brought about by a realization of how they all naturally fall into place, that truly brings about a genuine concern for all of the diverse elements of life. Human beings such as Abraham and the thousands of other righteous people over the ages, were not sent by the Creator as Messengers simply to teach mankind what shape to trim their beards, what shade of cloth to cover their heads with, or how to seek salvation through empty rituals. Ever since the dawn of recorded history, they had been laying down guidelines for us as to how to lead a peaceful, happy, healthy and useful life in this world—useful not only to ourselves but also to everything else on Earth. In the hadith collection of Sahih Bukhari 1:10, the Prophet was asked as to whose application of Islam would be deemed the best: He replied that the best applicability would be that of the one who avoided verbally or physically harming those who are in submission to God. In this connection, there is, in the Qur'an, a passage that speaks of the effect of words, both good and bad. Words have different effects over time depending on their qualitative nature:

> Do you not see how God sets forth a parable of a good word as a good tree, whose root is firm and whose branches reach out into the sky, yielding its fruit in every season by permission of its Sustainer? God sets forth parables for people that they may cause remembrance. (14:24, 25)

The parable of a bad word is that of a bad tree, torn up onto the face of the Earth, wholly unable to endure. A close study of the Qur'an would confirm that a system of life based on the 'good word' would help us to achieve understanding and righteousness through worldly life rather than by one's renunciation from it. The respect for the environment is cultivated by the realization of one's possible future state that is connected to behaviour in this life. In this aspect, the following supplication is well-known and oft-repeated in the daily prayers:

> Our Lord! Give us good in this world as well as good in the Hereafter and save us from the chastisement of the fire. (2:25)

And the Prophet Muhammad advises that one should: 'Work for the affairs in this world as if you were going to live forever; work for the next world as if you were going to die tomorrow,' (as stated in a hadith collection by Darimi,

Sunan-al-Darimi). In order to deal with the environment we need to develop an outlook which is well-interconnected and does not therefore bifurcate knowledge into sacred and non-sacred, for concern towards the environment makes everything sacred, in the sense of respecting nature, as it is a creation of God. This means that the social structure in a truly Islamic society and the definition of knowledge does not take on the usual mystical[297] or atheistic connotations. With such a rational, workable and wholesome approach to the whole of life, monasticism and a clergy or clerical system of any kind—official or non-official—is expressly forbidden in Islam. Obedience to any authoritative human being who does not make sense—and who abides by that for which there is no evidence—is as good as worshiping that individual, which leads to the worst kind of harm. Because of the integration of knowledge, priest-like *mullahs* or priest-like *ulema* are alien to Islam. Knowledge includes knowledge of the environment and nature, with the realization of the Creator as the ultimate one to which a human submits. Indeed, in the passage which speaks of the signs of nature (Qur'an 35:27) it is stipulated in the concluding sentence that only those who fear God, lest they go astray, are the *ulema* (the knowledgeable ones). The fear has components of: knowing that actions going contrary to the Qur'anic principles and/or the Equigenic Principle will lead to harmful consequences and retribution from God after death. God is not perceived as an unfair tyrant, but as the most just who loves us all and wants us to act aright for our own self-development. Consequently, *ulema* is not an institution but an intellectual *constitution*—it is a descriptor of how you behave and whom you ultimately submit to. The Qur'anic concept of *ulema* is thus a far cry from priesthood which comes part and parcel with the separation of knowledge into secular or non-secular and/or mystical and non-mystical.

In fact, the developments we see today that have led to the evolution of a quasi-clergy, dressed in special garbs, issuing inconsistent proclamations from ornate pulpits are in clear violation of the egalitarian methodology and principles of the Qur'an. The Prophet Muhammad did not distinguish himself as being above others by wearing special clothes or by being seated on a pedestal, literally or figuratively. He was with the people, both physically and mentally, trying to solve their problems be they social and environmental. Indeed, in those days, if one were to enter a room with a group of people seated on the same level, one would not have been able to discern as to which of them was the Prophet. Now if

---

297. It is a plain and blatant fact that no separation exists between newly realized scientific facts and the Qur'an, as an over-abundant number of verses in the Qur'an attest.

the Prophet was that way, then it confounds us as to how many adherents in the nominal Islamic communities have deviated from this natural and exemplary form of behaviour, by erecting false complexes, classes and hierarchical structures in society. It is therefore not surprising that the well-being of animals and nature are not even given a second thought, when even fellow human beings are treated with discrimination. Islam, in actual fact, came to sever the mental and physical subjugation of both man over fellow man, as well as man over nature. Islam came to sever all forms of slavery. Anything short of this is not Islam but a mere label. The Qur'an itself is completely anti-labeling as is clearly illustrated in 2:62 because in this verse it states that *anyone* who believes in one God (strict monotheism) and the Hereafter and does good-intention based deeds is on the proper path, which means the truth, and hence is in submission to God (that is, is a *Muslim*, in everything other than the Arabic name). Unfortunately, many of those who label themselves Muslims do not understand this point about de-labeling.

In order to acquire a full understanding of the principles of life on Earth, in our worldly life, it is necessary to understand and respect the laws of nature as laid down by the Creator of this universe through a change in our character—in the way we think and act. However, this change cannot be imposed from without. This change can only emanate from within, by an objective extrospection and introspection of life. It can be actualized by an individual only by examining the evidences in the universe and within that individual as a free thinker. It is only through this process that the laws of nature can be understood as applicable to human beings in relation to ecology. Many rules and regulations passed by governments are obeyed unwillingly by people out of fear of prosecution. Yet, only through an understanding of a more globally interconnected worldview, as espoused in the Qur'an, can a change in heart and a revolution in consciousness be brought about, without any compulsion.

Given choices as opposed to compulsion, the Qur'anic view beckons man to strive for optimum globality. But what exactly is globality? Globality, as defined in this book, stands for interconnectivity, and interconnectivity implies non-contradiction. This, in actuality, is the pre-eminent position of Islam— the zenith of its rationality. However, could there be problems associated with being rational? Indeed, is being too rational our main problem when it comes to dealing with the Earth? There is a growing view, especially in the West, that we must return to native myths and mystical symbolism in order to become more 'spiritual' and thus save our planet. There is assumption here, that in the West, we have been too rational and that this is what has caused all the problems—one needs a bit of mystification, pantheism, or perhaps even quasi-animism in order to develop a sense of respect for nature. From the Islamic perspective, however, it is precisely these myths that have caused the problems—not rationality. The Qur'anic perspective sees the universe governed by cause and effect in all spheres, be they biological, sociological or ecological, and all these levels too are interlinked by cause and effect. If one thinks one's function is to dominate nature, or, for example, that the mode of economical advancement has nothing to do with environmental damage, a position which has been greatly prevalent in the West—then one is not actually being rational because one is neglecting the interconnected evidences which reveal exactly where man is placed in nature—in a state of rational participatory coexistence. In other words, the structure of nature tells us that we must be cooperative participants in the maintenance of nature's pre-designed balances, the proof being in the signs of nature. The Islamic position would, therefore, regard the overbearing posture of man toward the natural world, that is, of man as a Titan—so prevalent in the West and which the East is blindly copying—as the greatest of all myths and perhaps the Titan of all myths. Therefore, it is completely counter-rational as opposed to being rational.

In contrast to the Titan, various indigenous native cultures, who are supposed to be 'primitive' do not damage the ecosystem in their way of life and are closer to the Islamic concept of nature if they interconnect things in their environment and respect those interconnections which correspond with reality. For example, they realize that if they overkill some animals for food then this could have adverse consequences for both themselves and the animals and plants. They, therefore, manage their areas sustainably. They have recognized and are mindful of globality—the nexus between cause and effect—to a fuller extent than many other peoples. A lot of these societies have creation myths and many have incorporated animistic tendencies. These myths are harmful if they develop a pattern of thinking that takes them away from examining cause and effect relationships in a rationally interconnected way and if they violate the basic concept of the oneness of the Creator.

The lack of a fully rational basis in many such tribes and civilizations has contributed to, not only their downfall, but even to their utter extinction, because in some cases they reacted in a superstitious way toward outside invasion by the Western nations. These latter nations have tragically decimated their populations, either physically or culturally, over the last five hundred years, by the use of force, or by various inducements including Old World weeds, animals and diseases which gradually spread, upsetting too, the ecological balances.[298]

The principle of globality not only demands complete internal and external consistency in one's thinking, but it also demands that one must not contradict one's self in one's actions and in one's sayings and doings. This principle not only implies that sociological issues cannot be divorced from ecological issues, but that, in addition, one's mental pollution (immorality and indecency) cannot be separated from environmental pollution, for, somewhere along the branching network of cause and effect interrelationships, one type of pollutant will inevitably lead to the other. Such contradictions have even been shockingly apparent, among those who are at the forefront of environmental movements—those who are supposed to be setting the best examples. For example, many rallies of environmental activists, who are supposed to be proponents for environmental protection, leave so much junk littered on the ground that it becomes an ideal subject for derision by the popular media. Indeed, the principle of globality, which is the methodological foundation of Islam, implies, for example, that one cannot support the welfare of a particular animal in some 'foreign country', and yet be a racist and hate the common people of that particular innocent country. In fact, such racism or nationalism—with all its political machinations and ramifications—may lead to war, which is the greatest of all ecological destroyers. Such militarism would not only destroy the people, but would also ironically annihilate the animals and ecology—the very things which the oxymoronic 'racist-environmentalist' would have been so concerned about in the first place!

Globality implies interconnectivity, and interconnectivity in turn also implies completeness. One of the reasons why society has moved away from ecological balance is because there is no balance in the other spheres of life. To employ an analogy: Imagine if there were an oversized carpet laid out in a room. It would inevitably cause a crease or a bump to show. No matter how hard you might try to eliminate that crease, it will just not disappear. One can, at best, only displace the crease from one place to the other on the carpet. Now imagine that very same oversized carpet being sectioned into different regions, by marking boundaries. Let these sections be demarcated into the economical, sociological, environmental and technological zones. If a crease were to

298. Crosby, Alfred W. (1986), *Ecological Imperialism: The Biological Expansion of Europe*, pp. 900–1900.

develop in the environmental zone, it would just end up being pushed into another zone, such as the adjacent sociological section, in an effort to smooth out the bulge. In fact, all that is happening in this analogical scenario is transfer of the problem not an elimination. If one used reason, though, one would try to replace the oversized carpet with a new one which would snugly fit the room. What is therefore required is precisely the realization of such a replacement; indeed, this is the global solution, in all senses of the word.

The Qur'an emphasizes reality in our daily pursuits, where we are not dwelling amidst the whimsical fabrications of manufactured fantasies. We are in the real world and as was briefly discussed in the last chapter, there is hardly any balance or justice in the social realm where 'third world' governments are under pressure in the 'economic sphere' or zone—to recapitulate the above-mentioned analogy. According to the Qur'an, a balanced economic system is one where lenders and borrowers share in the profit and loss—they are partners in the whole scheme—one not being the exploiter of the other and where no monopolization or hoarding is allowed. If the world banks and even national financial institutions were to base their economic dealings on a workable interest free cooperative model, it would assuredly start to reduce pressure on society and in turn help the ecological sphere. This is only one example of such an interplay between 'economics and ecology' based on Qur'anic precepts. If society's laws were based on the balance of nature—on the equigenic rights, then logically speaking such laws would not be *ad hoc* or relative, but would be based on the principles and the realization of balance and globality, to ensure true justice for the whole of creation in this world. As humans we can gradually move toward this envisioned balance if we just start to realize this point of view; however, if we do not, then we will uncontrollably continue to drift away, into the cauldron of socio-environmental dysfunctionalities.

Despite the suicidal direction in which the ark of humanity is adrift into, the media and institutions, in general, are not designed to make us think in such a relational way about the introduction of such an integrated ecologically based system. On the contrary, a great many among humanity have become entrapped by crusader-like mentalities fostered by false historic ties and 'straw man fallacies'. Such mentalities, from cradle to grave, are easily prone to manipulative injections for vested interests. Should it be surprising for us when an elite class controls a country's wealth, that there should be concern only about personal, familial or corporate profits and not about ecology? There has to be something madly wrong with those who are not concerned or are actively against social and environmental welfare, who give no thought to facts such as that 3 billion people in the world earn less than $2.00 per day, and pontificate obtusely about spreading democracy from the so-called magnanimous West (who have, in the first place caused more than half the problems in the world through the effects of colonialism, neo-colonialism and now post-neo-colonialism)! Such elitist organizations wield tremendous power: a great many of their controllers hold the reins of multiple directorships with major media networks that are obsessively transfixed on narrow vested interests.[299] Would these transnational conglomerates be willing to put a stop to ecological devastation, by for example, advertising against their very own publicly unspoken mandates to plunder the Earth, or by having programs which truly educate the public against local, national or international projects which, if stopped or modified would decrease their profits and hamper competitiveness? Will most governments and politicians, who often collude with such corporate interests, be willing to take real action instead of preparing reports on whether they should be preparing reports on environmental assessments—by which time the projects are already well near underway or have even been completed! Will things, as a whole, really change for the better, unless we change our worldview? When will the mind-sets, which foster the pogroms and holocausts against nature, and commit nature-cleansing, cease?

The Qur'an is completely opposed to a monopolistic economic system controlled by any group. This is really why many individuals and groups are averse to Islam. Similarly, Islam is against an unaccountable bureaucracy, or corporate entities, who would have to abide by the norms of the balance as applied to every citizen and not behave as pathological plunderers who can get away under government legislation influenced by the power brokers that control the so-called present democracies.[300] Islam does, though, encourage trade in socio-ecologically sound products, and does incorporate private property with certain provisions. In Islam, no one is above the law because superiority or inferiority is not based on skin colour, being male or female, young or old or by one's job status. The theme which repeatedly keeps coming up in the Qur'an is: How could there be such distinctions if we all emanate from

299. Herman, Edward S. and Chomsky, Noam. (1988), *Manufacturing Consent: The Politics of the Mass Media.* Chapter 1, entitled 'A Propaganda Model' reveals how the large corporations exercise powers. In 1985, WNET lost its corporate funding after this station aired the documentary 'Hungry for Profit', which contained information disclosing detrimental corporate activities in so-called Third World countries.
300. See Joel E. Cohen's book and DVD: *The Corporation* (whose reference is in the Bibliography).

a common origin and have ultimately been derived from the very same dust of the Earth? In Islam, there is no elite class. It establishes a system structured to hold individuals in corporations accountable not only to the people, but also to animals and nature through co-integrated *Equigenic Rights*. This system is not an unachievable Utopian Dream: a society such as this was certainly established 1,400 years ago in Medina, the City of the Prophet, during the Prophet's time and during the period of the first four nominated or chosen successors after him. In fact, the second Caliph after the Prophet, that is, Umar ibn Al-Khattab, was so sensitive to the well-being of animals, let alone human beings, that he was afraid that the pot-holes on the roads would be injurious for the roaming creatures in distant lands under his administration. Whilst he was situated so far from Iraq, Umar said: 'If a she-mule was to stumble in Iraq I would be responsible in the eyes of God for having omitted to pave the road for it.'

Universal justice, in Islam, means justice to all entities, for it takes the stance that it is not enough for us just to be humans, but rather to be *just* humans. However, it must be stressed that this can only be achieved to its maximal potential if our worldview changes on a global basis, where industry becomes not simply profit-oriented with a devil-may-care attitude, but one which is oriented towards the Creator. This would lead to far-flung implications, for this type of compassionate society would think in terms of space and time not only globally, but also the consequences of their actions to their own selves beyond this immediate world to eternity. We need to develop a society in which individuals think of origins, ends, processes and interconnectivities. This is the reason why the Qur'anic outlook is so critical for mankind at this stage.

It is claimed by many that 'all major religions and sects are diverse paths leading to God' even if they veer from the concept of the oneness of God and that the socio-environmental issues can be solved by any path that seeks to 'do good'. However, what 'good' means is never usually well-defined and may mean many things to many people. Indeed, what is the measure of 'good' and can there only be one truth if we can get a precise measure for 'good'? As we have thus far tried to illustrate in this book, the Qur'an emphasizes the uniqueness of the truth. However, truth is not something which one carries around like a banner—serving as a mere label. From the Qur'anic perspective, it is not what you call yourself but what you actually submit to in your daily actions which leads you to a harmonization with nature and the Creator of nature. The universality of Islam with respect to its anti-dogmatic and invitationally challengeable claim to being the message for all times and places is at the outset a necessary logical prerequisite for something claiming to be the truth, since the truth itself must be timeless. As discussed previously, from the Qur'anic view, a great many of the 'world religions' have remnants of Islam left in them, since they diverged from the single truth of there being one and only one true Creator. The Qur'anic view, therefore, is that there is only one path or methodology to the truth which is based on building upon what one knows for sure. This naturally entails using reason and the evidences in nature and within oneself. In fact, from the Qur'anic language itself, no separation is made between the 'sacred' and the 'profane', for everything is a creation of God who is its Owner and ultimate inheritor. An Islamic concern for nature proceeds and expands upon this fundamental principle with respect to its all-encompassing ethical system based on linkages. But what exactly are these 'linkages'?

By observing nature, one will realize that there is a balance. This balance maintained is the basis of justice. Peace is a concomitant result of justice, at the fountainhead of which is the consciousness of the Creator (who has in the first place been confirmed as a concretely existing unseen Intelligence). There is, thus, a unique linkage between balance, justice and peace. They all flow from and into each other. Now if anyone breaks this chain or linkage of reasoning then we cannot proceed to realize any of the other links in the chain—that is the various relations (i.e. confirmation of one God through design and other signs leads to peace which is connected to justice, which is connected to so on and so forth). And if we cannot realize these relations then they cannot be actualized. Consequently, any system that does not follow this relational linkage in its belief structure cannot lead to overall peace for man and nature. Secondly, the ultimate form of 'good' human behaviour is that which results from the acute awareness of a singular omniscient God as the watcher of all actions—no matter how small they are. This awareness leads to the ultimate form of human behaviour because even if one is alone, even under severe temptation, one will not engage in harmful actions against oneself, others and nature—a level of consciousness unattainable by any other means. Thirdly, the 'diversity of paths approach' or cultural relativism presupposes that all one needs to do is 'do good' and all religions hold this. There is at least one major problem with this view, the foremost being that 'doing good' is a relative term. In this view, one man's good may be another man's evil, and most significantly, it utterly fails to answer the question: what exactly is the measure of good?

We need an absolute measure and what better measure than the universal laws of cause and effect as encapsulated by the Equigenic Principle, which coincides perfectly with the Qur'anic and natural methodology used to view nature and man's role in it to the specifications of the Creator. Indeed, the application of this principle is the prime law that we have been created to follow as beings endowed with rationality. In summarization, what is being claimed here is that there is only one path to the truth and that one can verify, by natural cause and effect evidence, that there assuredly must be only one path. Logically, rationally, evidentially and sensibly, there can be only one straight path to the truth, left up to the individual's honesty to verify. The question that might remain is: Are we being honest that we are being honest in our search for the meaning of life, our place in it and our proper use of it?

In the wider political realm, from the Islamic perspective, all humans have a common and unique origin, being one nation or community. In Islam, human beings were supposed to have realized this 1,400 years ago with the advent of the Qur'an. We should also have realized that other species are communities unto themselves like us and the whole of sentient creation is a supracommunity—a community of communities in peace with the One that originated all life. Unfortunately, we have developed a basic sense of insecurity, greed and selfishness, caused by an illusion of artificially created needs. These needs have no overall benefit to oneself or one's surroundings. By the invisible hand of pathological consumerism and materialism, many humans have supported the creation of classes and nations, each entranced by their own golden-calf. The result is a fragmented human community, which does not even have a sense of community. How can sane ecological policies be implemented or even planned, which benefit the supra-community, when even the basic family unit is being rent asunder, when nations are fighting nations and brothers are fighting brothers, in a madness which essentially benefits no one?

The technological prowess and the irrational disposition of conventional laws and systems worldwide are bound to cause destruction. However, we must not migrate into dark caves, forsaking all technology, or live in this world with a dark cave mentality. The present reactionary 'solution' presented by mystics—no matter what 'tradition' they say they do belong to—many of which are essentially pantheistic, be they Neoplatonic, or Neoplatonic-like, does not give global interconnected rationality its proper place, and discredits the potentiality of human thinking. This is because of the fact that the Creator's teleological universe and His transcendence, is not seen in all its glory. Concomitantly, the absolute distinction between the Creator and man, which in reality brings about our realization of the unimaginable greatness of the Creator as a totally separate and 'other' reality and hence gratitude is mutated. The denial of teleological reasoning, brought about by the emphasis on the purpose in nature, of course may lead to an inordinate blanket discreditation of technology, which is nothing but the use of nature. Furthermore, technology itself is nothing but applied science. If—through teleological thought—it is realized that there is no separation between science and a belief system based on nature, then the application of science itself will be tantamount to the application of that very belief system itself, as there would be no separation between the two. It would be part of the very same movement. The application of an environmentally sound technology, based on such a framework, would therefore not create socio-ecological problems brought about by imbalances.

Some scientists and thinkers deeply hold the personal view that science and religion are not in conflict. Others on the other hand, are not quite so sure, for when they survey most religions they discover that there are indeed great areas of major conflict. From this, they draw incorrect conclusions and make the fundamental inductive error of concluding that *all* religions are in such an intractable conflict. They then become inimical to any 'religion'. However, there is now a growing affirmation among many, even though it may not have been fully concretized, that there is some sort of a rational religion somewhere, in thought or in space, which coincides with science. It is worth quoting the mathematical physicist Paul Davies, to get an idea of this direction. He concludes in his book *The Mind of God: The Scientific Basis for a Rational World* that:

> The central theme that I have explored in this book is that, through science, we human beings are able to grasp at least some of nature's secrets ... Why this should be, just why we Homo Sapiens should carry the spark of rationality that provides the key to the universe, is a deep enigma ... I cannot believe that our existence in this universe is a mere quirk of fate, an accident of history, an accidental blip in the great cosmic drama ... Through conscious beings the universe has generated

self-awareness. This can be no trivial detail, no minor by-product of mindless, purposeless forces. We are truly meant to be here.[301]

Indeed, an increasing number of scientists have begun to develop a distaste for the religion of atheism, founded on relativism, which is being realized to be nothing but a brand of self-referentially defeating dogmatic, absolutism especially with deeper realizations in the cosmology of origins and the resurfacing teleology of evolutionary biology. After almost four hundred pages of considering in great detail, on the molecular levels as well, the optimality of biological, chemical and physical systems in terms of their fitness to originate, produce and nourish sentient life, biosciences researcher Michael J. Denton, who is certainly no creationist, concludes that:

> In the discoveries of science ... as [it] penetrates ever more deeply into the order of nature, the cosmos appears to be a vast system finely tuned to generate life and organisms of biology very similar, perhaps identical, to ourselves. All the evidence available in the biological sciences supports the core proposition of traditional natural theology—that the cosmos is specially designed whole with life and mankind as its fundamental goal and purpose, a whole in which all facets of reality, from the size of galaxies to the thermal capacity of water, have their meaning and explanation in this central fact.[302]

Denton further adds a point, which Al-Jahiz, the Muslim scientist and writer of the first known theory of teleological macro-evolution, over one thousand years ago, would today sanction as a worthy extension of the ideas he wrote about. Denton states that:

> Today the whole situation with regard to the possibility of directed evolution has been dramatically transformed... The concept of directed evolution is... no longer an anomaly in a nonbiocentric world. On the contrary, it is merely a logical deduction from a rapidly emerging new teleological world-view. ...[it has become viable now to speculate]...as to how the whole pattern of evolution might have been written into the DNA script from the beginning.[303]

301. Davies, Paul. (1992), *The Mind of God: The Scientific Basis for a Rational World*, p. 232. Another very informative book is: *Cosmos, Bios, Theos*, (1992), edited by Henry Margenau and Roy Abraham Varghese. In it, one hundred eminent scientists are interviewed and asked a number of standardized questions on 'God', the universe, the origin of life, etc.
302. Denton, Michael J. (1998), *Nature's Destiny: How the Laws of Biology Reveal Purpose in the Universe*, p. 280.
303. Ibid. p. 281.

Seeing the infernal state of our planet, many such individuals feel that if the world is devoid of a wholly rational system, then one had better be devised very soon, for all the 'ologies and 'isms have utterly failed us. The ultimate question, with these considerations is: if we were to use our reason and all the best minds and resources that we could possibly muster, would we eventually culminate in the Qur'anic outlook towards life, where there would be absolutely no conflict with scientific facts? Would we arrive at the Qur'anic outlook, mutually based on a methodology built to serve both the environment and man, each without the expense of the other? Could the cosmology of peace that many individuals are desperately searching for, be near at hand, requiring only objective inspection, free from any prepossessions or biases? It is worth quoting the yearning search for a system which embodies that 'cosmology of peace' which Thomas Berry talks about in his book *The Dream of the Earth*, some aspects of which coincide with the approach we have been discussing throughout this book:

> The greatest single need at present is the completion of the story, as told in its physical dimensions by science, by the more integral account that includes the numinous and consciousness dimensions of the emergent universe from its primordial moment. Once that is done, a meaningful universe, a functional cosmology, is available as a foundation for the total range of activities in the ecological age.[304]

In the *Wisdom of the Elders* the noted environmentalists, David Suzuki and Peter Knudtson elaborate upon a similar point:

> In his thoughtful philosophical essays, Roger Sperry, the Nobel Prize-Winning brain biologist, has discussed society's desperate need to reconcile the electrifying insights of modern science with the compatible value systems that honor and protect the natural world. He suggests that to facilitate this search for a new global ethos by which we can navigate the ecologically turbulent seas of our times, each of us should engage in an intriguing thought experiment. Our challenge is, by a leap of the imagination, to divine what environmental values the wisest spiritual leaders of the world's great religious traditions might be publicly proposing if they were alive and were scientifically well informed. The task, muses Sperry, can be likened in some respects to that of trying to deduce what form of religion the teachings of Christ, Mohammed, Buddha, Confucius,

304. Berry, Thomas. (1990), *The Dream of the Earth*, p. 120.

and other founders... might have taken if Copernicus, Darwin, Einstein, and all the rest had come before their time instead of after.[305]

There is indeed a profound irony of tragic proportions in Roger Sperry's statement, especially in terms of the great lack of awareness of the Qur'anic contents amongst Western and Eastern scientists and others. This is because the Qur'an appeared *before* the scientists mentioned, yet contains ideas and descriptions about the natural processes that have pre-empted the discoveries and ideas by almost one and a half thousand years! Unbeknownst to most people on Earth at the present time, the 'thought experiment' suggested by Sperry, already corresponds with an actually existent belief system fully described in the Qur'an. All that is required is communication and confirmation through a proper understanding of understanding. It was perhaps in this vein that the social activist/reformer Leo Tolstoy remarked (loosely translated from Russian) that: 'The highest wisdom has but one science—the science of explaining the whole creation and man's place in it.'

There is now a gradual recognition and presentation of the facts in non-Muslim contemporary literature. In *Science and Religion,* the historian of science, John Hedley Brooke of the University of Lancaster explains quite rightly that:

> Cultural chauvinism can have insidious effects on the historiography of science. Even when they have not been beating the religious drum, Western historians have been censured for their myopia in treating modern science as if it were an exclusively Western phenomenon. Significant contributions... are easily overlooked. In the centuries preceding the scientific renaissance in the West, Muslim scholars did far more than merely reproduce their heritage from the Greeks... Not surprisingly, Muslim scholars see in the sixteenth century Europe not a renaissance but a reactivation.[306]

It is worth lengthily quoting historian and writer, Robert Briffault, who wrote a remarkable book entitled *The Making of Humanity*, in 1919, during a period in Europe in which colonialism and blatant imperialism was rampant and when there was an even greater ignorance about Islam:

> It was under the influence of the Arabian and Moorish [Islamic] revival of culture, and not in the fifteenth century, that the real Renaissance took place. [Muslim] Spain, not Italy, was the cradle of the birth of

305. Knudtson, Peter and Suzuki, David. (1992), *Wisdom of the Elders*, pp. 182–183.
306. Brooke, John Hedley. (1991), *Science and Religion*, p. 43.

Europe. After steadily sinking lower and lower into barbarism, it had reached the darkest depths of ignorance and degradation when the cities of the [Islamic] Saracenic world, Baghdad, Cairo, Cordova, Toledo, were growing centers of civilization and intellectual activity. It was there that new life arose which was to grow into a new phase of human evolution.

From the time when the influence of their culture made itself felt, began the stirring of a new life. The fact has been set forth again and again. But it has been nevertheless stubbornly ignored and persistently minimized. The debt of Europe to the 'heathen dog' could, of course, find no place in the scheme of Christian history, and garbled falsification has imposed itself on all subsequent conceptions.

...What we call science, arose in Europe, as a result of a new spirit of inquiry, of new methods of investigation, of the method of experiment, observation, measurement, of the development of mathematics unknown to Greeks. That spirit and those methods were introduced into the European world by Arabs [Muslims].[307]

Professor Thierry Hentsch, reflectively discusses the deep psychological basis of the distortion of Islam in a more recent book, *Imagining the Middle East*:

Our view of the Other [Islamic civilization and society] cannot—in all lucidity—set itself the objective of knowing it [Islam] 'in and of itself...' We must, henceforth, know that through it we seek ourselves. Since the image [created by distortion, and reflecting nothing but the mentality of the agent of distortion] is not a particularly flattering one, many Western intellectuals will persist in their refusal to awaken to the implications of our inevitable ethnocentrism—so unbearable do they find the notion that there may be truth in what the Other says about us.[308]

According to the overall globally consistent approach advocated in the Qur'an, it is deducible, by the process of elimination, that the answer to all our self-created and multifaceted problems on Earth rests on man's voluntary submission to the will of God. For the God of Islam, 'submission' does not mean following an empty set of dogmatic rituals, but entails the trying of our level best to carry out such a Creator's will as expressed through using the laws in nature

307. Briffault, Robert. (1919), *The Making of Humanity*, pp. 188–191.
308. Hentsch, Thierry. (1992), *Imagining the Middle East*, p. 205.

that lead to non-harm, naturally synonymous with the Qur'anic injunctions. No other approach to our problems will work for us, because no other approach even approaches globality—the interconnectivity, non-contradiction and completeness—so essential for a complete and sustainable resolution. Having regard for globality, means that an Islamic concern for ecology is contained within an all-embracive concern for the totality of the environment, that is, the notion of the environment in the widest possible sense. The Qur'an certainly deals with all spheres of life and has an interwoven structure for creating a healthy *supra community* in which all the economic, sociological, legal, technological systems are integrated in the proper way. These interlinked systems would evolve from a socio-ecological foundation based on the concept of the balance (*mizan*)—the prime factor which the Qur'an is inviting man to both realize and thereby implement. By being truly honest with oneself, one could utilize reason to become conscious of the Creator of the universe and the inherent balances in nature, of the apprehension in disobeying His equigenic laws, thereby significantly elevating our behaviour toward nature.

> As for those who would argue about God after He has been acknowledged, all their arguments are null and void in their Sustainer's sight... it is God who has sent down the book in the truth and the balance. (42:16, 17)

It is only through the realization and restoration of the upset balances that we would be able to establish justice, and it is only through this kind of justice, the only real justice, that we would be able to live in overall peace and security. In fact, looking at it the other way around, it is this very security also which maintains the balance. For it is with such security that our needs are not skewed by desires which would, at the very outset, tend to create the desires for harmful commodities, subservience to irrational authorities or reliance on disconnective belief systems that would disrupt the balances leading to peace. Consider the following passage from the Qur'an:

> Consider the night as it veils in darkness, and the day as it rises bright! Consider the process of the creation of the male and the female! Verily, you (mankind) aim at most divergent ends! Thus [consider this immutable psychological law]: for the person who gives [for a just cause] and is conscious of God, and believes in the highest good—for such an individual We shall facilitate the path towards ease [in terms of peace of mind]. In contrast, for the niggardly person, who considers

> himself or herself to be self-sufficient, and calls the ultimate good a lie, for such an individual We shall facilitate the path towards adversity [in terms of, at the least, psychological torment]—and of what use will such a person's wealth be when he or she goes down? (92:1–11)

True freedom leads to a concern for nature. We often talk of peace in terms of freedom from strife and hostilities among ethnic groups and nations. However, fighting in the battlefields, or strife in the cultural, economic and political arenas, are not the real cause of discord in human relationships. They are the effect of inner discord within our minds, prompted by greed, insecurity and fear. We shall never succeed in establishing lasting peace on Earth without removing the social, economic and political causes of conflict. To achieve this, we shall have to learn how to engender within ourselves, individually, a state of tranquillity and repose—a state of mind at peace with itself. Only those who are at peace with themselves can truly be at peace with the world at large. This state of peace, envisioned and reflected by the word Islam, is that peace which results from the lack of inconsistency between one's thoughts and things as they are, and likewise, between the sayings and the doings in one's life: it is a peace concordant with concrete reality and certainty. Peace itself can be imposed neither by stick nor by carrot; it has to be won through the altruistic magnanimity of the mind and the heart. Freedom is a prerequisite of peace—freedom from want, indignity, fear and most of all freedom of self-determination, of expression. Freedom could, however, become a double-edged weapon without the fine distinction between the purity of rational freedom and the emotional relativity of libertinism where one is shackled to the chains of one's whims. It needs always to be kept in mind that one person's capricious freedom could become another person's bane. Being truly free means being able to survey and explore the options rationally, to arrive at the best global solution for the maintenance of the integrative realm of nature, which includes both humans and non-humans, so that the dynamic flux of socio-ecological equilibrium is always preserved. One cannot truly be free and arrive at such global solutions if one is held captive by one's own passions, where the element of concern for creation simply does not even arise. Indeed, without such freedom, true peace is unachievable.

In this day and age, when the naturalists have started laying bare the secrets of the animal and ecological world, a plea of ignorance is no longer a valid excuse. It is high time that we acknowledged the biological fact that we humans are just one of innumerable other species on Earth. Until we learn to live with these others, our prayers for world peace ring hollow. One of the reasons for man's creation is a test to see how he deals with that balance according to the Qur'an; the way the universe is configured is precisely to test man's sensitivity towards the balance.[309] But what exactly does that mean? What is the nature and purpose of the test? And a test implies accountability. How is accountability related to maintaining the balance of nature? In the Qur'an it is stressed repeatedly in various contexts that this life has been created for a higher form of existence, and that man's status in the next life is dependent upon how he conducts his affairs in this life: there is an afterlife in which all human beings will have to answer to their Creator. Those whose harmful actions outweigh their good deeds, based on intentions, will suffer the most severe repercussions. On the other hand, those whose good deeds outweigh their evil actions will be amply rewarded in the next life as their Creator wills. There are numerous verses in the Qur'an on this issue. The Day of Judgment will follow the cataclysmic destruction of the entire universe, although the Qur'an deals with the description of the last phases of the Earth in some detail:

> When the Earth is shaken up by its cataclysm, and the Earth throws out its burdens, and man enquires: 'What has come over it?' That day it will narrate its annals as your Lord will have inspired it to do. That day people will proceed separately to be shown their deeds. Whosoever will have done even an atom's weight of good will behold it: And whosoever has done even an atom's weight of evil will behold that. (99, 1–8)

Anyone who has studied the Qur'an will note that it is most accurate when it talks of origins—such as the Big Bang, etc. Could it also be as accurate about 'the End' given the accuracy of its description of the beginning of our concept of space and time, when that was not realizable by humankind? How will the end of nature occur? Summarizing numerous verses and chapters on this in the Qur'an, basically, it states that: This universe's termination will occur suddenly, with stars being scattered, mountains being reduced to dust, with the Earth casting out its subterranean contents and so on as the fabric of the physical laws change, or are entirely disintegrated in a universal cataclysm. The Creator would, in this termination process roll up the universe like a recorder rolls up (closes) a written scroll, and as the first universe was originated, so shall it be recreated. We know how our universe began with the Big Bang. The Earth and

309. Qur'an 57:25.

the rest of the universe will be changed into another universe not based on the laws and structures that we know.[310]

Those who have forgotten the purpose of this universe—which is nothing but a testing ground for the human psyche for the growth of knowledge through experience—will suffer the consequences of their misdeeds. Everything in nature has been created to test mankind:

> We have made whatever exists on the Earth its adornment to test and try them—to know who acts better. Verily, We will (eventually) reduce all that is on it to dust. (18:7)

Ending up in an unenviable situation, however, is a concomitant product of wayward desires:

> Mutual rivalry for plenitude keeps you pre-occupied until you finally end up being deposited into the grave. But it is then that you will come to know—yes, indeed, you will then come to know. If you could but realize it with that knowledge which results from having gained certainty, you will behold hell with the certainty of observation itself. And, on that day, you will be asked to account for the joys of life. (102: 1–8)

For such people do not realize that:

> Instead, you ought to worship only one God and be among the grateful. They do not esteem God as they ought to. (39:66)

Lest all this seems far-fetched superstitious nonsense, the Qur'an repeatedly lets man ponder on the first creation—his humble origins:

> Let man then consider what he was created of: spurting fluid issuing from between the vertebral column and the ribs.[311] He (God) can bring him back to life on the Day when all secrets are laid bare. (86:5–9)

> Does not man see that We created him from a drop of fluid? Even then he becomes an open contender, and applies comparisons to Us, having forgotten his origin, and says: 'Who can put life into decayed bones?' Say: 'He who created you for the first time. He has knowledge of every creation. He is the one who gave you fire from the green tree

---

310. See Qur'an: 47:18; 56:5,6; 81:1–14; 82:1–5; 99:1–8; 101:1–11; 78:17–20; 70:8,9. 'Closure' of the cosmos: 21:104.

311. This refers to the gonads that become differentiated into the male and female ones by the seventh and eighth weeks, after which they start their descent in the embryo and was unknown until the 20th century C.E.

with which you are able to ignite the flame.' Is then He who created the universe and the Earth therein, not able to create others like them? Yes, indeed—for He is the all-knowing Creator. When he wills a thing he has only to say: 'Be', and it is [i.e. it instantaneously comes into being or does so evolvingly]. So all glory to Him who holds dominion over everything, to whom you will go back in the end. (36:77–83)

From the few verses highlighted, we can see that part of the awareness of the Creator's presence as the Owner of nature has an obverse and complementary side to it—that of retribution—of setting the balance aright completely after death through total justice, where nothing will be left out. There are literally hundreds of verses in the Qur'an dealing with this theme. Some of the verses describe what happens after death through similitudes because we cannot comprehend the next universe through the frame of reference of this universe—it is not identical in structure and processes. For one thing there is no decay or entropy. In essence, existence comprises creation and re-creation and there is a purpose to man's creation; man was built for re-creation not recreation.

The Prophet had said that there are two main reminders for us—the Qur'an and death. The proper realization of the true nature of these has the potentiality to transform and mold human behaviour to become congruous with the rest of nature—to live naturally in submission to the Creator. In reality, though, it must be noted that earthly death is not real death but is only a relative term. Death or passing away of the human psyche from the regular interaction with our familiar space and time is merely the continuation of an individual's life unfolding into a new life—a new system. Death is simply a gateway for the continuum of human growth. Life is indeed such a continuum, but in the Qur'an it is pointed out poignantly that human beings forget their humble origins in nature and become open contenders,[312] thereby defeating the very purpose for them being cast into the universe in the first place. Consider the following similarities: in the womb, as developing prenatal entities we were in another 'universe' in terms of space and time perception, even though we were developing physically. Like the womb, this universe is the pointing to this very fact. We have been provided with everything to realize: God sent down the Balance (that is, nature's equilibrium, order and consistency) and the Qur'an, two signs, so that we may be able to establish justice.[313] As has been discussed before, each of these concepts: evidence, balance, justice and the Qur'an are linked to form a cohesive whole in

312. Qur'an 36:4.
313. Qur'an 57:25.

the thought structure of one who has recognized the meaning of the evidences in nature. The only viable and sensible methodology by which this vision and its empowerment can be realized is by the usage of reason and evidence:

> Do not follow that of which you have no knowledge; for you will certainly be held accountable for your hearing, seeing, thinking—all of these. (17:36)

So it is that by using our faculties we are to behave in this universe in such a way as to achieve individual and collective growth, knowing that this temporary, entropic and equigenic universe has been optimally designed for this very purpose. The core of this design includes the knife edged balance in nature found in the ecosystem, biology and human psychology. The balance has been created to see who would keep the equilibrium and who would weigh things justly. In other words, such an *equilibrium sensitive system*—which encompasses a vast spectrum, from the interrelated food web to the sensitive balances in the human body, was necessary and sufficient in order to test mankind—the unique entity possessing 'freewill'.

In the Qur'an, it is explained in numerous passages that when you die you are really born into a new system in an afterlife (you are *not* reincarnated)![314] Whether your growth is stunted, retrogressive, constant or exponential depends on your behaviour in this life and what you take with you of your deeds as well as the traces you leave behind. The truly dead are those who are deaf and blind in the sense that they do not pay heed to the signs in the universe pointing to the Creator as the ultimate Owner, and act on the implications of those signs.[315] In this vein, with reference to animal welfare and the growth of the self (*nafs*), consider the following Qur'anic verses:

> Consider the Self, and how it is formed in accordance with what it is meant to be, and how it is imbued with moral failings as well as with consciousness of God. To a happy state shall indeed attain he who causes this [self] to grow in purity, but truly lost is he who buries it. To this truth gave the lie, in their overweening arrogance, [the tribe of] Thamud, when that most hapless wretch from among them rushed forward [to commit his evil deed], although God's apostle had instructed them, 'It is a she camel belonging to God, so let her drink [and do her no harm]!' But they denied him, and cruelly slaughtered her, due

314. Qur'an 80:19–22.
315. Qur'an 6:122.

to their misdeed, their Sustainer, visited them with utter destruction, leveling them, for He does not fear its consequences. (91:7–15)

In the Qur'an then, it is stated that God is the owner of the universe so that He may test our interactions in the universe. But it also states that those who are unjust reject the signs of God. This is the ultimate significance of the reason why the universe has been structured the way it is and why complaining about death and the potentiality of suffering misses the whole point of the nature of its existence and its direction:

> ... God has created the universe and the Earth in the truth, in order to reward every human being for what he or she has earned—none shall be wronged. (45:22)

The story of Adam in the Qur'an, is the story of the hope for humankind—a story of paramount significance. It is not a mythical story but a true one of mankind's nature as exhibited by events which transpired at the dawn of human civilization. The Qur'anic story of Adam has profound implications with respect to the development of ecological thinking and it is significantly different to the Biblical story. Firstly, it must be borne in mind, in the Qur'an, it is related that Adam was commanded by the Creator not to approach the tree:

> When we said to the angels: 'Bow before Adam,' they all bowed but Iblis (Satan), who refused and gloried in his arrogance and thus he became one of those who deny the truth. So we said; 'O Adam, he is truly your enemy and your wife's. Do not let him have you turned out of the Garden and come to grief.' (2:117)
>
> ... do not approach this tree, or you will become iniquitous. (7:19)
>
> 'Verily you will have no hunger or nakedness there, nor thirst, nor exposure to the sun.' But then Satan tempted him by saying: 'O Adam, shall I show you the tree of immortality, and a kingdom that will never show any wane?' (20:120)
>
> [Satan/Iblis said] Your lord has but forbidden you this tree lest you become angels, or lest you become immortal. (7:20)

In the Qur'an, Adam was explicitly commanded not to even *approach* the tree. Such a stricture goes a stride further than would a commandment prohibiting eating from the tree. This is because by keeping a distance, the probability of engaging in harmful actions diminishes. In fact, this is the behavioral principle man is supposed to follow in order to remain pure. However, it must be remembered that, we are not to deny ourselves those things which are conducive to our psycho-physical growth:

> O Children of Adam! Adorn yourselves for every act of worship, and eat and drink, but do not waste: verily, He does not love the wasteful! Say: 'Who is there to forbid the adornment which God has brought forth for His creatures, and the good means of sustenance?' ... (7:32)
>
> Say: 'Verily, my Sustainer has forbidden only shameful deeds be they open or secret, sin, rebellion against what is just, and ascribing divinity to aught beside Him—since He has never issued this from on high—and attributing unto God that of which you have no knowledge.' (7:33)

The state of the garden represents the state of perfect *earthly* socio-ecological equilibrium. Adam and Eve were on the garden of Earth and not in 'Heaven' as is often mistakenly assumed. This is easily realizable because of the way they were tempted to eat from the tree. Iblis (Satan)—the external entity doing the tempting—induced them into doing so by claiming that God did not want them to gain eternal life on Earth, the only thing that they did not possess in an otherwise earthly though socio-ecologically perfect scheme of a universe designed for a higher universe after death. If they were in the paradise of 'Heaven' then they would have had eternal life and hence would not need to be induced in this way. So the prime reason why they left this state of the 'garden' was that they disobeyed the Creator—the sign in this case was a direct instruction from God. Adam and Eve were influenced by external pressures and forced to transgress the limits and also by their own misplaced desires. There is, consequently, a potential to disobey God because of the capacity of humankind to select among various options of action and not because 'sin' is transferred generationally. Actually, in Islam, the concept of original sin is non-existent, as each human bears his own burden. Indeed, each human being is born in the state of perfect submission, as a 'sinless' human being. The implication of all this is that in order to return to that ideal temporal system in this life one must strive for the opposite of all that which led away from the Garden. From the genetic and 'paleocultural evidence' it seems that the true (and not symbolic) story of Adam well reflects human cognitive evolution by which time man was able to name all things and be God's vicegerent/trustee/successor[316] on the Earth, and become responsible

---

316. To see who Adam was 'succeeding', refer to: Haque, Nadeem. (2012), 'Future Implications of a Pre-Adamic, Global and High Ancient Civilization', *Scientific GOD Journal*, pp. 20–40.

for the proper utilization of it in accordance with his uniquely endowed capacity. In such very early settled societies, hereafter, God would send messengers in the form of men to persuade humans to move away from such socially and ecologically destructive behaviour in settled and agrarian communities. Now although Adam had disobeyed his Lord and went astray, he also did repent for his 'slip', and was therefore forgiven, and there is no 'original sin' handed down generationally, or of a snake being portrayed as the evil tempter of Adam and Eve:

> Thereupon Adam received words from his Sustainer, and He (God) accepted his repentance: for verily, He alone is the accepter of repentance: the dispenser of grace. (2:37)

As before, God wants us to follow true and confirmed revelation and avoid Adam's grievous mistake:

> That is why We have sent down this [Qur'an] ... and have given therein many facets to all manner of warnings so that people may remain conscious of Us, or that it may give rise to remembrance in them ...We had commanded Adam before, but he disregarded it; We found him lacking in resolution. (20:113, 115)

In summation, the garden is an ideal metaphor for the perfect and beautiful interaction between the 'man-made' and the natural—an achievable state on Earth. What is required to establish this garden is a realization of the singular Creator's existence, and ultimately knowing for sure that this universe is a testing ground for a higher universe, where we shall all be held accountable for upsetting the balances and rewarded for upholding them, be they in any of the interconnected spheres of life. We need to confirm the reality of both a Creator, and the next life, as these two form the poles of the circuit in which flows the consciousness of God (taqwa) maintained and fostered, with the signs—nature and the Qur'an—being the batteries of that circuit and our will to look into these, the chargers of those batteries. Every human being will be judged according to the scales on their individual balance of good versus harmful actions (Qur'an 21:47). Having realized the beginning and the end of things and that which created them, the Creator wants us, unlike Adam's initial 'slip', to remain steadfast in holding onto the Qur'an to help us achieve universal justice through the maintenance of the balance. This holding on to the Qur'an is not a dogmatic act, for nothing meaningful, inter-connectively useful and indeed eternal can arise from dogma and blind faith. What is required is evidence and this is what the Qur'an stands for as the innumerable verses in it attest[317] so that we can indeed establish a society based on the foundation of nature, a system based on the constitution of the Qur'an and the Equigenic Principle.

From the preceding discussions it must be clear that we need a change in our system of dealing with our fellow human beings and nature which is one not merely of *degree*, but rather of *kind*. Although this may be considered by many who want to cling to various blindly fideistic or atheistic traditions as rocking the boat too much, it is better to rock the boat while we still have one. Indeed, we need to address the root of the illness, not the symptoms. Anything short of this threshold is bound to fail in fundamentally resolving anything. In this book it has been argued all along that unless humanity, both individually and collectively, starts to move towards an understanding based on the global approach, it will never move towards any fundamental resolutions. In fact, the crux of the whole issue is that no matter how many conferences are convened or protocols set up to address the local and global environmental and related developmental issues, the overall situation will just keep worsening every year, every decade and every century.

Yet, despite such a 'doom and gloom' scenario, it is still not too late to reverse our downward slide into an abyss of ubiquitous socio-ecological destruction and depravity, where 'peace' has fast become just an inane five-letter word. The changes which would start from each individual within, towards that integrated outlook which is espoused in the Qur'an, will naturally be extended without, once individuals open themselves to critical, rational and uninhibited global thinking. What will be required for a true global transformation in human societies then will be that very realization, regarding both the natural world's relation with man and the relation of both, in connection to their mutual Originator, specifically the kind of Originator we have been discussing all along in this book. Once a critical mass has been reached in the number of human beings thinking in this way, the process of change would start to accelerate via a natural momentum propelled by reason. This would usher in the ecological age which was slowly being ushered in the early 19th century through a unitarian natural philosophy in the West and would have merged with Islam in the 20th century, but got set off-course through chance-based ideas of evolution, intense colonialistic subjugation through various techniques, the rise of relativism as a counter-reaction to mysticism, and a misunderstanding of space and time brought about by wrong

317. For instance see the Qur'an: 2:44; 3:190, 191; 16:90; 8:22; 4:82; 17:36; 28:49; 23:17; 31:15; 18:5; 67:10.

interpretations of quantum mechanics and general relativity which has kept the realization of a unitary God behind closed doors. This merging trend towards such an ecological age is now well underway, though through subtle, ultimately unstoppable, staged processes, one of which is the correspondence between the Qur'an and new scientific discoveries, despite frequent blockages, cover-ups and wilful or mistaken understandings.

The prerequisite for achieving this global transformation can only be through real education which deals with the totality of reality through full integration. The Qur'anic view would be that the stark necessity of such an education cannot and must not be underestimated at this crucial juncture in our history on Earth. This is due to the fact that humanity has already witnessed and experienced hundreds upon hundreds of years of socio-ecological damage, with only a few islands of sanity situated in the flowing stream of time. Looking at the issue objectively, is it not high time that we, as human beings, realized our waywardness and the true nature of our potential? Do we human beings really want to continue along the same path of destruction, due to our personal dogmatic intransigence, or are we ready to tackle our myths and false notions at a fundamental level, where all the problems are rooted? Getting to the root of the matter, the ultimate question is: Are we ready to emancipate ourselves into the embrace of a natural system, where we have nothing to lose but our ignorance towards humanity and the natural world? Or are we shackled to the unnatural world by societal pressures which we feel we must cling onto by 'accident or birth' and a false sense of societal or communal 'comfort'?

We can see that our detrimental perceptions of life have been at the root of both reversible and irreversible destruction. Directed by an exceedingly destructive way of thinking, we human beings are responsible for the wounds of our own making. Yet, is there some kind of prognostication of hope emanating from the Qur'an in the following passage?

> Corruption has appeared over both land and water because of what the
> hands of man have wrought. God has allowed this to transpire in order
> to give them a taste of their own misdeeds so that, hopefully, they might
> return [to the true and natural belief system]. (30: 41)[318]

We have seen that no dichotomy exists between the basic inbuilt nature of man and the nature of the Qur'anic guidance, in which the human being

---

318. Note that God lets us *taste* our misdoings and sets a limit on the actual harmful effects that could be cast upon us.

is asked to reflect, by reason, upon the nature of Nature. In fact, these four—human nature, reason, the book of the universe and the Qur'an—are, in their true essence, perfectly interweaving strands in the seamless fabric of a teleological and *equigenical* cosmos. By following an intervolved approach as explicated in the Qur'an, we can always return to, or remain indissolubly associated with our true and innate, pure nature, which is the nature of the universe itself. This is precisely the theme that the following verse of the Qur'an refers to when it directly addresses every human being to:

> Direct your face towards the upright way of life, which is the nature of God, upon which He has framed the creation of humankind. No change is permissible in God's creation; this is the proper way of life and yet, most people do not even know it. (30:30)

We have examined various concepts in this book and from these it can be concluded that: the post-nihilistic equilibrium dynamics of a supra community, having a direct monotheistic connection through the Qur'an and evidential based thinking, is what would form the essence of a global socio-ecological order for the 21st century and beyond, towards establishing *eco*librium—true ecological equilibrium, the balanced dwelling place for all species, including man. It is this deep yearning to evolve a society built on the realization of such a realistic interrelationship with nature, that is echoed by social historian Lewis Mumford. Indeed, it could be characterized as the Rise of the Ecological Age:

> The cycle of the machine is now coming to an end ... man is at last in a position to transcend the machine, and to create a new biological and social environment, in which the highest possibilities of human existence will be realized, not for the strong and the lucky alone, but for all co-operating and understanding groups, associates and communities.[319]

When we realize the essence of what socio-environmentalism ought to be, we realize that the sacred balance in Islam *is* Ecolibrium. With these sentient thoughts in mind, let us earnestly try to grasp the true essence of nature in man, before it becomes too late for man in nature.

---

319. Edwards, Tryon. (1959), *The New Dictionary of Thoughts: A Cyclopedia of Quotation*, p. 380.

Bibliography

Abubaker, Ahmad, (1989), *Africa and the Challenge of Development: Acquiescence and Dependency Versus Freedom and Development*, Praeger Books, New York.

Ali, Syed Irtifaq, 'Hima—The Protected Area Concept in Islam', *Islamic Thought and Scientific Creativity*, March 1996, Volume 7, No. 1.

Al-Jahiz, (1909), Kitab al-Hayawan, Cairo.

Amin, Mohammed, (1945), *Wisdom of the Prophet Muhammad*, The Lion Press, Lahore, Pakistan.

Arabia—The Islamic World Review, (1985), Vol. 4, No. 49, Slough, England.

Attenborough, David, (1984), *The Living Planet*, Fontana/Collins, BBC, London.

Attenborough, David, (1990), *The Trials of Life: A Natural History of Animal Behaviour*, Little, Brown and Company, London.

Augros, Robert and Stanciu, George, (1988), *The New Biology: Discovering the Wisdom in Nature*, New Science Library, London.

Averroes, (1967), *On the Harmony of Religion and Philosophy*, (translated by Hourani, George Faido), Luzac, London.

Banaei, Mehran and Haque, Nadeem, (1995), *From Facts to Values: Certainty, Order, Balance and their Universal Implications*, Optagon Publications Ltd., Toronto.

Bakan, Joel, (2005), *The Corporation: The Pathological Pursuit of Profit and Power*, Free Press.

Batchelor, Martin and Brown, Kerry, (1992), *Buddhism and Ecology*, Cassell, New York.

Bayrakdar, M., (1983), 'Al-Jahiz and the Rise of Biological Evolutionism', *The Islamic Quarterly*, Third Quarter, Volume 27, No. 3.

Bennett, Jon and George, Susan, (1987), *The Hunger Machine*, CBC Enterprises, Toronto.

Bernard, Claude, (1957), *An Introduction to the Study of Experimental Medicine*, translated by Henry Copley Greene, Dover Publications Inc., New York.

Berry, Thomas, (1990), *The Dream of the Earth*, Sierra Club Books, San Francisco.

Billings, W.D., (1978), *Plants and the Ecosystem*, Wadsworth Publishing Company Inc., Belmont, California.

Blair, J. A. and Johnson, R.H., (1983), *Logical Self Defense*, McGraw-Hill Ryerson Ltd., Toronto.

Bockris, John O'M., Veziroglu, T. Nejat and Smith, Debbie, (1991), *Solar Hydrogen Energy: The Power to Save the Earth*, Optima, London

Bookchin, Murray, (1990), *The Philosophy of Social Ecology: Essays on Dialectical Naturalism*, Black Rose Books, Montreal.

Brady, Kevin, Noble, Duncan and Young, Steven B., (2001), *Engineering Dimensions*, 'Greenhouse gas emissions: A systems approach', May/June, Professional Engineers Ontario.

Briffault, Robert, (1919), *The Making of Humanity*, Allen, London.

Bright, Michael, (1984), *Animal Language*, BBC, London.

Brooke, John Hedley, (1991), *Science and Religion: Some Historical Perspectives*, The Cambridge History of Science Series, Cambridge University Press.

Brown, James H., Whitham, Thomas G., Ernest, S.K. Morgan and Gehring, Catherine A., (2001), *Science*, 'Ecology Through Time: Complex Species Interactions and the Dynamics of Ecological Systems: Long Term Experiments', Volume 293, Number 5530.

Brown, Lester et al., (1990), *State of the World*, W.W. Norton and Company, New York.

Brown, Nick and Press, Malcolm, (1992), 'Logging Forest the Natural Way?' *New Scientist*, pp. 25–29. March 14, 1812.

Bucaille, Maurice, (1979), *The Bible, the Qur'an and Science: The Holy Scriptures Examined in the Light of Modern Knowledge*, North American Trust Publications, Indianapolis, Indiana.

Burke, James, (1985), *The Day the Universe Changed*, Little, Brown and Company., London.

Chapple, Christopher, *Animal Sacrifices: Religious Perspectives on the Use of Animals in Science*, 'Noninjury to Animals: Jaina and Buddhist Perspectives', edited by Tom Regan, Temple University Press, Philadelphia, 1986.

Chomsky, Noam, (1993), *Year 501: The Conquest Continues*, Black Rose Books, New York.

Chomsky, Noam, (1988), *Manufacturing Consent: The Politics of the Mass Media*, Pantheon Books, New York.

Cohen, Joel E., (1996), *How Many People Can the Earth Support?*

Colborn, Theo, Dumanoski, Dianne; Myers, John Peterson, (1996), *Our Stolen Future: Are We Threatening Our Fertility, Intelligence and Survival? A Scientific Detective Story*, Dutton, New York.

Crews, David, (1987), 'Courtship in Unisexual Lizards: A Model for Brain Evolution', *Scientific American*, December, Vol. 257, No. 6, pp. 116–121.

Crosby, Alfred, (1986), *Ecological Imperialism: The Biological Expansion of Europe 900–1900*, Cambridge University Press, New York.

Day, David, (1989), *The Eco Wars: True Tales of Environmental Madness*, Key Porter Books, Toronto.

Denton, Michael J., (1998), *Nature's Destiny: How the Laws of Biology Reveal Purpose in the Universe*, The Free Press, Toronto.

Diamond, Jared, (1997), *Guns, Germs, and Steel: The Fates of Human Societies*, W.W. Norton and Company, New York/London, 1997

Dice, Lee R., (1962), *Natural Communities*, Anne Arbor: University of Michigan Press.

Dobson, Andrew, (1992), *Natural History*, 'Withering Heats', Vol. 101, No. 9, September 9.

Douthwaite, Richard, (1993), *The Growth Illusion*, Council Oak Books, Tulsa, Oklahoma.

Easlea, Brian, (1973), *Liberation and the Aims of Science: An Essay on Obstacles to the Building of a Beautiful World*, Sussex University Press, London.

Edwards, Tryon, (1959), *The New Dictionary of Thoughts: A Cyclopedia of Quotation*, Standard Book Company, U.S.A.

Ewart, Neil, (1983), *Everyday Phrases: Their Origins and Meanings*, Blandford Press Ltd.

Ferre, Frederick, (1991), 'Theodicy and the Status of Animals', *Contemporary Classics in Philosophy of Religion*, Open Court, Chicago.

Foltz, Richard C., Denny, Frederick M., Baharuddin, Azizan, eds., (2003), *Islam and Ecology: A Bestowed Trust*, Harvard University Press.

Fairley, Peter, (2020), 'The H_2 Solution', *Scientific American*, February Issue, Volume 322, Number 2.

Foltz, R. C., (2006), *Animals in the Islamic Tradition and Muslim cultures*, Oxford: Oneworld.

Gelbspan, Ross, (1997), *The Heat is On: The High Stakes Battle over Earth's Threatened Climate*, Reading, Mass.: Addison-Wesley Publishing Company.

George, Susan, (1992), *The Debt Boomerang: How the Third World Debt Harms Us All*, London: Pluto Press w/Transnational Institute.

George, Susan, (1980), *Feeding the Few: Corporate Control of Food*, Institute for Policy Studies, Washington, D.C.

George, Susan, (1988), *A Fate Worse Than Debt*, Penguin Books, London.

Giller, Paul S. (1984), *Community Structure and Niche*, Chapman and Hall, New York.

Goldstein, Thomas, (1980), *Dawn of Modern Science: From the Arabs to Leonardo da Vinci*, Houghton Mifflin, Boston.

Grant, Wyn, (1991), *The Dairy Industry: An International Comparison*, Dartmonth, England.

Griffin, Donald R., (1992), *Animal Minds*, The University of Chicago Press, Chicago.

Hallowell, Christopher, (1997), 'Will the World Go Hungry?', *Time Magazine: Our Precious Planet*, Special Issue, November.

Hansell, Michael H., (1984), *Animal Architecture and Building Behaviour*, Longman Inc., New York.

Haque, Nadeem and Muslim, M., (2007), *From Microbits to Everything: Universe of the Imaginator: Volume 2: The Philosophical Implications,* Optagon Publications Ltd., Toronto.

Haque, N, (2009), *From Microbits to Everything: Beyond Darwinism and Creationism, Volume 3: The evolutionary implications.* Toronto: Optagon Publications Ltd.

Haque, N. and Masri. B.A., (2011), 'Principles of Animal Advocacy in Islam: Four Integrated Ecognitions', *Society & Animals* 19, 279–290.

Haque, N. (2011), 'Al-Hafiz B. A. Masri: Muslim, scholar, activist—Rebel with a just cause.' In A. J. Nocella II & L. Kemmerer (Eds.), *Call to compassion: Religious perspectives on animal advocacy.* New York: Lantern Books.

Haque, Nadeem, (2012), 'Future Implications of a Pre-Adamic, Global and High Ancient Civilization', *Scientific GOD Journal.*

Haque, Nadeem and Shahbaz, Zeshan, (2015), 'Extraterrestrials in Islam', *Nexus,* Vol 22, No. 5 (August-September).

Hartmann, Thom., (January 30, 2004), 'How Global Warming May Cause the Next Ice Age'. http://www.amazon.com/exec/obidos/ASIN/1400051576/common-dreams-20/ref=nosim/ and http://www.thomhartmann.com

Hellyer, Paul, (1999), *Stop: Think,* Chimo Media, Toronto.

Hentsch, Thierry, (1992), *Imagining the Middle East,* Montreal/New York, Black Rose Books.

Hill, Donald, (1984), *A History of Engineering in Classical and Medieval Times,* Open Court, La Salle, Illinois.

Houghton, J.T. ed., (1996), Intergovernmental Panel on Climate Change *Climate Change 1995.* Contribution of working group I to the second assessment report of IPCC, *et al,* Cambridge University Press.

Hoyt, John A., (1994), *Animals in Peril: How 'Sustainable Use' is Wiping out the World's Wildlife,* Avery Publishing Group, New York.

Hutchinson, G.E., (1948) 'Circular causal systems in ecology', Annals of the New York Academy of Sciences, Vol. 50, pp. 221–246.

Isabella, Jude, 'The Natural World is an Elephant World', *Nautilis*

Jacobi, Herman, (1973), cf. *Jaina Sutra,* Motilal Banasides, Dehli

Jackson, B.C. Jeremy, et al., (2001), *Science,* 'Ecology Through Time: Historical Overfishing and the Recent Collapse of Coastal Ecosystems', Volume 293, Number 5530.

Jacobson, Jodi, (1988), 'Environmental Refugees: Yardstick of Habitability', *World Watch,* Paper No. 86.

Kant, Immanuel, (1963), *Lecture on Ethics*, translated by Louis Infield, Harper Torch-Books, New York.

Kemmerer, L., (2012) *Animals and World Religions*, Oxford: Oxford University Press.

Kemmerer, Lisa, (2018), 'Africa, animals, and the Almighty: A Christian call to the cause of animal liberation', Ed. Rainer Ebert and Anteneh Roba, *Africa and her animals: Philosophical and Practical Perspectives*, Unisa Press, Pretoria.

Kerr, Richard A., (Dec. 3, 1999), 'Will the Arctic Ocean Lose All its Ice?', *Science*.

Knudtson, Peter and Suzuki, David, (1992), *Wisdom of the Elders*, Stoddart, Toronto.

Kormondy, Edward J., (1969), *Concepts of Ecology*, Prentice Hall Inc., Englewood Cliffs, New Jersey.

Kowalski, Gary, (1991), *The Souls of Animals*, Stillpoint, Walpole, USA

Kruuk, Hans, (1972), *The Spotted Hyena: A Study of Predation and Social Behaviour*, The University of Chicago Press, Chicago.

Lappe, Francis Moore and Collins, Joseph, (1986), *World Hunger: Twelve Myths*, A Food First Book, Grove Press Inc., New York.

Larsen, Janet, (January 22, 2004), 'Glaciers and Sea Ice Endangered by Rising Temperatures', *Earth-Policy News*, , http://www.Earth-policy.org/Updates/Update32.htm

Lassailly-Jacob, Veronique, (1992), 'Environmental Refugees', *Refuge*, Vol. 12, No. 1.

Leakey, Richard and Lewin, Roger, (1995), *The Sixth Extinction: Biodiversity and its Survival*, Weidenfield and Nicolson, London.

Lomborg, Bjorn, (2001), *The Skeptical Environmentalist: Measuring the Real State of the World*, Cambridge University Press Cambridge, Cambridge.

Lovelock, James, (1988), *The Ages of Gaia*, W.W. Norton and Co., New York..

Lovelock, James, (1991), *Healing Gaia*, Harmony Books, New York.

Lunde, Paul, (1982), 'Book of Animals', *Aramco World Magazine*, Vol. 33, No. 3, p. 17. The quote is from Al-Jahiz's *Book of Animals*.

Malik, Aamina H., Ziermann, Janine M., and Diogo, Rui, (2018), 'An Untold Story in Biology: The Historical Continuity of Evolutionary Ideas of Muslim Scholars from the 8th century to Darwin's Time', *Qur'anicosmos*, Volume 1, Issue 3, Institute of Higher Reasoning.

Margenau, Henry and Varghese, Roy A., (1991), *Cosmos, Bios, Theos: Scientists Reflect on Science, God, and the Origins of the Universe, Life, and Homo Sapiens*, Open Court Publishing Company.

Margules, C.R., Pressey, R.L., (11 May, 2000), 'Review Article: Systematic conservation planning', *Nature*, Vol. 405.

Masri, B. A., (1989), *Animals in Islam*, The Athene Trust, Petersfield, England.

McCann, Kevin Shear, (11 May, 2000), 'Review Article: The diversity-stability debate', *Nature*, Vol. 405.

Mohammed, Ovey N., (1984), *Averroes' Doctrine of Immortality: A Matter of Controversy*, Wilfred Laurier University Press, Kitchener, Ontario.

Mokhiber, Russell and Weissman, Robert, (1999), *Corporate Predators: The Hunt for Mega-Profits and the Attack on Democracy*, Common Courage Press, Monroe, Maine.

Mokhiber, Russell, (1988), *Corporate Crime and Violence: Big Business Power and the Abuse of the Public Trust*, Sierra Club Books, San Francisco.

Moore, Keith L., and Persaud, T.V.N., (1998), *The Developing Human: Clinically Oriented Embryology, 6th Edition*, W.B. Saunders and Company, Philadelphia.

Morris, Desmond, (1990), *Animal Watching: A Field Guide to Animal Behaviour*, Jonathan Cape, London.

Morton, Eugene S. and Page, Jake, (1992), *Animal Talk: Science and Voices in Nature*, Random House, New York.

Myers, Norman, (1984), *Gaia Atlas of Planet Management*, Anchor Books, Doubleday, New York.

Nash, Madeline J., (April 10, 2000), 'Will We Control the Weather?', *Time: Visions of Space and Science*, Vol. 155, No. 14.

Naylor, R.L., (1996), 'Invasions in agriculture: assessing the cost of the golden apple snail in Asia', *Ambio*, Vol. 25.

Ola, Johannnsen M., Shalina, Elena V., Miles, Martin W., (Dec. 3, 1999), 'Satellite Evidence for an Arctic Sea Ice Cover in Transformation', *Science.*

Penrose, Roger, (1989), *The Emperor's New Mind: Concerning Computers, Minds and The Laws of Physics*, Oxford University Press, New York/Oxford.

Pellat, Charles, (1969), *The Life and Works of Jahiz: Translation of Selected Texts*, (translated from the French by D.M. Hawke), London, Routledge and Kegan Paul.

Pepperberg, Irene M., 'Talking with Alex: Logic and Speech in Parrots', *Scientific American Presents: Exploring Intelligence, Quarterly*, Vol. 9, No. 4, Winter 1998.

Perkins, John, (2004), *Confessions of an Economic Hit Man*, Plume.

Perspectives of American Voters on the Cairo Agenda: A Report to PrepCom III, (1994), from survey and focus group research conducted for the Pew Global Stewardship Initiative, April 20.

Philander, George S., (1998), Is the Temperature Rising? *The Uncertain Science of Global Warming*, Princeton, Princeton University Press.

Pimm, Stuart L., (1991), *The Balance of Nature? Ecological Issues in the Conservation of Species and Communities*, The University of Chicago Press, Chicago.

Porritt, Jonathon, (1991), *Save the Earth*, McClelland and Stewart Inc., Toronto.

Porter, J.H., Parry, M.L.and Carter, T.R., (1991), 'The potential effects of climatic change on agricultural insect pests', *Agric. For. Meteorol.*, Vol. 57.

Postel, S.L., Daily, G.C. & Ehrlich, P.R., (1996), 'Human appropriation of renewable fresh water.' *Science*, Vol. 271.

Rahim, Ata-ur, (1991), *Jesus, Prophet of Islam*, Tahrike Tarsile Qur'an, Inc., New York.

Ebert, Rainer and Roba, Anteneh (Editors), (2018), *Africa and her animals: Philosophical and Practical Perspectives*, Unisa Press, Pretoria.

Regan, Tom, (1986), *Animal Sacrifices*, Temple University Press, Philadelphia, Pennsylvania.

Reice, Seth R., (1994), 'Non-equilibrium Determinants of Biological Community Structure', *American Scientist*, Sept 94, Issue 5, Triangle Park.

Reppert, S.M., Guerra, P.A. & Merlin, C., (2016) 'Neurobiology of Monarch Butterfly Migration', *Annual Review of Entomology*, 61:25–42

Repetto, Roberto, (June, 1992), 'Accounting for Environmental Assets', *Scientific American*, Vol. 266, Issue 6.

Rifkin, Jeremy, (1991), *Biosphere Politics: A New Consciousness for a New Century*, Crown Publishers, New York.

Romm, Joseph J., (1999), *Cool Companies: How the Best Businesses Boost Profit and Productivity by Cutting Greenhouse Gas Emission*, Island Press, Washington D.C.

Sandage, Charles and Fryburger, V., (1960), *The Role of Advertising*, Richard Irwin Publications, Homewood, Ill.

Ryn, Sim Van Der and Cowan, Stuart, (1996), *Ecological Design*, Island Press, Washington D.C.

Schacht, Joseph and Bosworth, C.E., Editors, (1974), *The Legacy of Islam*, Oxford at the Clarendon Press, London.

Schneider, Stephen H., (1997). *Laboratory Earth: The Planetary Gamble We Can't Afford to Lose*, New York, BasicBooks.

Scott, Jo, (1969), *Hunger: Man's Struggle to Feed Himself*, Parents' Magazine Press, New York.

Seamon, David and Zajonc, Arthur, (1998), *Goethe's Way of Science: A Phenomenology of Nature*, State University of New York Press, Albany, New York.

Shiva, Vandana, (1997), *Biopiracy: The Plunder of Nature and Knowledge*, Between the Lines, Toronto.

Singer, Peter, (1990), *Animal Liberation*, Avon Books, New York.

Skidelsky, Robert, (2018), *Money and Government: A Challenge to Mainstream Economics*, Penguin, Random House, UK.

Snow, Nancy, (1998), *Propaganda: Selling American Culture to the World*, Open Media, New York.

Steingraber, Sandra, (1997), *Living Downstream: An Ecologist looks at Cancer and the Environment*, A Merloyd Lawrence Book, Addison-Wesley Publishing Company, Inc.

Thayer, H.S., (1953), *Newton's Philosophy of Nature: Selections from his Writings*, Hafner Publishing, New York.

Retallack, Simon, Editor, (November 2001), *The Ecologist Report: Climate Change*.

Thomson, Ahmad, (1989), *Blood on the Cross*, London, Ta-Ha Publishers.

Timberlake, L., (1988), *African Crisis: The Causes, the Cures of Environmental Bankruptcy*, Earthscan Publications, London.

Time Special Edition, Earth Day 2000, 'How to save the Earth', Vol. 155, No. 17, April–May 2000, pp. 18–21.

Timmerman, Peter, (1989), 'God is Closer to You Than Your Jugular Vein', *Probe Post*, Spring Issue.

Tlilli, Sarra, (2012), *Animals in the Qur'an*, Cambridge University Press.

Vaclav, Havel, (1997), *The Art of the Impossible: Politics as Morality in Practice*, Alfred A. Knopf, New York, Toronto.

Robson, J. (Translator), (1963), *Mishkat al-Masabih*, Lahore, Pakistan: Sh. Muhammad Ashraf.

Robson, John M. (Editor), (1987), *Origin and Evolution of the Universe: Evidence for Design*, McGill-Queen's University Press, Kingston and Montreal.

Vinnikov Y., Konstantin, Robock, Alan, Stouffer, Ronald J., Walsh, John, E., Parkinson, Claire L., Cavalieri, J. Donald, Mitchell, John F.B., Garrett, Donald, Zakharov, Victor F., (Dec. 3, 1999) 'Global Warming and Northern Hemisphere Sea Ice Extent', *Science*.

Von Frisch, Karl, (1974), *Animal Architecture*, Harcourt Brace Janovich, New York.

Wadia, Koshlya, (1974), cf. *The Conception of Animals in Indian Thought*, Varanasi, Bharata Manisha.

Watkins, Mel, (1971), Preface to Levitt: *Silent Surrender: The American Economic Empire in Canada*, Liveright, New York.

Wilson, Edward O., (1992), *The Diversity of Life*, The Belknap Press of Harvard University Press, Massachusetts.

Woodbury, Richard, Wosnitza, Regine, (April–May, 2000) 'How to save the Earth', *Time Special Edition, Earth Day 2000*, Vol. 155, No. 17.

Woods, G.D., (1966), *Foreign Affairs*, January Issue.

Wohlleben, Peter, (2017), *The Secret Wisdom of Nature: Trees, Animals, and the Extraordinary Balance of All Living Things Stories from Science and Observation*, Greystone Books.

Wright, Robert, (1988), *Three Scientists and their Gods: Looking for meaning in an age of Information*, Times Book, New York.

Index

S

sakhkhara 70, 71
Saleh 126
samawati 54, 75
Sidelsky, Robert 182
Slaughter 152
Slaughter of Animals for Food 152
solar-hydrogen couplings 105
Solomon 52, 53, 119, 120, 127, 170, 171

T

taqwa 77, 125, 178, 221
technology vi, 20, 27, 56, 87, 88, 89, 91, 96, 97, 99, 100, 102, 103, 104, 105, 137,
      147, 164, 185, 186, 187, 188, 207, 208
teleology 44, 72, 209
theodicy 9, 157, 158, 164
Tobias, Michael 185
Total Fertility Rate 185

U

Utilitarians 12

W

wada-'ahaa 74
wahi 55, 60, 196
water 2–3, 18, 22, 54–56, 66, 73, 77, 78, 81–83, 85, 87, 91–92, 100, 103–105, 118,
      126, 144, 149, 150, 153–154, 163, 193–194, 209, 223–234

Z

zulm 90, 180–181

BV - #0063 - 150722 - C0 - 234/156/15 - PB - 9781912356973 - Gloss Lamination